MONSTROUS BODIES/
POLITICAL
MONSTROSITIES

MONSTROUS BODIES/ POLITICAL MONSTROSITIES

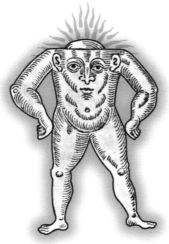

IN EARLY MODERN EUROPE

EDITED BY
LAURA LUNGER KNOPPERS AND JOAN B. LANDES

CORNELL UNIVERSITY PRESS
Ithaca and London

First published 2004 by Cornell University Press
First printing, Cornell Paperbacks, 2004

Printed in the United States of America

Design by Scott Levine

Library of Congress Cataloging-in-Publication Data

Monstrous bodies/political monstrosities in early modern Europe / edited
by Laura Lunger Knoppers and Joan B. Landes.—1st ed.
    p. cm.
Includes bibliographical references and index.
    ISBN 0-8014-4176-5 (cloth : alk. paper) — ISBN 0-8014-8901-6 (pbk. :
alk. paper)
    1. Europe—History—1492-1648—Psychological aspects. 2.
Europe—History—1648-1789—Psychological aspects. 3 National
characteristics, European—History. 4. Monsters—Symbolic
aspects—Europe—History. 5. Monsters in literature. I. Knoppers,
Laura Lunger. II. Landes, Joan B., 1946–
    D231.M66 2004
    001.944'094'0903—dc22

                                        2003020743

Cornell University Press strives to use environmentally responsible
suppliers and materials to the fullest extent possible in the publishing
of its books. Such materials include vegetable-based, low-VOC inks
and acid-free papers that are recycled, totally chlorine-free, or partly
composed of nonwood fibers. For further information, visit our web-
site at www.cornellpress.cornell.edu.

Cloth printing   10 9 8 7 6 5 4 3 2 1
Paperback printing   10 9 8 7 6 5 4 3 2 1

CONTENTS

ILLUSTRATIONS

Illustrations

Illustrations

ACKNOWLEDGMENTS

This book is the result of a new interdisciplinary initiative in early modern studies at Penn State University. In recent years, the Committee on Early Modern Studies has sponsored lecture series, symposia, and workshops, and helped to facilitate a National Endowment for the Humanities Summer Institute. This initiative has created a space for dialogue and intellectual exchange between faculty and students from a wide range of departments within the arts and humanities. The lecture series and symposium on monstrosities, from which this volume derived, were generously funded by the Humanities Consortium, under the aegis of Susan Welch, Dean of the College of the Liberal Arts, and Raymond Lombra, Associate Dean for Research and Graduate Studies. From the beginning, A. Gregg Roeber, Head of the Department of History, has been a close colleague and enthusiastic supporter of our efforts. In addition to the Department of History, we thank the Department of English and in particular Robert Caserio, Head, for help with funding the final preparation of the manuscript.

We are grateful to our contributors for their good-natured collaboration on this project and for their generous responses to our editorial prods. It was a pleasure to work with Catherine Rice, our editor at Cornell, who has skillfully and attentively guided this project to completion. Two anonymous readers for Cornell University Press offered incisive comments as well as a much appreciated endorsement of the project. Professor Christophe Deguerce, curator of the Musée Fragonard of L'École Vétérinaire d'Alfort and Professor Pierre Buisseret of the Muséum national d'Histoire naturelle graciously assisted with the acquisition of photographs from the collections in their museums. For their help with obtaining and processing images, Sue Reighard and Ryan Patton at Penn State's Institute for the Arts and Humanities deserve special mention. For their patience when this book project—like its monstrous subject—threatened to grow out of all bounds, and for their loving assistance in so many other ways, we thank our families: Gary, Theresa, and David; Ted and Eleanor.

MONSTROUS BODIES/
POLITICAL
MONSTROSITIES

INTRODUCTION

LAURA LUNGER KNOPPERS AND JOAN B. LANDES

A 1727 Portuguese tract, *Emblema Vivente, ou, Noticia de hum Portentoso Monstro,* features both a striking woodcut (figure 1) and an extended verbal account of an early modern monster.[1] The tract, taking the form of a letter written for the enjoyment (*divertimento*) of a friend, recounts an event that had taken place the year before. The author tells the tale of a monster that emerged from the forest of Anatolia during the reign of the Turks. The creature had the shape of a man, but of a monstrous man, and measured fifteen palms high. Its head, topped by a crescent, had human features, including big round eyes, a wide sloped nose, and a mouth in which a hard thin bone stood in the place of teeth. The creature was asexual, neither male nor female, with only a single orifice for the needs of nature. It had human arms but from each shoulder came out a long neck with an eagle's head. Its upper legs were covered with a gray matter, also found elsewhere on its body, and its lower legs were covered by gray scaly skin. But perhaps most remarkable, when the creature breathed, a light emanated from its chest, and in the chest was the figure of a cross.

Captured by the forces of the provincial governor where it was found and brought to the sultan of Constantinople, the creature would not eat any

1

Figure 1. *Emblema Vivente, ou, Noticia de hum Portentoso Monstro* (1727). Reproduced with the permission of Rare Books and Manuscripts, Special Collections Library, the Pennsylvania State University.

human food, nor did it seem to speak any language. A hermit whose advice was sought gave a dismal prophecy about the disobedience of the Turks, who had not properly followed Islam. The presence of the monster indicated that the Ottoman Empire would come to an end, to be conquered by Christianity. Although the monster was eventually killed, its ominous meaning as portent or living emblem continued to resonate, provoking denials by the Turks who did not want to give the Christians cause for hope.

Published in 1727, a century after Francis Bacon's call for the empirical study of monstrosity within a naturalist frame, and contemporaneous with the opening salvos in a decades-long dispute on the monstrous within the French Académie Royale des Sciences, *Emblema Vivente* presents an eloquent example of a truly portentous monster, one who cohabited a world in which rational men were seeking to inaugurate a disinterested inquiry into the problem of abnormal births.[2] The tract blurs the boundaries of science and religion, politics and ethnography. It titillates the reader with a detailed description of the monster's bodily traits, a composite of human and animal features, while also evoking the tradition of monster as portent and sign of God's displeasure. The word "monster" itself has a complex etymology: from the Latin *monere* (to warn), to *monstrum* (that which is worthy of warning), to *monstrare* (to point to that which is worthy of warning).[3] On the boundaries between belief and wonder, credulity and skepticism, the tract evinces seemingly contradictory attitudes toward the nature and meaning of the monstrous.

The Anatolian monster also serves as omen, replete with political and religious meaning. Upon the malformed body of the creature from the forest are written the transgressions of the ethnic Other, the Turks. According to the prophet who interprets the portent, the creature's head, crowned by a moon, is a sign of the Ottoman Empire, oppressed between the German and Russian empires, signified by the eagle heads. While the double eagles conventionally face in opposite directions, eastward toward Byzantium and westward toward Rome (as in the emblem of the Holy Roman Empire), here they are depicted looking at one other, thus signaling the unification of the neighboring Christian forces against the Turks. Interestingly, the Turks are indicted not as non-believers but actually for their failure to follow Islam: for their toleration of Christians, attacks on fellow Muslims, and violation of the Qur'an. As the prophet exclaims, before offering his dire interpretation of the monster to the Sultan: "Oh Ottoman Empire! How I fear your impending fall!"[4]

Emblema Vivente shows the conflation of attitudes toward the monstrous in the early modern period: at a time when the monstrous was allegedly being rationalized, made the subject of anatomy and embryology, and moved away from its status as portent or warning, the creature emerges from the forest in Asia Minor, exposed by the light in its chest, which looks like intermittent lightning or a giant firelight, but turns out to be emitted from the sign of a cross. Despite the creature's alterity, it is marked by the dominant sign of Christianity and its body can be read as affirming both the aberrations of the Turks and the normative values of Catholicism. The Ottoman Empire, failing by the seventeenth century to keep pace with the commercial, technological, mercantile, and educational advances in Western Europe, is depicted not as a threatening rival, but as an empire in decline: the Turks bungle attempts to capture and later to kill the monster and are doomed by their own faithlessness.[5] Although the Portuguese author in some respects distances himself from the content of the tale, its political and religious propaganda value is clear.

Yet this monster cannot be dismissed as mere fantasy simply because of its provenance in Asia Minor or its place within anti-Ottoman Christian polemics. For even in the writings of the century's most skeptical, not to say scientific minds, one finds talk of hybrid creatures and fantastical births. Thus, Voltaire entertains the existence of satyrs and speculates on how monkeys in torrid zones might mate with abducted human females, and he reports having seen a four-breasted woman with a cow's tail on her chest at a fair.[6] Linnaeus countenances dragons, and includes genera of troglodytes, satyrs, and pygmies, as well as six monstrous varieties of *Homo sapiens,* in his *Systema naturae;* and Joseph-François Lafitau credits Iroquois testimony about the existence of anencephalous (headless) men as confirmation of his monogenetic theory, according to which the New World was populated by a migration from Asia, the home of the (headless) Blemmyae in the ancient sources.[7]

Overall, the interest taken in monsters in eighteenth-century savant society compares favorably to the attention they received among learned and unlearned alike in former times. Michael Hagner identifies new categories for the monstrous in the eighteenth century as well as strong continuities with earlier beliefs: "Living monsters continued to be displayed in public shows and marketplaces. They were exhibited in natural cabinets and provided the subject matter for countless case studies in erudite journals. In fact, the eighteenth century witnessed a massive increase in the representations of monsters."[8] As Andrew Curran and Patrick Graille observe, the monster in the eighteenth century is "a fluctuating beast, a hybrid occupying an ambiguous position in Enlightenment thought somewhere between the limits of empirical knowledge and the territory of fantasy."[9] Most noticeable for Curran and Graille is the lack of a single, coherent definition for the monstrous in the supposedly rationalized eighteenth century.

Reminiscent of the disquieting monsters populating Goya's *Caprichos* at century's end, monstrosity in *Emblema Vivente* escapes scientific or rational containment. The writer takes care to narrate the story of the monster in precise, empirical detail, attesting thereby to its veracity and providing a fictionalized experience in which the reader can participate.[10] The woodcut gives concrete form to the creature, underscoring the importance of the visual in exhibiting and verifying the early modern monstrous.[11] And yet the language of description is slippery and marked by recourse to multiple resemblance: the creature's nose is "like the beak of an eagle" (*como bico de Aguia*); the down of its face and beard is "like a bird's" (*como as aves*); the color of its eyes is "like copper wire" (*como cor de alambre*); its toenails are "like some four-footed animals" (*como alguns animaes quadrupedes*).[12] Even the visual image brings not understanding or explanation, but wonder ("all of those who saw him were at awe at the sight of his horrible body, unlike anything ever seen")[13] and the writer expects that his friend will also wonder at the figure in paper he is sending.[14]

Similarly, the writer's apparent skepticism is unstable, overly self-conscious, and contradictory. While he acknowledges that the tale seems like a fable ("fabula") and claims to be writing only to amuse his friend, the writer insists that the account is as true as many historical works. He questions the veracity of classical teratology—pointing out that present-day travelers have found no traces of the dog-headed Cynocephalos, of the one-eyed Monocles, of the Fanesios with ears so long they cover the body, of the Monopodes with only one foot, or of any other monstrous race. And yet these observations serve not to relegate the present creature to the realm of fantasy but to remark on the facts that monsters do not reproduce themselves and that the one in this story is one of the strangest ever known to man. Notwithstanding the ways in which science could be mobilized to defeat the most fabulous and credulous claims, texts such as *Emblema Vivente* also point to the rhetorical purposes to which monstrous imagery continued to be put: defining religious, ethnic, and national boundaries; legitimating faith; asserting cultural identity; or reinscribing anomalous, strange, and aberrant experiences.

This book frames the study of the monster in early modern Europe. A more destabilizing term than the contained categories of "medieval," "Renaissance," "baroque," "Reformation," or "Enlightenment," "early modern" blurs boundaries, gesturing both forward and backward.[15] Monsters blur boundaries as well, transgressing, violating, polluting, and mixing what ought to be kept apart.[16] The "early modern monstrous" calls attention to the rational and scientific, but at the same time undermines confidence in wholly rational explanations. Similarly, the category "early" implies a knowledge that is stamped as incomplete and unfulfilled. As a heuristic, "early modern" bridges centuries as well as territories once treated independently. It encompasses exploration and colonialism, political centralization and revolution, transformations in print and communication, religious schism and scientific investigation. It is an important period for defining ethnic, religious, national, and sexual identities and boundaries. At the same time, Europe itself was not one homogeneous, undifferentiated whole. Oppositions between Europeans could be played out in the discourses of monstrosity, as were those between Europeans and non-Europeans. Monsters emerge in the early modern period as just such crucial definitional Others in the processes of European self and nation formation; at the same time, they constantly threaten the very identities they help to define.

In recent years, scholars have begun to challenge the long-standing view of a progressive rationalization and naturalization of monstrosity, which is said to have culminated in the nineteenth-century science of teratology: the scientific study of visible conditions caused by the interruption or alteration of normal growth.[17] Yet such narratives are not easily dispelled, for they tell the story of how, in the shift from omen and fable to comparative anatomy and embryology, the monster came to be tamed, analyzed, dissected, and ordered. Thus, unlike the early moderns, for whom monstrosity set others apart, as a being against nature, moderns are presumed to have come to accept or normalize the monster.[18] Culminating an era marked by superstition, the eighteenth century has been identified as a transitional age, "marking the necessary passage," as Jean-Louis Fischer states, "between the end of a fabulous representation of the monster and the beginnings of a science of anomalies, malformations, and monstrosities."[19] In the words of another scholar, "Monstrosities in general, a lot of monsters in particular, have today a complete explanation."[20] Their difference from the norm is seen as an instance of species variation within the world of nature.

Still, the question arises, normalization to what end? Even as the subject of embryology or comparative anatomy, according to Georges Canguilhem, the monster remains "the living example of negative value," whose purpose is to reinforce a dynamic and polemical concept of normality.[21] As Michel Foucault elaborates, "the norm carries with it at the same time a principle of qualification and a principle of correction. The function of the norm is not to exclude, to reject. It is, on the contrary, always allied to a positive technique of intervention and transformation, a sort of normative project."[22] And, in a related manner, Michael Hagner charts the shifting epistemic spaces in which monsters changed from collectable but unclassifiable items of wonder and display to dissectable specimens within the evolving life sciences. He concludes that "the instrumentalization of monsters" during the Enlightenment produced "a new chapter in the highly problematic relation between 'deformation' and the order of life. The subordination of the 'natural' under the rule of autocratic reason [as spelled out by Max Horkheimer and Theodor Adorno in *The Dialectic of Enlightenment*] changed: the scientific notion of deformations as representatives of older and more primitive biological forms of existence that did not reach the defined standard created new monsters."[23]

Foucault also underscores changes in the privileged locus of monstrosity. Thus, medieval Europeans were captivated by the bestial man; during the sixteenth and seventeenth centuries conjoined twins—either a head with two bodies, or a body with two heads—came to the fore, as monstrosity was imbued with religious or political significance; and this was followed by a fascination with the hermaphrodite in the late eighteenth and early nineteenth centuries.[24] Calling attention to monstrosity's normative and biological features, Foucault argues that monstrosity is fundamentally a "juridical-natural concept." In the eighteenth century, he claims, one discovers the monster "at the point of the conjunction of nature and law. It carries with it natural transgression, the mixture of species, the confusion of limits and characters. But it is only a monster because it is also a juridical labyrinth, a violation and troubling of the law, a transgression and indeterminacy at the level of law."[25]

Thus, the progressive narrative, in which the monstrous moves from portent to science, undervalues the political, polemical, and juridical uses of monstrous imagery throughout the early modern period. Monstrous bodies carry the weight of political, social, and sexual aberration or transgression: the borders of the known and the acceptable are marked by the construction of the monstrous Other.[26] As in the Portuguese tract *Emblema Vivente*, religious, ethnic, and national identities, societal and political norms are instantiated and enforced by the construction of monstrous bodies. Monsters are used and reused to inscribe religious values from the Reformation through civil and religious conflict in seventeenth- and eighteenth-century Europe. With the advent of early modern science, monsters not only move into the realm of medical pathology but also appear in political and legal debate and comprise a topic of discussion within newly constituted scientific and cultural public spheres.[27] Monstrous bodies reflect the felt upheaval and disorder of political revolution. Facilitated by the print revolution that characterized the early modern period, the dissemination of the monstrous—not merely as text but as printed image—retains its rhetorical and symbolic efficacy, not least as a weapon in political and religious propaganda and debate.

This interdisciplinary volume of essays features new links between the monstrous and the political. Appearing in multiple discourses and forging connections between them, monsters are a rich subject for not only the history of science, but also for political and religious history, literary studies, art history, and history of popular culture. The use and representation of the monstrous is affected by the rise of science but also by religious and political conflict, transformations in print, and the rise of the nation-state. The early modern period has been traditionally viewed as the origin of the modern, the turning point for the rise of individualism and of political states and national identities. Such overarching metahistorical schemas are now treated with increasing skepticism, and the alleged rationality of the professed age of reason has been widely challenged. Even so, a great deal of the scholarship on monstrosity continues to assume a secularizing teleology.

This reflects, in good measure, the wide impact of Katharine Park and Lorraine Daston's ground-breaking 1981 article, which located an epistemological shift during the sixteenth and seventeenth centuries "from monsters as prodigies to monsters as examples of medical pathology."[28] Park and Daston identified three main strands in thinking about the monstrous in classical and Christian antiquity.[29] These were first, the scientific investigation of biological anomalies, stemming from Aristotle and his followers; second, the view of the monster as portent or divine sign, credited to Cicero and later shaped by Augustine in Christian thought; and finally, the cosmographical and ethnographic approach to the study of monstrous races, associated with Pliny and Solinus.[30] Views of the monster as divine portent, as Park and Daston showed, continued in the Reformation as both reformers such as Luther and Melanchthon and their opponents used monsters in religious polemic, to signify monstrous aberration in the Church. But, according to Park and Daston, the apocalyptic and religious resonance of monstrous imagery declined with the diminution of religious conflict. Over time, they likewise note "the 'withdrawal' of high from popular culture (the 'great' from the 'little' tradition)."[31] And, most emphatically, they suggest that as a result of natural scientific investigations of monstrosity, from Francis Bacon and the Royal Society in England to the French Académie des Sciences, monstrosity ultimately became a feature of nineteenth-century teratological taxonomies.[32] Earlier attitudes—monsters as prodigies or portents, frightening signs of divine wrath—survived in popular literature and settings: ballads, broadsides, wonder books, and the public fair.[33] However, what remained of the older tradition was principally accounted for by the notion of popular superstition.

Park and Daston's original framework helped to shape a now vibrant and thriving field of study on marvels, wonders, and monsters from the high Middle Ages to the eighteenth century.[34] At the same time, their own continuing studies culminated in a major monograph, published in 1998, in which they proposed a reformulation of their earlier perspective. In *Wonders and the Order of Nature, 1150–1750,* Park and Daston write that "we now reject this teleological model, organized as a progress toward rationalization and naturalization."[35] In place of successive stages culminating in the rationalization and naturalization of the monster, they posit three separate complexes—horror, pleasure, and repugnance—and attempt to address the ways in which cognitive and emotional response to anomalous births overlapped and coexisted within the early modern period:

As portents signifying divine wrath and imminent catastrophe, monsters evoked horror: they were *contra naturam,* violations of both the natural and moral orders. As marvels, they elicited wondering pleasure: they were *praeter naturam,* rare, but not menacing, reflecting an aesthetic of variety and ingenuity in nature as well as art. As deformities or natural errors, monsters inspired repugnance: they were neither ominous nor admirable but regrettable, the occasional price to be paid for the very simplicity and regularity in nature from which they so shockingly deviated.[36]

Wonders and the Order of Nature is a marvelously rich, lavishly illustrated account of the relationship between wonder and science in the early modern period. Yet in substituting a more complicated, or what they term "undulatory," movement for an explicitly linear account, Park and Daston nevertheless continue to tell a story about the rise and decline of wonder in relationship to early modern science.[37] Their argument remains tied to a progressive epistemological shift insofar as the supernatural is supplanted by the natural, and magical explanations give way to rational accounts. While such a narrative maps important shifts in scientific explanations, it does not wholly account for the wide range of metaphorical and political uses of the monstrous.

Since Park and Daston's earliest contribution, our understanding of the scientific culture of monstrosity in early modern Europe has been greatly enriched, especially by literary scholars' examinations of the intersections of literature with medicine, science, and technology. In *Monstrous Imagination*, Marie-Hélène Huet highlights the important role played by maternal imagination in early modern theories of monstrosity. She shows how imaginationist explanations—according to which the improper excitation of a mother's imagination could result in a monstrous birth—came to be discredited in the medical sciences of embryology and heredity: "Like the maternal imagination, the teratogenist *modifies* by intervention, a process that left undisturbed would have produced normal progeny."[38] By modifying the embryo's evolution, Huet explains, the scientist assumes both visible paternity of monstrosities and the maternal role in generation: "The laboratory has fully and successfully replaced the womb, and rational, male intervention has been substituted for the female imagination."[39] In Romanticism, Huet locates a corresponding displacement of maternalist theories of generation, with male artists "duplicating in [their] own terms the field of teratogeny." Not only did Romantic artists turn to tales of monstrosity, but by reflecting on the "dark desire to reproduce without the other . . . [they] rehabilitated the resulting monstrosity as a troubling but unique work of art."[40] In another creative synthesis of literary and scientific culture, Dennis Todd looks at the popular interest generated by the alleged birth of seventeen rabbits to one Mary Toft, with implications for the treatment of imagination, monstrosity, and personal identity in the writings of Jonathan Swift and Alexander Pope.[41] Similarly, a volume edited by Peter Platt presents the variety of discursive practices that employed wonder and the marvelous to challenge, rather than affirm, epistemological or scientific certainty and aesthetic wholeness.[42]

Other scholars exploit the interpenetration of literary and scientific accounts of monstrosity to further our understanding of the limits of Enlightenment notions of progress. Julia Douthwaite looks at the double-edged promise of science in relation to the *Homines feri:* potentially reclaimable, the wild child also brought disturbing reminders of the despotism of the human passions. Observers wondered whether wild children were a separate genus of mankind or monsters, perfectible or degenerate, models of uncorrupted nature or uncouth savages.[43] Patrick Graille investigates the "monstrous" nature of hermaphrodites, exploring their destabilizing effects within classical and enlightened discourses of literature, mythology, history, philosophy, anthropology, law, religion, natural science, and medicine.[44] Andrew Curran's study of physical monstrosity in Diderot's works highlights the *philosophe*'s vacillation between physiological fact and speculative fantasy. Charting the monster through Diderot's philosophical, literary, and scientific writings, Curran challenges "the chronicle of monstrosity's progressive de-sacralisation."[45] Echoing themes in Park and Daston's account, Zakiya Hanafi is interested as well in the influence of science in displacing magical and sacred ways of looking at the world. Far from disappearing, she insists that the monster became a machine under the impact of the Scientific Revolution during the period 1550 to 1750 in Italy. The monster moved from the formaldehyde jars of curiosity cabinets and museum shelves to take up residence within the self, in the sciences and machines of man's own creations, but also in the metaphors and witticisms of Baroque literary culture. "Metaphors," Hanafi suggests, "are monstrous be-

cause they impair reasoning and lure us into a pleasurable state of indo-
lence."[46]

By focusing on the political and rhetorical use of the monstrous, particularly on the grotesque body, this volume complements both earlier history of
science approaches and studies more concerned with the literary. Our interest
in monstrosity and representation allows us to raise a number of questions. To
what extent or in what ways does monstrous language become rhetorical,
polemical? What is the effect of the use and reuse of the language of monstrosity, and what is the significance of the multiple appropriations of monstrous bodies? What emotional responses do monsters call up, and how do
myths of monstrosity figure in understandings of self and other? How do political exigencies—as much as epistemological frameworks—shape and produce the monstrous?

Each of four sets of paired essays explores themes central to the construction and deployment of monstrous bodies through verbal and visual texts. By
highlighting polemical and rhetorical uses of the monstrous, particularly gendered, bestial, and grotesque bodies, we feature the multiple uses to which
printed words and images were put to convey monstrosity. The contributors
are concerned not so much with natural, biological bodies as with bodies constructed through discourse, bodies implicated in structures of power and
knowledge.[47] In particular, monstrous bodies carry the weight of political, social, sexual, or religious aberration or transgression. They link the individual
body to the body politic.[48] They offer a standpoint from which to understand
the rise of individualism, modern political state structures, and national identities.

The print revolution greatly facilitated the dissemination and circulation
of monstrous representations in texts as well as images.[49] In either respect,
monstrous bodies retain their efficacy as a form of symbolic representation, as
a rhetorical weapon in political and religious polemic and debate. Monstrous
bodies mark the boundaries of nations and depict abnormalities in the body
politic as literally grotesque and deformed. They reflect the felt upheaval and

disorder of political revolution. They provide the language through which Catholics and Protestants in Reformation Europe portray their enemies. Similarly, in the shift from the ordered body politic of monarchy to the headless parliamentary state, absolutists and republicans accuse one another of bringing forth monsters, in both "fact" and "fiction." Analysis of the use and representation of monstrous bodies, in particular to convey the cataclysmic disorder of political revolution and change, complicates a progressive teleology in which the fabulous, portentous, or strange is supplanted by medical, scientific, or normative explanations. In these accounts, the supernatural does not so much disappear as transform and reemerge in a politicized form.

The first pair of essays in our volume, in Part 1, "Monstrous Races, Boundaries, and Nationhood," traces the early modern incorporation and politicization of the monstrous bodies of classical teratology. While recent scholars have debated the relation between the monstrous races marking the margins of the unknown and modern ideas of race and colonialism, these two essays show how the classical monstrous was redeployed inside early modern Europe.[50] The grotesque and deformed physical abnormalities that characterized the monstrous races of Herodotus and Pliny served in the early modern period not only to define European selves against non-European Others, but also— as these essays show—to set boundaries between and within European nations. Both the essays show how monstrous bodies were appropriated and revised, either to define the emerging nation state against other cultural and national identities—"monstrosities" seen as morally, politically, and socially inferior to one's own nation—or to police hierarchical relations of gender and religion within a given nation-state.

Peter Burke's essay shows how the language of classical teratology resurfaces in the metaphorical name-calling of inter-European stereotypes and rivalries. In the early seventeenth century, the monstrous races are not so much rationalized as appropriated for political uses, defining European selves and national character. Burke traces in particular how the monstrous races and the language of national character converge as Europeans label other Europeans as various kinds of animals. Monsters mark not only the boundaries of the unknown, but also the boundaries between European selves and nations. Political use of monstrous difference—aligning other Europeans with the bestial and nonhuman—shows the reappropriation rather than the rationalization or gradual discarding, of the language of the monstrous.

Focusing on two published accounts of monstrous births in 1640s England, David Cressy explores the trope of monstrosity and the deployment of classical monsters in response to the religious, social, and political tensions of the English civil war. The two tracts—recounting the birth of headless babies to a popish recusant and to a dissenting radical—show the monstrous results of female resistance to authority in home, Church, and state: in each case, disregard of the proper boundaries leads to a headless baby, linked with the general upheaval in the (about to become) headless body politic. Here, "true and faithful" relations attested by witnesses recount the most marvelous of events, drawing on a tradition of teratology while at the same time responding to immediate circumstances in the particular local environments. Cressy's essay shows the importance of print and representation in uses of monstrous bodies as propaganda against gender disorder, religious extremism (whether papist or Puritan), and unwise speaking in a time of political upheaval and change.

While this first set of essays brings to the scholarly fore new, politicized, and intra-European uses of the monstrous races long recognized as one important strand of the monstrous in defining outer European boundaries, the two essays following look at reuses of another traditional theme—the monster as omen or divine portent. Part 2, "Apocalypticism, Bestiality, and Monstrous Polemics," explores uses of the monster as portent in the midst of political and religious controversy and crisis. While Park and Daston do point to the crises of Reformation Germany as invigorating interest in the monstrous, less attention has been given to monstrous polemic and religious conflict than to scientific, literary, and imaginative uses, and indeed biblical figures of the monstrous seem to have escaped notice almost altogether.[51] These two essays, however, look at intertwined political and religious appropriations of monstrous bodies to read apocalyptic significance into historical time and events. From early Reformation polemic in Germany to the later political and religious debates in seventeenth-century England and the United Provinces, bestial, monstrous, and feminine bodies are the sites of struggle and resistance, of apocalyptic hopes and warnings.

In the first essay, R. Po-chia Hsia traces Protestant-Catholic uses of monstrous births in sixteenth-century Germany, noting how the eschatological stress of the Reformers differed from Catholic confessional polemics that employed the monstrous to evoke repugnance of heresy. Both Luther and his adversaries take up the language of the monstrous to depict the body of Christendom torn asunder. Tracing monstrous propaganda from Sebastian Brant on the 1495 birth of conjoined twins in Worms, through various Protestant and Catholic uses of the papal Ass of Rome, the monk-calf of Saxony, and other monstrous births, Hsia explores how the language of monstrosity becomes part of a struggle for power and legitimacy in Reformation Germany. In this context, Hsia argues, the language of the monstrous first multiplies and then ultimately becomes depleted of meaning, replaced by a new language of discipline and sin.

Laura Knoppers then shows how the binaries of the apocalyptic monstrous become fragmented and contested in the turmoil of mid-seventeenth-century English politics. The tradition of the apocalyptic monstrous, drawn from the Book of Revelation and part of the visual and verbal legacy of the Reformation, is variously appropriated to support—or violently attack—the controversial figure of Oliver Cromwell. From the Fifth Monarchist attack on Cromwell as "the Antichrist, the Babilon, the great dragon," to Andrew Marvell's counter-image of an "Angelique *Cromwell* who outwings the wind," to a Dutch Catholic representation of "Crom-ghewelt" ("Crooked Violence") as crooked Beast and Whore, to a late engraving that shows Cromwell in heroic state, standing upon the bodies of the transgressive woman and her serpentine counterpart, seventeenth-century texts deploy and fiercely contest the meaning of the apocalyptic monstrous. While usually associated with the grotesque, aberrant, or deformed, the most dangerous monstrosity turns out to be that which cannot be seen: these polemical texts charge that the heroism of Oliver Cromwell is as false and deceptive as the beauty of the Whore of Babylon.

While the monster as portent has been a recognized phenomenon since the time of Cicero, and was given a Christian providentialist cast by Augustine, Hsia's and Knoppers's essays trace particular instances of monstrous polemic related to religious schism and political change. Monstrous births signal the rupture of the body of Christendom, while grotesque bodies reflect deformities of the body politic. These authors—as with Burke and Cressy preceding—trace conversations and practices that transcend national boundaries, although they may be used to shape nationhood. Hence, the classical monstrous races are redeployed in and against various European nations, while apocalyptic discourse and biblical figures also cross national boundaries.

The essays in Part 3, "Medical Knowledge, Grotesque Anatomies, and the Body Politic," likewise treat knowledge and practices deployed in and by a number of nations: science, medicine, and anatomy. They explore the place of the monstrous in the production of medical knowledge and the extension of that knowledge from anatomical abnormality to aberration in the body politic. Both essays boldly revise our understanding of the scientific and medical: whether to show the merged boundaries of the natural and the supernatural that marked early modern medicine, or to show the rhetorical resonance of anatomical practice among contending parties in revolutionary France. Both essays also show how appropriations of the body in medicine and anatomy destabilized the very domain they were meant to secure. Linked with monstrosity, the body is seen through its malformations, through its excessive sexual functions. Figured this way, the body is always marked by a monstrous excess that cannot be contained in the rationalizing gestures of early modern science and medicine.

Marie-Hélène Huet complicates the trajectory of secularization and medicalization by showing how medicine itself is closely aligned with the monstrous. The Renaissance art of identifying and curing diseases straddled the normal boundaries of the natural and the supernatural; the physician did not simply make empirical observations, but was a reader of signs, and the source of the physician's knowledge was seen as in part divine. Indeed, Huet argues, the origins of disease and of the monstrous overlap. If monsters were subjected to the medical gaze, that gaze partook of the natural and divine and was both a physics and a metaphysics. Although medical science slowly divested itself of religious belief, refocusing on the human body and integrating monstrous births into its empirical knowledge of the body, that process of divestiture was more uneven and complex than has been recognized.

In the essay following, Joan B. Landes investigates another dimension of medical and veterinary science. She explores how anatomical routines—dealing with the body, corporeality, corpses, and death—figure in revolutionary polemics, whether to dissect the corrupt body politic of old regime France or to arouse revulsion and horror against the deeds of republicans. While Gillray's satiric images metaphorically anatomize the revolution, dissecting its monstrous appetites, prints from the Terror demonstrate the monstrous utility of the body part and dismemberment in both revolutionary and counterrevolutionary consciousness. Against this background, Landes considers the anatomist Honoré Fragonard's series of lifesize écorchés, composed from preserved human and animal cadavers, as objects situated on the borders between idealized and grotesque expression, medical science and voyeuristic display.

While Huet and Landes ultimately evoke a tradition of the monstrous as natural phenomenon stretching back to Aristotle, they—like our earlier contributors—show both the instability and the revolutionary potential of the monstrous body in the early modern period. Visuality and the grotesque come to the fore in Landes's essay, while interpretations of the body as sign mark Huet's. Landes's interest in the French Revolution and the language of the monstrous recalls both the English Revolution explored earlier by Cressy and the deformed English body politic as treated by Knoppers. Landes's essay also adds to our volume's ongoing interest in the monster as a visual phenomenon. From the illustrated *Völkertafel* examined by Burke to the crude woodcuts of headless babies in Cressy's study, to the graphic images of Pope-Ass, monk-calf, and other monstrous births in Hsia's account, to Knoppers's interest in the many iterations of the Whore of Babylon, visuality can be seen as a central component in constructing the early modern monstrous. Both Landes and Huet return, furthermore, to issues of gender: Marie Antoinette as particularly the object of revulsion and female sexuality fixed under the medical gaze.[52] As such, their commentary intersects with Cressy's concern with female resistance to authority in the home and Church and Knoppers's exploration of the beautiful but dangerous Whore of Babylon and the cross-dressed Oliver Cromwell of polemical print.

The final interpretive essays in our volume, while referencing the nation, Catholic-Protestant polemics, and the dangers of science that are central to the earlier essays, also move into literary texts and questions of figuration and representation. The contributors to Part 4, "Displacing Monsters: Sign, Allegory, and Myth," foreground issues of representation, tracing how the forms of texts themselves and the rhetorical figures that they employ are shaped by ideas of the monstrous. In particular, each essay points to the importance of the monstrous as a site through which new possibilities of representation are opened up: whether in the early Renaissance, as traditional allegorical ways of seeing begin to break down, or in the period of Enlightenment, as the epistemological assumptions of modernity challenge the grounding of both monstrosity and myth.

Timothy Hampton focuses on the tension between analogy and allegory in the representation of monsters in sixteenth-century French literature. Hampton begins with Pierre Boaistuau's use of the Ravenna monster, then moves to Aristotle's theory of generation of animals, to consider the implications of the convergence of allegory and similitude by which the monstrous comes to reflect a larger meaning. Turning to Rabelais, Hampton shows how the rhetorical slippage from similitude to descriptive identity in depictions of the monstrous in the *Quart livre* of the adventures of Pantagruel has broader implications for the political and religious struggles in sixteenth-century France. While Boaistuau uses simile to stabilize, Rabelais uses it to unsettle meaning, to represent the familiar as something unfamiliar. For Rabelais, any attempt to ascribe fixed meaning to the monstrous Other runs the risk of misprision that may degenerate into calumny (John Calvin's attack on Lent and on Rabelais himself as a monster) or violence (Pantagruel's encounter with the sausages, who mistake him for their enemy). Montaigne, in turn, retreats from political allegory in his reading of the monstrous, perhaps aware of the dangers of attempts to establish definitive meaning.

In turn, David Armitage argues that modernity's earliest and most enduring myth of monstrosity, Mary Shelley's *Frankenstein, or The Modern Prometheus* (1818), was, in part, a lineal descendant of early modern mythography. Armitage begins with a traditional trajectory and view of science and medicine: by the late eighteenth century, monsters seem to be both dissected and discarded, part of pathology and embryology. Mythology follows a similar trajectory. Yet, in contrast to the less successful attempts of her contemporaries, John Polidori and William Hazlitt, Mary Shelley employs an eclectic and syncretic use of myth to create a powerful figure of the modern monstrous. Shelley's monster is identifiably modern in its debt to the Scientific Revolution and Enlightenment, but equally early modern in its debt to Renaissance mythography; therein, Armitage suggests, lies Frankenstein's lasting appeal as a myth at once novel and renovated.

Both Hampton and Armitage treat canonical literary authors and texts: Rabelais' *Quart Livre* and Mary Shelley's *Frankenstein.* But while Bakhtin's influential reading of the grotesque has dominated discussions of Rabelais and the monstrous,[53] and nineteenth-century science has been a recurrent topic in criticism of *Frankenstein,*[54] both essays in Part 4 come up with a new set of questions, reminding us that monstrosity remains an open-ended topic. Hampton focuses not on the grotesque body but on figuration of the monstrous, the slippage from simile to identity, while Armitage takes us back to myth, but also looks ahead to a modernity in which the monstrous finds an equivocal place.

As the essays in this volume attest, then, the uses of monstrous in the early modern period were rich and various. In particular, the deformed and grotesque body—whether drawn from the monstrous races of classical teratology, appropriated from medical science and such practices as anatomy, posited in empirical accounts of alleged portents or monstrous births, or engendered in political polemic in time of revolution—was inscribed with political, religious, moral, and cultural meanings, long after its alleged rationalization and secularization. The monstrous Other served to define (European, white, male, Christian) selves and nations. But that Other both marked and violated boundaries, threatening the very identities it served to define.

The strange creature from *Emblema Vivente* points to the multifaceted and highly contested uses of monstrous bodies to depict (variously defined) political monstrosities in the early modern period. The tract recounts a rich tale of an emblematic monster, whose cross under a crescent moon both shows the Turks and warns them of their imminent destruction by Christian forces. The creature's story is one of many, told with differing degrees of credulity and skepticism and used for diverse rhetorical, literary, and polemical purposes. But it underscores, finally, that the monstrous cannot be contained.

In the narrative of *Emblema Vivente,* the Anatolian monster quite literally escapes confinement. To hide from his people the dire prediction of doom, the sultan orders that the monster be taken to the highest cliffs of the Black Sea and thrown, still inside its cage, to death in the waters below. Yet the creature manages to escape, climbing out of the cage, which has caught upon a cliffside rather than falling into the sea and which the Turks foolishly break open by pelting it with rocks. Having left the creature behind for dead, the Turks suddenly find it behind them, raging ("furiosas"). Far from contained, caged, or destroyed, the monster tears apart terrified horses and Spahis; fiercely attacks the three hundred heavily armed Janissaries sent to destroy it; and—even in dying—fatally wounds many others, whose rapidly rotting bodies spread a great pestilence.

Nor is the meaning of the monster, ultimately, deciphered for the reader of *Emblema Vivente.* As we have seen, the labile, shifting comparisons defy attempts to pin down meaning. Is the creature man, woman, or beast? Like a bird or quadruped? Hero or villain of its own romance-like story? Even the meaning of the portentous cross is unstable, moving from a seemingly certain prophecy of doom—"Providence has given this calamity to our age"[55]—to qualification and the potential for change: "But God is great, full of mercy and compassion; let us seek, my Lord, his mercy."[56]

Far from definitively categorizing, labeling, or deciphering the monster, *Emblema Vivente* recounts a series of failures of explanation, failures of containment. The tract thus reminds us that the struggle to shape and control the meaning and identity of the monstrous moves well beyond questions of (shifting) scientific investigation. Our contributors here show—in a rich array of texts and contexts—the multiplicity of political and rhetorical uses of monstrous bodies in early modern Europe. Constructed in political, religious, rhetorical, medical, and scientific contexts, the monsters move beyond their original homes and refuse—albeit not with the fury of the Anatolian monster—to stay in their intended places, to acquiesce in their projected purposes. Marking and violating boundaries, shifting territories, appearing and reappearing in polemic, the monsters explored in these essays refuse to be contained. As such, they provide a rich source of material for our interdisciplinary approach to the fraught and compelling politics, religion, and culture of early modern Europe.

PART I

MONSTROUS RACES, BOUNDARIES, AND NATIONHOOD

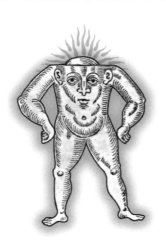

1

FRONTIERS OF THE MONSTROUS

Perceiving National Characters in Early Modern Europe

PETER BURKE

Monsters were and are often represented as combining elements from different normal bodies, whether animal or human. The fabulous griffin, for example, combined a lion with an eagle. In similar fashion this essay, located on the border of teratology, will link two themes in cultural history that have normally been considered apart.

The first theme is that of so-called "monstrous races," headless, dog-headed, one-legged, and so on, located at the edge between the human and the nonhuman, just as they were located at the edge of the world—that is, the world known to the writers. The second theme is that of early modern discussions of national character, a debate that grew out of a much older tradition of European stereotypes of Europeans. There is a tension between the two themes that I hope will be productive.

The two points to be emphasized at the start are complementary opposites. On the one side, the so-called "monstrous races" are best seen not as pure fantasies but rather as distorted and stereotyped perceptions of people—or sometimes of simians—from other regions and other cultures (Asians, Africans, and later Americans). Bernadette Bucher has noted the transformation of a printed description of an American people with "shoulders so high that the face seems to be in the chest" into literal Blemmyae.[1] The point applies not only to the more picturesque Blemmyae, Cynocephali, and Sciapods but also to amazons, androgyni, anthropophagi, giants (viewed as monstrously big), pygmies (viewed as monstrously small), troglodytes, and wild men or what Pliny described as the "people with tails," *homines caudati*.[2]

To make this point is not to deny that monsters may have been good to think with in other ways, as David Williams, for example, has suggested in his *Deformed Discourse*.[3] Take the case of the wild man or "woodwose," a recurrent figure in the Nuremberg Carnival in the fifteenth century. In this carnival context the woodwose may be interpreted as a symbol of the prohibited desires that were allowed expression at a time of license, in other words an image of what we have come to call the Id. What I want to suggest here, on the other hand, is that—however they originated in the collective imagination and whatever their other uses—some monsters came to be employed to mark the frontiers between self and Other, including national selves. They represent stereotyped perceptions of other cultures.

For—and this is the second point which will be emphasized in what follows—European stereotypes of other Europeans often contained a monstrous element. Like the inhabitants of other continents, these foreigners were frequently perceived as misshapen, absurdly skinny, or comically fat, just as they were described as "bestial" or "brutish." In the mild form of the stereotype, "they" were not proper people because they did not know how to behave. In the extreme form of the stereotype, they were completely dehumanized and identified with animals.

What follows then are some reflections on what has been called "ethno-anthropology" or "ethno-ethnology," or alternatively a study in "heterology" or "xenology," not to say xenophobia.[4] They will not neglect context but the emphasis, as is both inevitable and appropriate in an overview, will fall on cultural traditions rather than the situations in which they were reemployed (discussed, for example, in the case study by David Cressy, below). These reflections on texts and images are divided into two parts, concerned respectively with monstrous races and with national characters in Europe. A brief coda will attempt to view these European phenomena from a global perspective.

MONSTROUS RACES

To begin with "Monstrous Bodies." Beliefs in monstrous races can be found in a number of cultures. In the West, these beliefs can be documented from ancient Greek times, proceeding through Herodotus and Pliny, to Marco Polo and "Mandeville" via Augustine and Isidore of Seville, and continuing into the Renaissance (when the humanist Aeneas Sylvius Piccolomini, Pope Pius II, described the Scythians as descendants of a monster who was half woman and half snake).[5] Climate was thought to explain this variety of physical types and customs. Since Africa had an extreme climate, anthropophagi, troglodytes, and pygmies, for instance, were located there.

These beliefs or stereotypes survived into early modern times. They formed part of a larger system of stereotypes of the not quite human—werewolves, for example, witches (who turn into cats), or the Jews (associated, ironically enough, with the pigs they consider unclean).[6] Protestants, in the eyes of Catholics, were monkeys, as a sixteenth-century French painting of iconoclastic Huguenots testifies.[7] Jesuits were associated in the eyes of Protestants with swine, dogs, foxes, wolves, with spiders weaving webs, "dangerous flies," and with locusts or "Egyptian grasshoppers."[8]

Class prejudice as well as religious or ethnic prejudice was expressed in the language of monstrous bodies. Peasants, for instance, were perceived by townspeople as little removed from the animals they looked after.[9] King Henry VIII's response to the rebellion known as the Pilgrimage of Grace was to describe the common people of Lincolnshire as "one of the most brute and beastly of the whole realm."[10] Miners were perceived by outsiders as dwarves, pygmies or "gnomes" (a term recorded in English in the early 18th century). The use of "animal categories in verbal abuse," to quote the famous article by

Edmund Leach, was widespread at this time.[11] The animals who recur most often are the pig, the dog, the ape or monkey, the fox, and the wolf.

Despite many continuities with the Middle Ages, some changes are also visible in early modern times. In the first place was the well-known displacement of these stereotypes westwards and the relocation of the Plinian races in the New World. Columbus mentioned the Cynocephali whom he failed to see in the Antilles, the Cyclops whom he heard about, and the *homines caudati* of Cuba where "everyone is born with a tail." Sir Walter Raleigh searched for the Blemmyae in Guyana, and a member of his expedition inscribed them on a map of the region. Giants were sighted in Patagonia, Amazons on the Amazon, and androgynes among the Timucua. Images of the wild man and woman appear in the 1505 edition of Vespucci. Relocation was associated with more gradual changes in the language used to describe exotic others, notably the terms "cannibals," "savages," and "barbarians."[12]

For example, ancient anthropophagi turned into modern cannibals.[13] Eating people, especially babies, had long been a symbol of being less than human, associated with heretics and witches in particular and vividly illustrated in a Nuremberg Carnival image of a pig-headed man with an infant whom he is apparently about to devour.[14] Dog-headed cannibals were described and illustrated in the *Carta Marina* (1525) of Lorenz Fries. But there was a shift to a vision of cannibals such as the Tupinambá of Brazil, who were fearsome but human.

In similar fashion there was a shift from the concept of the wild man to that of the savage. In the Middle Ages, the woodwose, the wild man or woman (German *holzwib*), haunted the collective imagination.[15] This figure wears a coat of skins and leaves and often carries a club. He or she is sometimes represented with a tail, sometimes with a captive boy tied to a branch, as if to eat.[16] The wild man is located in the woods (the *selva*), hence known in Italian as the *uomo selvatico,* in Spanish as the *salvaje,* and hence the term "savage," which emerged in English around the year 1600.

An early example of the term, from William Camden's *Remains concerning Britain* (1605), is "a savage of America." Like cannibals, savages gradually became more human. They were sometimes viewed as irrational, sometimes as childlike, sometimes as lacking "civilization" (or in Montaigne's case, as lacking "our" civilization). The debate on the origins of the American Indians (Chinese, Jews, Carthaginians, Norwegians and so on) reminds us that—despite regular recourse to animal categories by colonists—they were regarded as human by European scholars.[17]

Like "savage," the term "barbarian" shifted its meaning, while continuing to imply cultural inferiority to the speaker. Barbarians were traditionally believed to be irrational, incapable of speech, making unintelligible sounds. In ancient Greek the *barbaroi* went "bababa," and in the Middle Ages they spoke "gabble" or "gibberish." Like Spenser's wild man in the *Faerie Queene,* the barbarian was supposed to lack speech and make "a soft murmur and confused sound / Of senseless words" (Book 6, Canto 4, lines 11–14).

In the ordinary language of early modern Europe, the concepts of monster, wild man, savage, and barbarian shaded into one another. However, in the work of two sixteenth-century Spanish clerics with direct experience of the New World, Bartolomé de Las Casas and José de Acosta, we find something more subtle.

Las Casas attempted to use the term "barbarian" in a more neutral way. In one sense of the term, according to him, the Amerindians were barbarians because they lacked writing. In another sense, "all the peoples of the world are men." In some ways, the Spaniards were more barbarous than the Indians because of the "cruel acts" they had carried out in the New World, a point that Montaigne would develop in one of his most famous essays.

For his part, Acosta refined the binary opposition between barbarous and civilized by distinguishing three kinds or degrees of barbarian. In the first place, those who are pagan but in other ways civilized, like the Chinese. Secondly, those who lack writing but live in organized states, among whom Acosta included the Mexicans and Peruvians. At the bottom of the ladder came those who lack any form of social organization, such as the Brazilians.[18] The example of Acosta reminds us that some people drew careful distinctions between the different categories of "Other." Another example is that of the

English antiquary John Aubrey, who adopted a comparative method in his researches and described the ancient Britons as "two or three degrees, I suppose, less savage than the Americans."[19]

However, the most important change in the conceptual system came with the development of zoology. There was a gradual shift from the idea of monstrous races to the idea of the races of the globe, once again differing in form because they live in different climates. The French physician, traveler, and philosopher François Bernier made what was apparently the first systematic attempt at classification in 1684, with his fourfold division into European, African, Asian, and Lapps.[20] In his *System of Nature* (1735), Linnaeus presented four domesticated species of human being, the *Europaeus albus,* governed by law; the *Americanus rubescus,* governed by custom; *the Asiaticus luridus,* governed by opinion; and the *Afer niger,* governed by masters. Buffon's *Histoire naturelle* (1779–89) made a sixfold division between Lapps, Tartars, South Asians, Europeans, Ethiopians, and Americans.

All the same, the survival of the idea of monstrous races in scientific circles should be noted. There was a quest for troglodytes, for example, for humans with tails, for pygmies, for the wild man. The wild man appeared to have been found at last in Borneo (another displacement to a newly explored region), in the form of the figure known locally as the "man of the woods," *orang-utan,* the equivalent in Far Eastern ethno-ethnology of the western woodwose. In other words, two stereotypes fused, one of them local and the other foreign.[21] Although Edward Tyson argued in 1699 that this *homo sylvestris* was a monkey, Linnaeus still found a place in his *System of Nature* for the *homo ferus* (four-footed, mute, and hairy), just as he found a place for the *homo monstruosus,* represented by Patagonian giants and Hottentot pygmies.[22] The debate would continue.

NATIONAL CHARACTER

Eighteenth-century discussions of national character reveal a similar approach to physical or cultural difference. These discussions developed out of a long tradition. The ancient Greeks had compared and contrasted the mores of different peoples, as in the case of Herodotus on the Greeks, Egyptians, Persians, and Scythians. Once again, climate was invoked to provide explanations of difference. In Europe, the rise of pejorative stereotypes has been linked to what has been called "the era of Latin Christendom's self-discovery in the late eleventh and twelfth centuries."[23]

For example, the French claimed that the English, like the wild men, have tails (and the English made the same point about the Cornish).[24] The Poles called the Germans the *Niemcy,* in other words, the people who do not speak: the equivalent of the ancient Greek *barbaroi.* The Italians were especially prone to call foreigners "barbarians," especially the French invaders from 1494 onwards, witness Julius II's famous cry, "Barbarians Out!" (*fuori i barbari*).[25] The habit spread. The French scholar Étienne Pasquier attacked the Italian historians who called the French "barbarians," but he himself called the Germans by the same name.[26] Eastern Europeans were particularly likely to be described as barbarians by travelers from regions to the west of them and to be viewed as descendants of the Scythians or the Huns.[27]

So, although the phrase "national character" was something of a novelty in the eighteenth century, the idea is much older. Around 1500, the Italian humanist Giovanni Pontano wrote about the customs of different nations, "de moribus nationum." In England, John Florio's verdict was that "the Carthaginians are false and deceivers . . . the Persians are gluttonous and drunkards, the Spaniards . . . disdainful and despisers, the Italians, proud and revengers . . . the Briton [Englishman] a busybody, the Irishman, wild."[28] Jean Bodin offers a good example of the Renaissance revival and adaptation of ancient Greek climate theory and the links between climate, physical types, and customs. According to Bodin, Europeans could be divided into two types associated with the Mediterranean and the Baltic: "The Mediterranean peoples . . . are cold, dry, hard, bald, swarthy, small in body, crisp of hair, black-eyed and clear-voiced. The Baltic peoples, on the other hand, are warm, wet, hairy, robust, white, large-bodied, soft-fleshed, with scanty beards, bluish gray eyes, and deep voices."[29]

At a time when the two peoples were frequently at war, contrasts between the manners of the French and the Spaniards were particularly common. "Such is the slowness in their speech, motion, walk and all actions," wrote Bodin of the Spaniards, "that they seem to languish from inertia. The French, on the other hand, do things so rapidly that they have finished the matter before the Spanish can begin planning."[30] Carlos Garcia wrote a whole book about the *contrariedades* between the customs of the two nations.[31] Formulaic descriptions such as the "courteous Frenchman," the "benevolent German," the "civil Italian," the "contemptuous Spaniard," and the "haughty Englishman," were in general circulation.[32]

Contrasts of this kind, as well as between individuals, formed part of the study of physiognomy, which was not limited to faces but examined other signs of character from ways of speaking to ways of walking. In the "digression concerning physiognomy" in his *Discourse on Medals* (1697), the English virtuoso John Evelyn had much to say about the "manner of nations." "The Polander," for example, "is very imperious, haughty, unquiet, liberal, superstitious." The Hungarian, "bellicose, brave, impatient of restraint." The Spaniards, "proud, ostentous, formal, affecting gravity, slow, deliberate, patient, constant, valiant, loyal, but extremely bigottish and superstitious, which renders them cruel." The Italian, "naturally cautious, prudent and frugal, temperate, polite, of an acute refined wit, amorous, jealous and vindictive of injuries." The French, "versatile, inconstant, loud; lovers of noise, ceremonious, prompt, confident . . . elated with the least success and as soon dejected upon the first repulse."[33]

In the eighteenth century, national character became an object of explicit debate, with rival explanations in terms of "physical causes" such as climate and "moral causes" (or, as we might say, "culture"). Montesquieu emphasized climate, while David Hume was more of a culturalist. Hume defined "national character" as "a peculiar set of manners," taking as an example the proposition that "the common people in Switzerland have probably more honesty than those of the same rank in Ireland." Hume argued for the importance of "moral causes" to explain such differences on the grounds that manners change over time.[34]

In this context it may be illuminating to consider a remarkable visual testimony from this period (figure 2). It is known as the *Völkertafel*, it comes from Styria (Steiermark), in the early eighteenth century, and it is now to be seen in the Museum für Volkskunde in Vienna, while copies or similar paintings and one print are to be found elsewhere in Austria. This comparative ethnography of Europe deserves a fuller analysis than is possible here. Ten nations are represented: Spanish, French, Italian, German, English, Swedish, Polish, Hungarian, Russian, and "Turkish or Greek" (the conflation of the last two nations and the absence of the Dutch should be noted). Comments on these ten nations are organized under no fewer than seventeen categories (morals, minds, costumes, illnesses, religions, excesses, pastimes and so on). This kind of classification has parallels elsewhere—a certain Zahn employed eighteen categories in his "Mirrors" of 1696 to describe the Germans, Spaniards, Italians, French, and English—but its visual expression is unusual, if not unique.[35]

Whether the *Völkertafel* really belongs in a museum of folklore may be doubted. Is it really an example of popular culture? On the one hand, the terminology is popular rather than scientific, with phrases such as "windbags" or "fickle as April weather." On the other, the layout resembles that of the "tables" which were coming into fashion in European bureaucracies in the eighteenth century, with neat columns and rows like soldiers drawn up on parade. Without knowing who made the "Table" or where it was originally displayed, it is difficult to know whether we should treat it as a joke or a parody, or take it seriously as an ethno-ethnography, elaborating popular traditions.[36]

XENOPHOBIA AND DEHUMANIZATION

John Evelyn compared the manners of nations to "the ferity and other qualities of those brute animals naturally bred among them."[37] The *Völkertafel* de-

Figure 2. *Völkertafel* (early eighteenth century). Courtesy of Österreichisches Museum für Volkskunde, Vienna.

votes one of its rows to animal comparisons. The Spaniards are compared to elephants, the French to foxes, the Italians to lynxes, the Germans to lions, the English to horses, the Swiss to oxen, the Poles to bears, the Hungarians to wolves, the Muscovites to donkeys, and the Turks to cats. It is time to turn to what might be described as "Political Monstrosities." According to Gibbon, Europe in his day was "one great republic whose various inhabitants have attained almost the same level of politeness and cultivation." But they did not always see one another in this way. There was no lack of pejorative stereotypes, in other words xenophobia. A Scottish visitor to England declared in

1763 that the English "will express their antipathy in such terms as these, a chattering French baboon, an Italian ape, a beastly Dutchman and a German hog."[38]

In the seventeenth century, in a context of war and economic rivalry, the English described the Dutch as herrings, sharks, frogs, and even maggots, while a broadside of 1691 showed *The Dutch Boare Dissected or a Description of Hogland*.[39] The Russian bear (replacing the Polish bear of the *Völkertafel*) was to be found in English prints from the 1730s onwards.[40] At the time of Cromwell's invasion of Ireland, some soldiers testified to seeing Irishmen with tails, and comparisons were made between Ireland and Borneo.[41]

The old idea that it was the English who had tails was still very much alive. In the early sixteenth century, the Scottish poet George Dundas alluded to this in a dispute with his English colleague John Skelton: "Anglicus a tergo / Caudam gerit / Est canis ergo." A little later, the writer John Bale complained that an Englishman could not travel abroad without it being "most contumeliously thrown in his face that all Englishmen have tails."[42] The poets Saint-Amant and Vondel in France and in the Dutch Republic also referred to the tails of the English, and a dragon's tail was shown in a Dutch cartoon of Oliver Cromwell (figure 3).[43]

One of the contexts into which these images should be placed is that of political, economic, or cultural hegemony, leading to a double reaction of xenophilia and xenophobia, as in the case of the Americanophilia and Americanophobia of the last century or so.[44] There were, of course, successive hegemonies in early modern Europe, notably those of Italy, Spain, the Dutch Republic, France, and England.[45]

The Italians, for example, were viewed as monsters because of their propensity to poison their enemies, a favorite theme in French and English literature and drama. They were accused of "bestiality," of using their women according to the "Italian manner," just as they were accused of effeminacy (linking them to the classical idea of the hermaphrodite as a type of monster).[46] The Italianate foreigner was regarded as an "ape," as in William Rankin's sixteenth century satire, *The English Ape*. The ape was a symbol of

DEN AFGRYSSELIKKEN START-MAN:
Gepaſt op den teegen woordijgen STAAT van ENGELANDT.

Figure 3. Dutch cartoon of Oliver Cromwell as horrible tail-man (1658). © Copyright
The British Museum.

mindless imitation, but the comparison may have other associations as well. It
is tempting to draw on the ideas of Mary Douglas to make the point that the
Italianate Englishman, for instance, was perceived as monstrous because he
was on the margin of two cultures, neither a real Englishman nor a real Italian, just as he was on the margin of two genders, an effeminate male.

In similar fashion, in their age of hegemony, the Spaniards were described
not only as "a proud, deceitful, cruel and treacherous nation" but as "inhuman." They were leeches "sucking the blood of the European Christians."[47]

36

Again, eighteenth century English prints show the French as foxes.[48] A German visitor in 1770 noted the English expressions "French bitch, son of a bitch or French dog."[49] The French were also viewed as frogs and as monkeys. A reference to a "chattering French baboon" has already been quoted. During the Napoleonic wars, English prints represented "the Monkey Race in danger," or a monkey in a revolutionary cap bearing the banner of atheism, or monkeys welcoming back Napoleon in 1815.[50]

BEYOND EARLY MODERN EUROPE

To sum up. By juxtaposing two kinds of image, this essay has attempted to show that monsters were good to think with in early modern Europe and in particular that they offered a means for people to define their identities and to confront cultural differences at a time when knowledge of these differences was becoming more widespread thanks to the spread of printing in general and printed maps and newspapers in particular. However, the views they encouraged were stereotyped and generally hostile to the Other, an obstacle rather than a means to international understanding.

Europeans were not of course unique in seeing others in monstrous terms. The Chinese, for instance, had their own version of the Plinian races, including the Blemmyae, illustrated in a printed book of 1667, Wu Jen-ch'en, *Shan-hai-ching kuang-chu* (The Book of Mountains and Seas, with Annotations). The Japanese of the Tokugawa era called Europeans "Southern barbarians" and sometimes described them as subhuman. Their slogan *joi* corresponds to the Italian *fuori i barbari*.[51] Japanese screen-paintings and other images of the Portuguese and later the Dutch show them as monstrously bloated in their western doublets and hose.

The "monstrous tradition," as we may call it, survived into nineteenth- and twentieth-century Europe, although a greater emphasis than before was now placed on the contrasts between the inhabitants of the different continents, an emphasis sometimes described as "race-thinking."[52] Taine's attempt to explain human history through the three factors of race, milieu, and mo-

THE IRISH FRANKENSTEIN.

Figure 4. John Tenniel, "The Irish Frankenstein or the Celtic Caliban." *The Tomahawk,* 18 December 1869.

ment was typical of its time, like Gobineau's stress on the inequality of races and the place of interbreeding in the decline of civilization. The terms "half-breed," "half-caste," or "mongrel" were all pejorative. Only in some parts of the Americas in the early twentieth century were *mestizos* and mulattoes viewed in a positive light.

Despite these changes, the continuities remain striking. The debate about the existence of a tailed tribe in Africa known as the Niam-Niam is a celebrated example of such continuities.[53] In the political context of the Irish struggle for independence by violence if necessary, images of the Irish as simians (like the French before them) or even as monsters appeared in the English press. A new situation led to the reactivation of a traditional image, or to variations on a traditional theme. John Tenniel's cartoon of "The Irish Frankenstein or the Celtic Caliban" (figure 4), which appeared in *The Tomahawk* in 1869, is the most notorious of these images. The reference to Frankenstein was particularly appropriate in the sense of implying that the English had played a part in the creation of the monster they now feared.[54]

More recently, when Harold Wilson was the British prime minister and was in dispute with Swiss banks, he made a reference in public to the "gnomes of Zürich," one more reminder of the political contexts in which stereotypes are either forged or reactivated. Even today, the monstrous races are far from extinct: they have simply been relocated yet again, this time in outer space and in the future.[55] Just as science fiction draws, consciously or unconsciously, on the tradition of the medieval romance, so it offers variations on the Plinian stereotypes and puts them to new uses in its images of "aliens."

2

LAMENTABLE, STRANGE, AND WONDERFUL

Headless Monsters in the English Revolution

DAVID CRESSY

Consideration of things lamentable, strange, and wonderful allows us to examine circumstances once thought extraordinary, and to anatomize phenomena that historical figures judged alarming, providential, or prodigious. It opens a way of sensing a past society's raw nerves. Accounts of monstrous births, in particular, lead us through family stories and community narratives into histories of sexual and religious deviance, on to the partisan and ideological concerns of the popular press. Demanding attention to language as well as physiology, to religion, morality, and medicine, monsters are good to think with. The trope of monstrosity is a much-traveled territory, with intercultural as well as interdisciplinary dimensions.

Even as recently as the autumn of 2000, it was hard to avoid the media attention given to the Maltese twins, the poor conjoined creatures Mary and Jody, in which the word "monster" was scrupulously avoided. Perhaps science is now the monster, making possible separations that were hitherto unthinkable. Bringing together expertise and opinion from medicine, the Church, and the law, and provoking a widespread popular debate about technology, ethics, and "the will of God," the Maltese twins episode may reveal as much about our own anxieties as did the discourse on monstrosity in the sixteenth and seventeenth centuries. Graphic and exploitative renderings of the twins in the popular tabloids look remarkably like some broadsheets of the 1560s, though the question today is what to do about the malformed creature rather that why the birth happened or what it might portend.[1]

My purpose here is to explore some of the problematic connotations of monstrosity within the conflicted religious culture of early modern England. I take as my primary point of entry two published accounts of monstrous births from the 1640s. By focusing on these printed reports, with their religious glosses and grotesque illustrations, I hope not only to illuminate the trope of monstrosity but also to shed fresh light on religious and cultural anxieties in the era of the English civil war. There are, then, two projects, inevitably entwined, rather like some of the dicephalous twins that feature in the literature. But rather than dwelling on many-headed monsters, like Christopher Hill's Hydra of revolution,[2] or the more common kind that sported just two, my discussion will deal with malformed human creatures whose most horrific feature was their lack of any head at all.

The first publication (figure 5) is titled *A Strange and Lamentable Accident that happened lately at Mears Ashby in Northamptonshire. 1642. Of one Mary Wilmore, wife to John Wilmore rough Mason, who was delivered of a Childe without a head, and credibly reported to have a firme Crosse on the brest, as this ensuing Story shall relate.* The second (figure 6), published four years later, is *A Declaration, of a strange and Wonderfull Monster: Born in Kirkham Parish in Lancashire (the Child of Mrs. Houghton, a Popish Gentlewoman) the face of it upon the breast, and without a head (after the mother had wished rather to bear a Childe without a head than a Roundhead) and had curst the Parliament.* The pamphlets follow the familiar 1640s format with an illustrated title page and five pages of text, and each was published in London. The Mears Ashby pamphlet, as I shall call it, was printed for Richard Harper and Thomas Wine, to be sold at the Bible and Harp in Smithfield. The Kirkham production was printed by Jane Coe, widow and successor of Andrew Coe, a prolific pro-Parliamentarian printer of the mid-1640s. A rare reference to them in the secondary literature is in Jerome Friedman's book on the pulp press in the En-

A
STRANGE
And Lamentable accident that happened lately at
Mearſ. Aſhby in Northamptonſhire. 1642.

Of one *Mary Wilmore*, wife to *Iohn Wilmore* rough M ſon, who was
deliver:d of a Childe without a head, and credibly reported
to have a firme Croſſe on the breſt, as this en-
ſuing Story ſhall relate.

Hor: *Miranda cano.*

Printed at London for *Rich: Harper* and *Thomas Wine*, and are to bee ſold
at the Bible and Harpe in Smithfield. 1642. *Aug. 23.*

Figure 5. Title page with woodcut of headless monster, *A Strange and Lamentable accident that happened lately at Mears Ashby in Northamptonshire* (1642). By permission of The British Library. Shelfmark E 113(15).

42

A DECLARATION, 20

Of a strange and Wonderfull MONSTER:

Born in KIRKHAM Parifh in LANCASHIRE (the Childe
of Mrs. *Haughton,* a Popifh Gentlewoman) the face of it upon the breaft,
and without a head (after the mother had wifhed rather to bear a
Childe without a head then a Roundhead) and had curft the
PARLIAMNET.

Attefted by Mr. FLEETWOOD, Minifter of the fame Pa-
rifh, under his own hand ; and Mrs. *Gattaker* the Mid-wife, and divers
other eye-witnefles : Whofe teftimony was brought up by a *Member* of the Houfe of Commons.

*Appointed to be printed according to Order : And defired to be publifhed in all the
Counties, Cities, Townes , and Parifhes in* England : *Being the fame
Copies that were prefented to the Parliament.*

march 3   London, Printed by *Jane Coe.* 1646.   1645

Figure 6. Title page with woodcut of monstrous birth, *A Declaration, of a strange and Wonderfull Monster: Born in Kirkham Parish in Lancashire* (1646). By permission of The British Library. Shelfmark E 325(20).

glish revolution, where the births are wrongly identified as taking place in Nottinghamshire and Leicestershire.[3] They are not normally mentioned in discussions of the English civil war.

These two pamphlets take us into a world of conflict, division, and distraction in which monstrosity and malignancy were combined. Perpetuating a tradition of sensational reportage which extended from before the beginnings of print (and which still continues), they contributed to the partisan frenzy of news, rumor, and opinion that accompanied the English civil wars. On one level, they draw on ancient traditions of teratology, the interpretation of portents, deep-rooted concerns with God's vengeance, and the perennial fascination with monstrous births. On another, they engage with questions of orthodoxy, discipline, and allegiance, and the moral and religious confusions of the English revolution. These authors are principally interested in human wickedness and divine retribution. But they are also concerned with social, professional, and gender hierarchies, the maintenance of clerical and husbandly authority, and the threat to these hierarchies posed by headstrong women. Among the many topics they touch on are normal and abnormal childbirth; mainstream, radical, and Recusant religion; different kinds of deviancy; and the construction of these issues in print. Monstrosity ties these topics together, commanding a kind of horrified attention.

I will begin with some brief mention of some kindred publications that preceded these two pamphlets, in order to establish their tradition. I will then examine the texts in more detail, in an attempt to illuminate the religious and rhetorical proclivities of their authors. Finally, believing that genre is only part of the story and mere textual analysis insufficient, I will try to get behind the texts as well as into them, to see how these episodes operated in the particular local environments of revolutionary England. I take it as my task to treat these works situationally as well as generically, to try to relate the words on the page to their immediate historical settings. I hope to be able to show how the horrors of monstrous birth related to the horrors of religious division in a country moving from the many-headed monster of rebellion to the revolutionary spectacle of a headless king.

The century before 1640 saw more than two dozen accounts of monstrous births presented to English readers. Many more could be viewed in continental sources, including a headless monster born in Gascony in 1562 whose form anticipates the lamentable accidents in Northamptonshire and Lancashire.[4] These malformations were generally attributed to the power of God rather than the caprice of nature, and most were accompanied with cries of woe and calls for repentance. They exhibited a world of unstable boundaries and providential interventions, in which things natural and supernatural could be dynamically engaged.

It was widely believed in early modern England that God could change the rules of nature and cause to be born a creature of disturbing monstrous form. God could cast up monstrous fish on the shore and cause the birth of strangely deformed pigs or calves. He could produce human babies with monstrous folds of skin like ruffs, masses, or molae of ill-shaped flesh, conjoined or half-made sets of twins, and even babies lacking vital parts such as heads. As one pamphlet writer of 1617 proclaimed, "This terrible God, I say, who created all of nothing, can as easily divert the usual and orderly course of procreation, into dreadful and hideous deformity."[5] He did this, so interpreters claimed, to send a warning or message, to shock Christians to attention. The monster was simultaneously an admonition or warning and a monstrance or demonstration of divine power and wrath.

Another belief, not necessarily incompatible, held that particular parents were to blame, visited with a monster on account of their monstrous, vicious, or irreligious activities. Women especially were believed to be responsible for the issue of their wombs, and were widely thought capable of imprinting their children with features seen, imagined, or discussed at the time of conception or during pregnancy. The sight of a black cat, for example, might result in a child's swarthy complexion, feline features, or cattish qualities, and in the most extreme case might explain an apparently miscegenated monster with claws and a tail.

A broadsheet of 1568 presented *The forme and shape of a Monstrous Child born at Maydstone in Kent, the xxiiii of October,* whose mother, Margaret Mere, "being unmarried, played the naughty pack." Characteristically, this misshaped monster was depicted as "a warning to England" as well as a judgment on its sinful mother. The creature provided a coded analogue of moral and political deformities, so that the "gasping mouth" challenged "ravine and oppression," the "gorging paunch" attacked greed, the fingerless stumps "set forth" idleness, and the foot climbing to the head chastised subjects "most vicious, that refuse to be lead."[6] Given the common trope of the "body politic" and the normal hierarchy of head and members, it is not surprising that writers in this genre presented obstetrical monstrosities as signs of a world turned upside down.[7]

Jacobean contributions to the genre included: *Strange Newes out of Kent, of a Monstrous and misshapen Child, borne in Olde Sandwich, upon the 10 of Iulie last* (1609); *A Wonder Woorth the reading, or, A True and faithfull Relation of a Woman, now dwelling in Kent Street, who, upon Thursday, being the 21 of August last, was deliuered of a prodigious and Monstrous Child* (1617); and *Gods Handyworke in Wonders. Miraculously shewen upon two Women, lately deliuered of two Monsters . . . within a quarter of a mile of Feuersham in Kent, the 25 of Iuly last, being S. Iames his day* (1615). More Elizabethan and Jacobean examples in this vein are cited in my *Travesties and Transgressions.*[8]

Typically these publications extracted the maximum moral meaning from unfortunate gynecological accidents and preached the generic religious message of reformation. It was hard to pin down what particular religious offense most angered God, but it was mostly to do with failures of charity or zeal, excessive swearing or lechery, and neglect of the Sabbath. Tales of monstrous birth were typically co-opted on behalf of a moderate godly agenda, not unlike the murder pamphlets examined by Peter Lake. But so understated was the Protestantism in their message—with barely a whiff of Calvinism—that they can be seen as continuing the trans-Reformation tradition of marvels and providences recently explored by Alexandra Walsham.[9]

A telling characteristic of these "true and faithful" relations was their insistence on the veracity of their report, and their reference to witnesses who could certify the details. This applied as much in the 1640s as in the 1560s. The fact of a story being printed was no guarantee of its truth for, then as now, the press was rife with inventions and lies. Sending his father "several printed papers to entertain you" in March 1642, Sir John Coke observed, "so many false reports are spread abroad that a man knows not what to believe." Pamphleteers regularly accused each other of making things up, and readers became inured to "false and foolish and unwitnessed fictions."[10] In the case of our two pamphlets, the authenticity of the Mears Ashby account was certified by the authority of its author, John Locke, cleric, who described himself as "a very honest and conformable man," as if that were sufficient. The truth of the Kirkham "declaration" was "attested by Mr. [Edward] Fleetwood, minister of the same parish, under his own hand, and Mrs. Gataker the midwife, and divers other eyewitnesses." Accompanied by "what proofs there are to make it appear to be truth," the pamphlet also claimed endorsement by members of the House of Commons. As Fleetwood assured his readers, "as we must tell no lie, so we should not conceal any truth, especially when it tends to God's glory."[11] But neither vehement assertion nor godly credentials assuage all doubts about the particular incidents that these authors describe.

By the early 1640s monstrosity was in the air, in the pulpits, on people's lips, and in the popular press. More than simply an abomination of tissue, monstrosity pointed to social pathology and religious failing, a disturbance of the natural order. The word provided another weapon with which to beat opponents. "Sure ye be monsters," claimed enemies of the Laudian bishops, who vilified the prelates as "ravenous harpies" or monsters "metamorphosed into ravenous wolves."[12] The bishops were judged guilty of a "monstrous design" against the Church. Their "etcetera oath" in the canons of 1640 was "a strange mis-shapen monster," one "happily stifled in the embryo . . . ere it could come to birth."[13] On the other side radical sectarians became "runagadoes, monsters eke," who had created a church "full of strange and monstrous shapes."[14] Conservatives characterized the Roundhead as "a monstrous beast," and later blamed themselves for "neglect[ing] the stifling this monster in its cradle."[15]

A common conceit was the connection between monstrous creation and monstrous behavior. Londoners on the eve of the Long Parliament were said to be "monstrously out of temper," involved in a "scandalous, headless insurrection."[16] Verses decried the Scots rebels and their English friends as "a monstrous body that will have no head."[17] The people themselves, within a few months, had become "a furious monster" engaged in "a monstrous frenzy."[18] Popular petitioning became "monstrous easy," thought the Wiltshire magistrate John Davers, making "authority decline."[19]

Radical pamphlets could be described as having their "monstrous and untimely birth from the womb of an ignoramus." Controversialists likened the proliferation of news and opinion to a monster out of control: "monster-like, she now hath many heads."[20] Papists, Cavaliers, Levellers and regicides all had the adjective "monstrous" attached to them. Parliament too could be deemed to be behaving monstrously, and at least two publications of the 1640 satirized "mistress parliament brought to bed of a monstrous child"—in one case, tellingly, "of a deformed shape, without a head."[21] The times were so disjointed, monstrosity and malignancy so rampant, that it would have been surprising if the civil wars had not been accompanied by monstrous births.[22]

The Mears Ashby pamphlet opened with the words "This kingdom," aligning England's errors and distresses with those of late imperial Rome. "This kingdom," it began, once happy and flourishing, was now "clouded and masked with various distractions" and become "a laughing stock and a scorn to all nations." The ferment of 1641 and the outbreak of war in 1642 provided a context in which the "strange and lamentable accident" of a headless child might be understood. The deviancy and disobedience of the parents, especially the mother, were exhibited as signs of the times. This was the setting for "this ensuing story of God's wrath and judgments."

> Mary Wilmore, wife of John Wilmore, rough mason, being great with child, [was] much perplexed in her mind to think that her child when it should be delivered should be baptized with the sign of the cross. The minister of the parish, being a very honest and conformable man, not suiting with the vain and erroneous sycophants, as there are too many thereabouts inhabiting, desires her husband to go to Hardwick, a village near adjoining, to one Master Baynard, a reverend divine, to know his opinion concerning the cross in baptism. Whose answer was, that it was no ways necessary to salvation, but an ancient, laudable and decent ceremony of the Church of England. Which answer being related to her from her husband, it is reported she should say, I had rather my child should be born without a head than to have a head to be signed with the cross.

Here, then, in the heart of England, among poor working commoners, was a continuation of the debate over Christian ceremony that had agitated reformers and divines since the early days of the Reformation. The sign of the cross in baptism was one of the most sensitive and controversial rituals, relished by ceremonialists, accepted by conformists, challenged by Puritans, and withheld, ignored, or rejected by the radicalized ministers who emerged amidst the shattering of the Laudian religious regime. The early 1640s saw dozens of local struggles over this ritual performance, with tumults in church and physical struggles across the font.[23] The reverend Mr. Baynard had caught the conundrum, "that it was no ways necessary to salvation, but an ancient, laudable and decent ceremony of the Church." The sign of the cross was not required by Christ, and had no sacramental efficacy, but was nonetheless properly maintained by authority and custom. Mary Wilmore, by contrast, espoused the radical opinion that the cross in baptism was "a pernicious, popish and idolatrous ceremony" to be avoided at all costs. Derision of the ceremony in these terms could be found in print dating back to the 1572 *Admonition* and beyond. But Mary Wilmore, an illiterate countrywoman, most likely absorbed her view from local nonconformists, described here as "conventicling sectaries," rather than from controversial books.[24]

Sectarian gatherings had sprung up all over England in 1641, some led by radicalized ministers, others by pious laymen. They drained the parochial congregations and undercut the authority of established clerics like the incumbents of Mears Ashby and Hardwick. Rejection of ritual, rejection of authority, condemnation of the prayer book, and schism from the Church of England were part of a pattern of rebellion that moderates and conservatives tended to describe as "monstrous." Mears Ashby's Mary Wilmore appears not to have been a Baptist, opposed to infant baptism, but rather an adherent of popular Puritanism shorn of popish ceremony.

The gender dimension is especially significant, for this is a story of a woman's headstrong opinion and its catastrophic obstetrical consequences. Mary Wilmore, the central character, rejected the authority of both her husband and her minister and upset the hierarchy of household and parish. It was "her weakness," her perplexity, and her reckless vaunting that caused the "lamentable accident." Misled by "vain babbling" and "conventicling sectaries," she followed her own opinion, raised her own voice, and brought destruction on her child. She too was monstrous for challenging God and drawing down his judgment on her womb.

For sure enough, the pamphlet continues, having announced her opinion, "it pleased God about a month after, she was accordingly delivered of a monster, *rudes indigestaque moles* [a crude ill-shapen mass], a child without a head, to the shame of the parents, in not having that part whereupon it might have been marked with that token whereof it should never after have been ashamed." Mary Wilmore had won, though at the price of her ill fame and the loss of her child. The title page of the pamphlet shows her just delivered in childbed, with gossips and midwife in attendance, the headless body pitilessly exposed. But no more of her personal history is given. Instead this monster is presented as the most recent example of the working of providence (among several cited) and as a dramatic demonstration of an active God siding firmly with the Book of Common Prayer. Mary Wilmore's folly is to be understood as a sign of the times, a message for the moment, a warning and judgment, in a kingdom wracked by religious division and war. The pamphlet ends by advocating the only way forward by prayers for harmony and peace.

We know somewhat more about Mrs. Houghton of Kirkham, whose social origins and religious opinions were so different from the wife of the Northamptonshire rough mason, but whose childbearing had such a comparable outcome. The problem in Lancashire was zealous attachment to popery rather than sectarianism, but it led to disturbingly similar results.

The Kirkham *Declaration* begins by announcing "This wonderful manifestation of God's anger," and frames its account by reference to ancient Israel rather than Rome, the Bible rather than the classics. The scene is set in a Lancashire that many would count among the dark corners of the land. According to the author of the *Declaration,* presumably Edward Fleetwood, "the people that live there are a mixed number, some precious godly people, but for the most part very bad. No parts of England hath had so many witches, none fuller of papists, and they were the chief instruments in seeking to have that wicked Book of Allowance for Sports on the Lord's day to be published, and it was set forth by their procurements, and the godly people amongst them have suffered very much under their reproaches and wicked malice." From Fleetwood's perspective, Kirkham was "a parish which God hath blessed with good ministers, and some godly people (though but few) in it, who by the malice of wicked and profane wretches have been much abused heretofore."

One of these wretches, he goes on, was a gentlewoman "both by birth and marriage." Her parents, both papists, "were of a very bitter disposition against godly people," and her mother, Mrs. Browne, "would usually call honest men roundheads and Puritans and heretics." Mrs. Houghton's mother was especially notorious for an anti-Protestant exploit that may have influenced her daughter. It was she, apparently, around 1640, who "took her cat and said that it must be made a roundhead like Burton, Prynne and Bastwick, and causing the ears to be cut off, called her cat Prynne (instead of Puss)." This was a celebrated and shocking incident that made the rounds in several publications.[25]

Mrs. Browne's daughter, Mrs. Houghton, was described as "a good, handsome, proportional, comely gentlewoman, young, and of a good complexion, of a merry disposition, and a healthful nature, well personed, had her conditions been suitable." In other circumstances, Fleetwood might even have admired her. She was married to a fellow Catholic, Mr. Houghton, "a gentleman descended of an ancient family, well known in those parts, and not altogether of such a bitter spirit as those he matched with, he hath been a gentleman well bred, only in a popish way educated." As in Northamptonshire, it seems it was the women who were especially unruly and outspoken, while their husbands maintained cordial relations with the religious authorities. The pamphlet presents gender disorder, religious extremism, and unwise speaking as a dangerous, indeed monstrous, compound.

An outspoken Catholic gentlewoman in an officially Protestant country, Mrs. Houghton flaunted religious pictures and crucifixes that Fleetwood described as "superstitious fooleries" and "popish trumpery." As a Royalist in the Civil War she baited Parliamentarians with assertions that "the king was in the right." She outraged Parliamentarian neighbors by railing against Roundheads, saying "that the Puritans and independents deserve[d] to be hanged." This was provocative talk, of a kind that may have been common in the course of the war,[26] but it paled besides the next conversation recorded. One of the Kirkham women apparently championed the Roundheads as "honest men, and in the right way of walking, and living like the people of God," and prayed that Mrs. Houghton might be more like them. Her response was emphatic and prophetic: "No, saith she, I had rather have no head nor life, I nor any of mine will ever be such." One of the women then wished that Mrs. Houghton's children, if she had any, might see the light, to which she made her awful vow: "I pray God, that rather than I shall be a roundhead or bear a roundhead I may bring forth a child without a head."

The pamphlet comments, "this was a fearful saying, and taken note of by divers of her neighbors that heard her speak it." And sure enough, when the time came, Mrs. Houghton's child, like Mary Wilmore's, was born without a head. "The midwife being sent for . . . delivered her," but "the child (or rather monster) was born but dead." The creature was exhibited for a few days and then buried in Kirkham churchyard, not without some suspicion that it had been attended by popish priests and friars. The midwife, Mrs. Gataker, "a godly woman," was so troubled by the incident that she reported the details to the incumbent Edward Fleetwood. Other women who had heard Mrs. Houghton's brag also came forward with their testimonies. The headless monster was seen as retribution and punishment for its mother's vaunting opinion, and a clear demonstration of "the hand of God." News spread quickly across Lancashire, and Colonel More, "an honest godly gentleman, a member of the House of Commons, and one of the [county] committee [for sequestrations]," wrote to Fleetwood "to know the certainty of it, whether it was truth or not."

This was no idle curiosity or prurient interest of Colonel More's. If the hand of God had indeed shown itself in Lancashire, if such a blow had been struck against popish pride, then the Parliamentary authorities needed to be informed. In response the minister reexamined the midwife, who confirmed her earlier report; "yet for further satisfaction, Mr. Fleetwood caused the grave to be opened and the child taken up and laid to view, and found there a body without an head, as the midwife had said, only the child had a face upon the breast of it, as you may see in the portraiture." Shown on the title page of the pamphlet, "as near as we could delineate" said Fleetwood, the headless monster stands four-square in the center, surrounded by scenes from the story and an array of popish elements—beads, crucifixes and tonsured priests. Cats feature prominently, as they do in other publications, suggestive of feminine folly, Catholic error, and witches' familiars.[27] Mrs. Brown is shown in the chair with her cropping shears and the disfigured moggies she named Burton, Bastwick, and Prynne. Exactly the same block, somewhat the worse for wear and with the popish elements excised, was used six years later to adorn the title page of *The Ranters Monster,* depicting "the ugliest ill-shapen monster that ever eyes beheld."[28] But intertextuality affected direct observation. Despite claims for its verisimilitude, the central image shares a likeness with descriptions of headless monsters familiar from Pliny's *Natural History* or Mandeville's *Travels,* with eyes in their shoulders and mouths in the middle of their breasts.[29]

The birth of headless babies to women who brought such judgments against themselves lay well beyond the normal range of experience. The "accident" at Mears Ashby, Northamptonshire, was described as "strange and lamentable," while the birth of the headless monster at Kirkham, Lancashire, was said to be "strange and wonderful." Readers were not only urged to acknowledge these accounts to be true but also to accept the authors' interpretation of them. The first invited reactions of sadness and indignation, the second of amazement and scorn. Both publications served as propaganda in the media battle accompanying the Civil War.

Both stories drew attention to the problem of controlling unruly women, at a time when patriarchal discipline, like other forms of authority, seemed to be crumbling. Popular pamphlets mocked the women who ran to conventicles and followed sectarian preachers, and accused the sisters of being loose with their bodies as well as their opinions. At a time when women were petitioning Parliament and arguing politics in the streets, misogynist authors such as John Taylor feared that "women shall wear the breeches and men petticoats," and classified "feminine divinity" as one "the diseases of the times."[30] The women "are up in arms already, like so many amazons," claimed "Pigg's Coranto" of 1640.[31] Nor were men the only ones alarmed, for the gentle Margaret Eure wrote to her nephew Ralph Verney in May 1642, "the women in this country begin to rise . . . I wish you all to take heed of women, for this very vermin have pulled down an enclosure."[32] Catholic women were commonly considered the devil's fifth column, allured by their weakness to popery and resistant to patriarchal discipline. So it should not be surprising that in the gender politics of the 1640s, social conflict, monstrosity, and religious deviance were constantly in a state of collision.

The Mears Ashby case was a warning of what might happen to those guilty of "contemning and slighting God's holy ordinances." It was an anti-Puritan story vindicating "honest and conformable" ministers against "babbling and erroneous" schismatics. As well as being the fruit of her folly, Mary Wilmore's monster was associated with "hatred, emulations, contentions, heresies, seditions, needless and unprofitable questions, which tend to rebellion and discord." The author used the occasion to call for uniformity and order: "as there is one Lord, one faith, and one baptism, one God and father of all, even so Lord grant that we may jointly agree in love, and that there remain amongst us a godly consent and concord." And the very final word of his pamphlet was "peace." One reason this story enjoyed relatively little circulation, compared to the episode at Kirkham, may have been that John Locke's moderate conformity was on the losing side.

The story of the Kirkham monster, by contrast, belonged to the Parliamentary victors. Even while the war was raging, they could cite it as a "wonderful manifestation of God's anger against wicked and profane people," conflating Royalists and papists. The certificate authenticating the event was ordered printed by the House of Commons, so that "all the kingdom might see the hand of God herein, to the comfort of his people and the terror of the wicked that deride and scorn them."[33]

The Kirkham story enjoyed wide circulation because of its political utility. It was recited in several Parliamentarian publications even before featuring in Edward Fleetwood's pamphlet. These including John Vicars, *A Looking-Glasse for Malignants* (1643), *Jehovah-Jireh, God in the Mount* (1644), and *Five Wonders Seen in England* (1646, also printed by Jane Coe). Some of these publications provide supplementary details, including the actual date of the birth, 20 June 1643, and a more particular description of the creature: "with no head, but yet having two ears, two eyes, and a mouth in the breast of it, the hands turning backwards to the elbows, with a cleft down the back, so as it was not discernable whether it were male or female." It had been buried, deceptively, with "a bundle of clouts" or cloths where its head should have been. The connection between the woman who gave birth to a monster and her own mother who had mutilated cats in mockery of Burton, Bastwick, and Prynne was irresistible. But the story of Mrs. Houghton's willingness to bear a child without a head did not appear in print before Fleetwood's version of 1645. To John Vicars, who seemed to revel in such things, "this prodigious birth" was "a direct judgment of the lord for desperate malignancy against the lord's choice ones."[34]

Indeed, to Vicars and his ilk, the story from Kirkham was a godsend. Vicars had been collecting reports of "prodigious signs and wonders" that warned of God's wrath against England, but he had more examples from "former ages" than from "these modern times." Until now the best he could offer was a monstrous birth in London in 1633 and reports from colonial New England. For someone searching for "visible footprints and impressions of God's highly conceived indignation," Mrs. Houghton's monster born in 1643 was almost too good to be true.[35]

Attempts to go beyond the pamphlets, to ground these accounts in the local histories that lay behind them, however, have been more frustrating than rewarding. It is not too difficult to reconstruct the major religious divisions, but most of the networks of interaction among the parties remain hidden.

Mears Ashby was an open field parish in the pasturelands of mid-Northamptonshire, astride the road from Northampton to Wellingborough. Edward Vaux was lord of the manor, and another gentleman, Thomas Clendon, rebuilt Mears Ashby Hall in 1637. Neither appears in our story. Besides the will of the Rev. Justinian Bracegirdle, providing in 1625 for the purchase of the advowson and for support of scholars at Oxford, little is known of the religious affairs in the parish. There was no known local radical tradition and nothing to offend the episcopal authorities. A survey of 1637 finds the church fabric in generally good order, though the font needed mending and the church wanted "beautifying."[36] Until the radical upheaval of 1641 the parish appears to have been quietly conformist, under its vicar George Lawson (who was later sequestered as a Royalist malignant).[37]

It would seem that "John Locke, cleric" was curate rather than incumbent.

One of this name matriculated at Emmanuel College, Cambridge, in 1624, B.A. in 1628, and was ordained at Peterborough in 1631. He tried for an usher's place at Oundle School but was rejected as "a very ignorant and illiterate man, much given to gaming and company keeping." He shows up in the 1630 Quarter Sessions as "nuper de Oundle," and may then have served as a curate at Thrapston before moving to Mears Ashby. One of this name was rector of Coney Weston, Suffolk, from 1644 to 1655, and of Alresford, Essex, from 1646 to 1661, though it is unlikely that a prayerbook conformist from Northamptonshire would find preferment in revolutionary East Anglia. Perhaps this was rather another John Locke who attended St. John's College, Cambridge, from 1628.[38] The pamphlet bespeaks a classical education in its author, as well as conformist opinions, for his description of the monster as "rudes indigestaque moles" is taken directly from Ovid's *Metamorphoses*.[39] His title page features a tag from Horace, and his text is sprinkled with Latin aphorisms. Here is proof, if proof were needed, that apparently "popular" pamphlets often belonged to a discourse among the elite.

As for the Rev. Baynard of Hardwick, the next village to the north, this was John Baynard, an Oxford man, rector since 1629. The worst that the Laudian visitors could say of him in 1637 was that his surplice was worn thin. Locke invokes Baynard for maintenance of traditional discipline, but his subsequent career shows him moving with the times. He was intruded minister at Burton Latimer in 1644, ejected in 1662, and eventually licensed as a Congregationalist preacher.[40] Of John and Mary Wilmore, the monster's parents, nothing more can be found. There is no Mears Ashby parish register before 1670, no churchwardens' accounts or bishops' transcripts. And they are absent from the manor court records.

Northamptonshire was a Parliamentary stronghold for most of the civil war, and the main Parliamentary army traversed the county twice in 1642 to and from the battle at Edgehill. Northampton itself was strongly garrisoned, and Castle Ashby was fortified for Parliament early in 1644. This did not stop Royalist incursions, leading to the battle of Cropredy in the south of the county in 1644 and the decisive battle of Naseby in the northwest in 1645. The parishioners of Mears Ashby, in the center, were frequently exposed to Parliamentary troopers and their Puritan chaplains, and though they may never have seen an actual Royalist in arms they would most likely have encountered soldiers who had purged parish churches of their sacramental accouterments.[41]

John Locke, the author of *A Strange and Lamentable Accident*, presents himself as a supporter of the prayerbook and an advocate for peace. His senior colleague and neighbor, Mr. Baynard, was equally conformist. Such men would have been threatened by Civil War militants, and alarmed at the influence of radicals on their congregations. Locke reports that "conventicling sectaries" had sprung up in the district by 1642, perhaps energized and led astray by firebrands in the army. His pamphlet, then, can be understood as a lament for a passing order, harnessing the story of Mary Wilmore's headless monster to the slippage of social and religious discipline and the demise of the old regime.

The continuation of that slippage may lie behind yet another report of a monstrous birth in Northamptonshire late in 1643. The Royalist newsletter *Mercurius Aulicus* reported as credible an account "from Rothwell in Northamptonshire of a woman . . . that hath brought forth a child marvelous to behold; the lower part like a wench, the breast as black as a crow, the mouth contrary, no eyes, the one ear like unto a hound, the other ear like unto the wattle of a hog, the head (round) like a cony, and the back like a fish." There was little more to say about this mix-up, which indicated the confusions of the Roundhead cause and the disorders of nature, except "that the woman is well known to people of credit in London" and to "leave the reader to make his inference."[42] There was no pamphlet by the minister of Rothwell explaining to readers how this accident should be understood.

Somewhat more can be learned about the background to the report of the second headless monster. Kirkham was a large spread-out parish comprised of seventeen separate townships in the Fylde of rural Lancashire. Kirkham town was the largest settlement, with 405 souls at the end of the seventeenth century in a total parish population of 4,161.[43] Early in the 1630s the plague had returned with a vengeance, killing, said chroniclers, "the more part of the people of the town."[44] An outbreak of suspected witchcraft in the region in 1635 added to social and supernatural tensions.[45]

Throughout the early Stuart era the parish suffered acute religious divisions, as Catholics and "church-papists" competed with Protestant reformers. The leading families oscillated between occasional conformity and popish delinquency, and conservatives controlled the tithes (leased from Christ Church, Oxford), the grammar school, and most local offices. The Houghtons (sometimes spelled Hoghton or Haughton) were well-documented Recusant landowners whose influence stretched back to the beginning of the sixteenth century. During most of Elizabeth's reign they were locked in disputes with successive vicars of Kirkham over tithes and ecclesiastical lands. The Mrs. Houghton at the center of this story was married to Mr. William Houghton of Prickmarsh in Kirkham in Layfield, and her mother, Mrs. Browne, was a notorious Catholic militant.[46] There was no religious census, of course, and estimates of the Catholic presence are likely to be wide of the mark, but the region was generally reckoned to be a bastion of the old religion. According to Edward Fleetwood, Protestant incumbent for most of Charles I's reign, the parish was "infested with popery," and this infestation lay behind the story of Mrs. Houghton.[47] When the Protestation came to Kirkham in March 1642 it was prominently signed by Edward Fleetwood, cleric, while Mr. William Houghton was among the several hundred refusers.[48]

Nor was this the only problem, for animosity between the vicar and lay elders, the "thirty sworn men," often brought parish proceedings to a halt. Edward Fleetwood, a southerner of gentle birth, became vicar in 1629. He was a self-regarding reformer, described by his own bishop as a "silly, willful man," and may have been out of his element if not out of his depth. Many of Fleetwood's parishioners were resistant to Protestant discipline, but the problem was aggravated by personal and cultural factors as well as religion. A prolonged struggle for control of the parish led to the minister intermittently locking the church door and excluding the congregation. "How good and joyful a thing it is for brethren to dwell together in unity," enthused the parish book in 1638, but for three years the vicar prevented the thirty men from meeting in church. At the height of the crisis Thomas Clifton, Esq., later identified as a popish delinquent, headed a petition of 483 parishioners to the bishop of Chester seeking to have Fleetwood censured. Bishop Bridgeman, the laziest of prelates, as usual prevaricated, but in 1639 Fleetwood faced charges before the Chester consistory court and although the dispute was about money and authority, he was forced to admit that he "sometimes omitted to use the surplice." A few years earlier he had been admonished at a metropolitical visitation for such minor professional irregularities as failing to read prayers on Wednesdays and Fridays and neglecting to wear a hood.[49] Early in 1641, at a time when Parliament was issuing orders against ceremonialist excesses, somebody broke into Kirkham church and stole the green communion cloth from the parish chest and other liturgical furnishings. Seeing the parish books "cast abroad in the church," Fleetwood took them into his possession, removed them to London, and for ten years denied parishioners access to their records. "Malicious words of slander" spoken against the vicar on this occasion were aired at the Easter 1641 Quarter Sessions, where one parishioner said that Fleetwood "will never be quiet with the parish" and another answered that he would be quiet "if the parish will be quiet with him."[50]

Fleetwood soon emerged as a prominent Presbyterian, becoming in 1646 a member of the Seventh Lancashire Classis. His writings suggest that he strongly supported the Parliamentary cause and ingratiated himself with Parliamentarian leaders. The deaths of his brother in March 1642, within weeks of the circulation of the Protestation, and of his seven-year-old son John in May 1643, just a month before the birth of Mrs. Houghton's monster, may have been acts of providence that were hard to understand.[51] Fleetwood continued his labors at Kirkham until 1649, when he answered the welcome call to a southern parish, and he died in 1667.

Mrs. Gataker, the midwife of the pamphlet, was really Mrs. Isabel Greenacres (née Tomlinson), widow to Arthur Greenacres who had been vicar of Kirkham from 1598 to his death in 1627. She was the minister's second wife, and had borne at least four children (the first in May 1616, within a month of getting married). Renowned as a godly woman and an able midwife, she lived until 1659. In March 1642 she subscribed the Protestation, on the same page as Edward Fleetwood.[52] Why the vicar should call her "Gataker" is a mystery. It cannot be that he had few dealings with the town midwife who was also his predecessor's widow, or that he was ill tuned to Lancastrian pronunciation. Most likely he, or his printer Jane Coe, unwittingly substituted the name of the prolific Presbyterian Thomas Gataker, a member of the Westminster Assembly. The misspelling is a clue, perhaps, that Fleetwood did not have full control of the publication of which he is the attributed author.

Colonel More, the "honest godly gentleman" whose inquiries brought the episode to the attention of Parliament, was John More (1599–1650), M.P. for Liverpool, a Presbyterian shipowner, and eventually a regicide. I have so far been unable to find his report to the House of Commons or the date of its submission.[53]

The Civil War further divided Kirkham. The conflict between Parliament and crown split families and communities, exacerbating the local tension between religious reformers and popish traditionalists. The king's willingness from September 1642 to allow Catholics in arms on his side transformed the recusant community from outlaws to partisans. As Fleetwood's *Declaration* reveals, there was lively debate, even among women, about the merits and demerits of Roundheads and Cavaliers. Each side's armies came through Kirkham several times, holding ground and raising troops before moving on. Preston, eight miles to the east, lay alternately under Parliamentary and Royalist control. During the war, locals reported, "the country was in a combustion." As elsewhere in such circumstances, soldiers intimidated civilians, Parliamentarians plundered Kirkham School, and families were forced from their homes.[54]

The months of Mrs. Houghton's pregnancy coincided with some of the fiercest and most confused local fighting of the war. The Houghtons, of course, were leading Royalists (or "prime malignants" according to one's loyalties), and a kinsman, Sir Gilbert Houghton, commanded the king's garrison at Preston. When Parliamentary forces took Preston in February 1643 Sir Gilbert escaped but his brother was killed, his nephew was captured, and his wife, Lady Houghton, was held hostage. The royal army under the Earl of Derby then occupied Kirkham, and all the men in the parish aged sixteen and over were summoned to present themselves "in their best weapons, to attend the king's service." A month later Preston was again under Royalist control, though not immune from periodic Parliamentary attacks. Throughout the spring and into the summer, exactly the time of Mrs. Houghton's pregnancy and parturition, Kirkham was a place of military maneuvers, quartering, and rendezvous, facing frequent alarms and occasional plunder. When the monstrous birth took place in June 1643 the community was more fractured then ever. Parliamentary forces again took Preston in August 1644 and the retreating royal army once more descended on Kirkham. Later in the year there was another skirmish in the parish, when a Cavalier raiding party, in league with some Kirkham householders, was sent packing by a group of women throwing stones from their aprons.[55] This was the context for Mrs. Houghton's vaunt, the horror of her headless baby, and the trumpeting of the news through the London press.

To conclude: the Mears Ashby pamphlet and the Kirkham *Declaration* belonged to the tail end of a tradition of Renaissance teratology publicized by the popular—or at least inexpensive—press. Whereas earlier reports tended to see monstrous births as general warnings against sinfulness, these accounts of the 1640s focused on the special providential punishment of notorious individual delinquents—in one instance a sectarian, in the other a papist—who were held personally responsible for the outcome. The focus in each case falls on a woman, a mother whose obstinate error and outspoken opinion, in defiance of both clerical and patriarchal authority, had catastrophic consequences. Common to both is the vaunting vow, the awful brag, the daring challenge to nature and to God, answered, inevitably, by horrors. The motif is familiar from folk tales, and is common in compilations of providences, where divine retribution both matches and illuminates the crime. For Mary

Wilmore and Elizabeth Houghton to bear headless babies was similar to the fate of other malefactors choking on stolen apples, crushed by sinfully erected maypoles, or otherwise hoist by their own petard. "As Adonibezec was repaid in his own kind, Haman hanged upon the same gallows he had prepared for Mordecai, and Pharoah and all his hosts drowned in the sea," it was, as Fleetwood said, "an example of the justice and equity of god in his judgments." To the extent that these things have been noted at all by historians, that is the preferred explanation.[56]

But the providential mileage in these stories was not limited to particular localities. Driven by partisan concerns, each pamphlet offered messages for the community at large, tied to the propaganda battles of the English civil wars. John Locke's report from Mears Ashby attempted to sustain prayerbook conformity against insurgent religious radicalism. Edward Fleetwood's account from Kirkham served the Presbyterian Parliamentary establishment against the powers of popish and Royalist malignancy. Each suggested graphically that extremist positions lead to unviable offspring. In an era of Roundheads and rattleheads, heads of proposals and heads of traitors, it was perhaps appropriate that these offspring should be headless. If the head signifies reason, guiding the members and governing the state, a headless monster could point to a commonwealth that had lost its way and lost its mind. "Times of distraction" are, after all, times when the world is out of its wits. But the head signifies authority as well as reason, and the crisis at Mears Ashby and Kirkham was about order as much as rationality. At a time when the head of the Church had lost his congregation, and the head of the state governed less than half a kingdom, a headless monster may have been the most appropriate emblem for a world turned upside down.

PART 2

APOCALYPTICISM, BESTIALITY, AND MONSTROUS POLEMICS

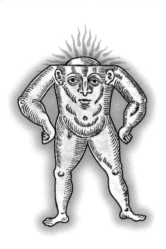

3

A TIME FOR MONSTERS

Monstrous Births, Propaganda, and the German Reformation

R. PO-CHIA HSIA

SEBASTIAN BRANT AND THE POLITICS OF PRODIGIES

On 10 September 1495, a set of twins, joined at the head, was stillborn in Worms. The event was reported in a single-leaf broadsheet with a woodcut illustrating the twins (figure 7), and verses written by the Strasbourg cathedral preacher Sebastian Brant, who was best known for his 1494 *The Ship of Fools,* a book of 112 chapters of verses that lambasted the foolishness of his times.[1] Brant hailed the birth of the conjoined twins as a good portent:

> *One has often seen the child*
> *Who has two heads on a body*
> *Which signifies as I have written*
> *That the princes here gathered*
> *Will be transformed into one body.*
> *And the twin heads of the secular world*
> *Shall come together as one*
> *And be brought together in one body.*[2]

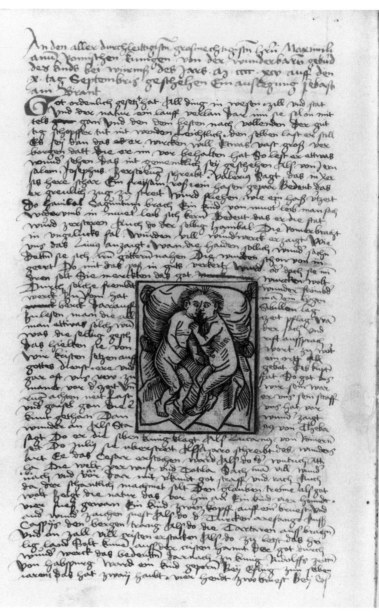

Figure 7. Sebastian Brant, broadsheet of stillborn twins (1495). Courtesy Staats- und Universitätsbibliothek Hamburg. Cod. Hist. 31e, fol. 413–14.

A Time for Monsters

The reference in Brant's verses to "the princes here gathered" was to the meeting of Emperor Maximilian I and the imperial Estates in that same year in the imperial city of Worms. Brant expands on the analogy between the twins and the Diet of Worms:

> *This is what I care about*
> *That Common Christendom*
> *Now meeting in the city of Worms*
> *May come together in peace and unity*
> *I think it has only one brain*
> *And one understanding in its head*
> *And I truly believe that*
> *God wants to bestow*
> *Unity to our Empire.*[3]

Alarmed by the advances of the Ottoman Turks in the Balkans and provoked by the invasion of northern Italy by the French in 1494, the Diet of Worms meant to address the weakness of the Holy Roman Empire which had proved helpless in stopping the French violation of Milan, a nominal imperial fief.[4] Under the leadership of Berthold von Henneberg, archbishop of Mainz and chancellor of the Holy Roman Empire, the imperial estates were eager to strengthen peace and order; concerned about granting excessive powers to the emperor, they advocated the establishment of an imperial council. Sharing some of these goals, Maximilian I hoped to use the Diet of Worms to strengthen the dynastic position of the Habsburgs and come to a series of compromises with the estates.[5] Among the institutional reforms adopted by the Diet, some—such as the creation of an Imperial Chamber Court as the highest court of appeal in the Empire—proved to be of long-standing success. Others—such as the institution of an empire-wide tax, the Common Penny, intended in part to finance defenses against the Ottomans—failed to win widespread compliance. Barely two years later in 1497, Berthold von Henneberg already pronounced the reforms a failure.[6]

Of the estates in the Empire, the Imperial Cities represented the force most desirous of peace and order, which were essential to the economic prosperity of the great urban centers. In his optimistic interpretation of the prodigy of the conjoined twins of 1495, Sebastian Brant was expressing precisely the sentiment of the urban elites: the coupling of emperor and Imperial Cities was very much the subtext of Brant's verses. In fact, the Strasbourg humanist would serve his native city as a delegate to the 1512 Imperial Diet of Trier that won Maximilian's confirmation of certain privileges for the Alsatian Imperial City.[7]

But what are we to make of Brant's 1495 prodigy, especially since he had earlier expressed hostility to popular prophecy in his 1494 *Ship of Fools?* In Chapter 11 of the latter work, entitled "Contempt of Scripture," Brant mocked the credulous multitude who flocked to the "circus" (*Affenspil*) of the Drummer of Niklashausen,[8] a shepherd boy in the vicinity of Würzburg who claimed in 1476 to have seen apparitions of the Virgin Mary and who preached repentance to a great gathering, before the increasingly anticlerical tone of his prophecies provoked a crackdown by the bishop of Würzburg.[9] Clearly, Brant was not so much against prodigies—the warnings sent by God in the signs of perturbed nature—but popular prophecy itself.[10] He wrote that "A fool is one who wonders / that the Lord God is punishing the world,"[11] for the world was already full of sins for the admonishing humanist. It was not the quality of the prophecy or prodigy that mattered, but the quality of the prophet. In other words, the proper response when faced with these admonitions of God was not "wonder," the pleasure of the foolish multitude and lower classes gaping, as it were, at "the acts of apes," but "fear": the terror of God's punishment of sins. The destruction of Jerusalem and Israel served as warnings for Christians of his day, as Brant conscientiously reminded his readers.[12]

Feelings of pleasure and fear, together with repugnance, constituted the spectrum of emotional and cognitive responses to the monstrous in early modern Europe, as Lorraine Daston and Katharine Park have suggested.[13] They have also reminded us that interest in monstrous prodigies depended on very specific historical contexts. Thus, the high-water mark of interest in prodigies in Italy between 1494 and 1530 coincided with the crisis of the French invasion and the Valois-Habsburg struggles.[14] A parallel preoccupation also reflected the crisis in the Holy Roman Empire. Similar to Italy, the 1490s witnessed the first wave of this intense concern with prodigies, as the publications of Sebastian Brant exemplified. But unlike in Italy, the crisis in the Holy Roman Empire persisted much longer, with the confessional conflicts unleashed by the Protestant Reformation feeding a discourse of monstrosities.

Of the three emotions that Daston and Park suggest were provoked by monsters, that of pleasure was very much lacking in the bitter and anxious climate of the German Reformation. The interpretation of monstrous prodigies in sixteenth-century Germany expressed fully the other two emotions: fear and repugnance. As I shall argue in the course of this essay, those emotions were generally split along confessional lines, with fear dominating the language of prodigy in the Lutheran discourse on monsters, except for the very early years of the evangelical movement, and repugnance being the chief characteristic of the Catholic discourse of monstrosity against the Protestant Reformation. An explanation for this difference may well lie in the emphasis on the apocalypse in the Lutheran Reformation and the repudiation of eschatology in Catholic polemic, which focused instead on the repugnance against heresy. The case study of Reformation Germany suggests that we need to understand the language of monstrosities not only as different emotional responses to wonders, as Daston and Park have argued, but also as political discourses in the struggle for power and legitimacy.

In the following sections, I will analyze the contending discourses on monsters by focusing on the following themes: Martin Luther and the language of births; the apocalypse and fear; Reformation propaganda and Catholic polemics; and the decline of monstrous discourse in Germany toward the end of the sixteenth century. I shall argue that the advent of the monstrous discourse on the eve of the Reformation reflected a profound anxiety about redemption, a fear fueled by the expectation of the end of time that resulted in the births of multiple bodies of Christendom. The intensification and multiplication of this monstrous discourse in the following decades mirrored this painful and prolonged labor. But once the unified *corpus christianum* was torn asunder in this violent monstrous birth, the language of monstrosities in sixteenth-century Germany, like the postpartum mother, was depleted and exhausted. A new language of discipline and sin would serve a new age of confessional churches in seventeenth-century Germany.

BEGETTING THE BODY OF CHRISTENDOM: MARTIN LUTHER
AND THE APOCALYPSE

If twins joined at the head signified unity of purpose, then a body with multiple heads could not but be a monster of discord. In a generation after the imperial reform at Worms, the empire itself almost broke apart on the question of religion. In the new century, a new religious fervor was on the rise, as the social and natural order seemed increasingly out of joint: new shrines and pilgrimages; a new wave of anti-Jewish violence; the endowment of chapels, preacherships, and masses; and the appearance of prophets and preachers, whether sanctioned or not by the Church, testified to a changing mood by the year 1500.[15] To many contemporaries, the Mystical Body of Christendom seemed ill and corrupt; and a host of heavenly signs brought portents of even greater travails. The Book of Nature and the Book of Scriptures both echoed the themes of sin and repentance; and many disasters prefigured the end of the world itself. As Luther would write a few decades later in his preface to the Book of Daniel: "This is now ours and the last age, when the Gospels are resounding, and crying out against the pope, so that he is desperate and knows not how and what he should do."[16] Divine power seemed on the verge of eruption: it would shower sinners with signs and portents, and intervene directly in human affairs. Prophets and preachers cried out for political and religious reforms in the Holy Roman Empire.

The author of Christian discord was, of course, Martin Luther, whose criticism of the sale of papal indulgences soon led to a storm of protests against the teachings and practices of the Roman Catholic Church. To the defenders of the old order, the Saxon monk and reformer was no less than a seven-headed monster, as in Johannes Cochlaeus's well-known image (figure 8).[17] The seven heads are, from left to right: doctor, Martin, Luther, ecclesiast, enthusiast, "Visitator," and Barrabas. The term "enthusiast" represented a name of abuse, applied usually by the Catholic Church (but also by the Protestant reformer himself) to Anabaptists and religious radicals of all sorts. Perhaps Cochlaeus was also mocking the practice of Protestant clergy visiting parishes to enforce Christian discipline. From left to right Luther's many heads gradually reveal him to be a rebel, as Barrabas was condemned to die as a rabble-rouser by the Romans but instead was freed and his place taken by Jesus at the crucifixion. Hence, Luther was an Antichrist. The sevenfold nature of Luther's head alluded of course both to the number of deadly sins in Catholic doctrine and to the seven-headed, ten-horned Beast from Revelation. Not to be outdone, a Lutheran antipapal polemic countered this with a woodcut of the "Seven-Headed Papal Monster" (figure 9). The verses point to his claws treading the Gospels underfoot and his lion's mouth—referring to Leo X—threatening nations with excommunication and swallowing up whole countries: the text ends with the verse "Gott geb das es gar get zu grund" or "May God send it straight to hell."[18]

Not only is the pope a seven-headed monster in Reformation propaganda, the clergy in general is monstrous. Collectively, they represent Leviathan, the sea monster in the Old Testament, shown in another satirical print (figure 10) in a monkish garb breathing fire, smoke, and sulfur from its mouth, menacing Luther, also in a monkish garb, depicted as an Old Testament prophet. This woodcut by Matthias Gnidias juxtaposed the monk-Leviathan with the monk-prophet (Luther).[19] The good friar Luther, holding the Scripture in his hands, will triumph over the monstrous fire of Leviathan, for the Latin caption states that the Lord will visit the earth with his sword and kill the Leviathan monster; that he will trample underfoot lions and dragons; and the dragon, with a halter around its nostrils, will be dragged away on a hook. Similarly, the opponents of the true prophet, Luther, the monkish and monstrous

Figure 8. Johannes Cochlaeus, Seven-headed Luther (1529). © Copyright The British Museum.

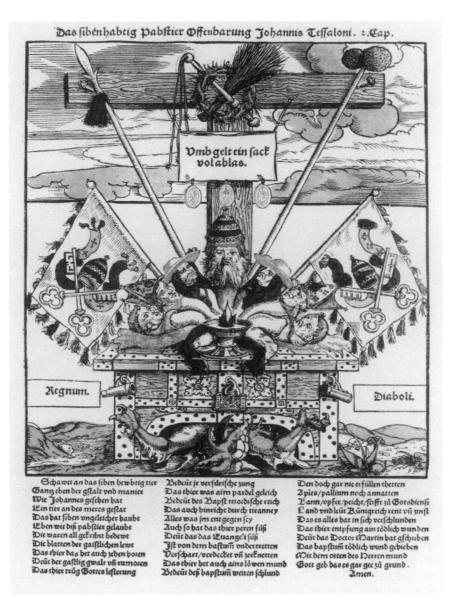

Figure 9. Seven-headed Papal Monster (1530). Courtesy of Kupferstichkabinett, Staatliche Museen zu Berlin.

Figure 10. Luther and Leviathan, from *Dialogi Murnarus leviathan vulgo dictus, Geltnar, oder Gensz Prediger* (Strasbourg, 1521). Courtesy of The Franciscan Institute Library, St. Bonaventure University.

defenders of the Roman Church, would meet their just punishment by an angry God.

If the appearance of the seven-headed papal monster and the Leviathan signify the apocalypse, the end of the world was already presaged in 1496 with the appearance of the papal ass of Rome (figure 11). Although this woodcut refers to the flooding of 1496, the particular representation of this monster owes its inspiration to the polemics of the early Reformation years.[20] Supposedly found on the banks of the Tiber after the flood waters had receded, this monster, whose representation here betrays a specific Reformation antipapal polemic, was interpreted by Melanchthon and Luther in the following way: the monster has the head of a donkey instead of having Christ as its head; the misshapen body is that of the Church; its scales signify the secular powers; the elephantine hand represents ecclesiastical repression while the other, human hand signifies pretensions to secular power; the claws and hoof of the monster also signify its pretension to both secular and spiritual powers; the feminine breasts and belly signify the sensuality of the cardinals and the ecclesiastical elites; the old man at the back represents a dying regime, with the dragon's head signifying the use of ecclesiastical bans as threats.

In the midst of this sulfurous swirl of polemics, generated by ardent partisans of Wittenberg and Rome with their images of the monstrous Reformer and Pope, Luther remained surprisingly serene. If the metaphoric language of monstrosities represented a new discourse of religious anxiety, Luther showed supreme confidence in his adherence to a traditional view. In several passages of his *Table Talk,* the Wittenberg reformer demonstrated a knowledge of Aristotle's theory of human generation: the development of limbs, the prominence of the head in the fetus, and the chorionic protection of the embryo.[21] Aristotle aside, human knowledge of the generation of life was limited. We cannot know the sex of our child in the fetus, Luther remarked in one of his conversations: "All of this is beyond our providence. My father and mother did not think that they would bring forth a Doctor Martin Luther. Creation is God's alone, something which we cannot perceive."[22] Echoing the Augus-

Der Bapstesel zu Rom

Figure 11. Woodcut of Papal Ass of Rome, from Philipp Melanchthon, *Deuttung der zwo grewlichen Figuren Bapstesels zu Rom und Munchkalbs* (Wittenberg, 1523). Courtesy of Rare Books Division, The New York Public Library, Astor, Lenox and Tilden Foundations.

tinian view, Luther refused to allow himself to be drawn into speculation about prodigious and monstrous events. In answering a letter from Nicolas von Amsdorf about "the monstrosity of foxes" on 3 June 1545—the original event is unclear as Amsdorf's letter is not extant—Luther refused to provide a theological interpretation except to agree that this was indeed an unnatural phenomenon.[23]

Birth and miscarriage provided a beautiful metaphor for Luther's evangelical message, but had no intrinsic prophetic significance. In a lyrical reflection, Luther compared the unborn child to the Christian Church:

The fruit in the mother's body is a representation and simile of the Church, as the baby in the womb is surrounded and wrapped with a thin skin, which in Greek is called *chorion* ... from which the fruit draws its sustenance. The *chorion* does not break until the fruit is ripe and timely and is brought forth into the light of the world. And thus also is the Church wrapped up and enclosed by the Word and seeks no other teaching of God's will, except what is revealed and shown in the very same Word, with which it is at peace, and remains steadfast through the faith until such a time that it will see in that other life God's light and countenance and hear God Himself preaching on the mysterious and now hidden things, which we have here in faith, but only there in beholding.[24]

For the Augustinian Luther, indebted to late medieval German mysticism, the *theologia deutsch*,[25] the true Church, the invisible Church, was a child waiting to be born. Yet Luther the reformer wished to play no part in hastening its birth. Continuing his metaphor of the embryonic Church, Luther disapproved of

those so frivolous and vainglorious that they rupture the *chorion* by premature movements (like the Anabaptists and other enthusiasts and hordes of rebellious spirits, who despised the preachership and wait for new signs and movements from heaven), and must therefore become premature fruit and dead children as aborted and premature matter. Therefore when the Church gazes upon this representation and simile, she should learn to be bound to the Word that she was given by God, from which she should not deviate a finger or hair.[26]

Aborted, premature mass; dead children; monstrous births: these seemed to have held little horror for Luther, who was calmly waiting for the Last Judgment. Sometime in the summer or autumn of 1532, Luther and his students were talking of monstrous beings that women sometimes gave birth to, among which was one that resembled a mouse that tried to run under a stool into a mousehole. Luther was supposed to have simply remarked on the power of the mind that it could even change the body.[27] And when somebody asked whether monstrosities of this kind ought to be baptized, Luther replied no because he believed they represented animal and not human life. And when someone else asked whether these monstrous beings possessed souls, Luther responded blithely: "I don't know. I haven't asked God about this."[28]

REFORMATION PROPAGANDA

Luther's refusal to specify the meaning of prodigies contrasted strongly with his contemporaries, who were eager to seek divine meaning in unnatural signs. But the language of monstrosity, as we shall see, is essentially unstable and slippery. Both Protestants and Catholics interpreted the same monstrous prodigies for their own advantage. For the Protestants, the 1522 monster of Freyberg, Saxony, born on 8 December, served as a portent for the depravity of the monastic estate (figure 12). The Protestant interpretation refers to the golden calf in a preaching position; he is blind and preaches with an outstretched tongue; his huge ear signifies the tyranny of the sacrament of confession; and his stiff neck the rigidity of the monkish estate.

However, as with the seven-headed monster, the monk-calf also has a Catholic interpretation. This was given by Pierre L'Estoile, a bourgeois of Paris, whose journals have been a major source for the study of the reign of Francis I:

> When Luther took Augustinian vows
> Taking human resemblance from that of a cow,
> His face, yet full of innocence
> He then polluted by his impudence
> For this monster demonstrates his presence
> To all humans difficult and strange
> For vices are wallowing in mud
> Therefore we come to know and recognize
> That the Saxons are harder than stones

Figure 12. Woodcut of Monk-Calf of Saxony, from Philipp Melanchthon, *Deuttung der zwo grewlichen Figuren Bapstesels zu Rom und Munchkalbs* (Wittenberg, 1523). Courtesy of Rare Books Division, The New York Public Library, Astor, Lenox and Tilden Foundations.

Who value this vain monster
And forsake not their sins bestial
Until they feel the hand of the judge celestial.[29]

What can one conclude from the different interpretations of the same signs? Religious polemics, it seems, used the same grammar, spoke the same language, and recognized the same signs. But if Catholics and Protestants saw different meanings in the same signs, the very stability of this language of monstrosities began to be undermined. In the multiple readings of confessional polemics, the principle of uncertainty has crept in; if God sends monsters as prodigies, as everyone agrees, does he favor the Protestant or the Catholic reading? How, precisely, does the language of monstrosity signify?

If discourses convey meaning through a three-part process of utterance, signifying, and interpretation, then the language of monsters is inherently ambiguous. True enough, God had spoken of his anger and displeasure in unnatural utterances of monstrous births. But were the conjoined twins, deformed fetuses, and vegetable matter understandable signs that communicated a specific divine intent, or simply audible utterances that reflected a generalized wrath? In other words, did monsters signify corruption of the Roman Church or the diabolical nature of her opponents? Did conjoined twins signify unity or discord? Since a sign cannot signify both something and its opposite, the act of interpretation was completely dependent on context to supply meaning. An interesting observation is that in the representation of Jews, the language of monstrous birth failed to convey the traditional anti-Jewish commonplaces.

Two single-leaf broadsheets of the late sixteenth century narrated monstrous births to Jewish women. The first, published in 1561 by the Augsburg printer Michael Moser, purported to report on the stillborn birth of a deformed infant, born with cow-like ears and with one leg each sticking out front and back. The unfortunate mother, Reitlin, gave birth on 18 December 1561 in the village of Lauterbrunnen outside of Augsburg. The author reported the event without any anti-Jewish rancor (perhaps even with a sympathetic tone) and simply remarked that the monstrous birth was another sign of the sins of the world and the Final Judgment as foretold by Christ. The fact that the mother was Jewish simply happened to be a detail of no significance.[30] The second broadsheet, published under a similar title ("True and Shocking Birth"), appeared in 1575 from the print shop of Michael Schirat in Heidelberg, and represented the German translation of an Italian text reporting on a monstrous birth on 26 May 1575 in Venice, where twins joined at the lower body were born alive to a Jewish mother.[31] Again, the accident of Jewish birth was not commented on. Again, the message was unnatural birth, the unmistakable and threatening utterance of God to repentance and Christian love. In these examples, the intended audience was Christian; and the two Jewish births were narrated in Lutheran, Catholic, and Calvinist milieus. Any attempt to construe an anti-Jewish interpretation would have subverted the original meaning of this discourse, whose signification only worked in the general Christian context and not in the specific field of anti-Semitism.

FROM ESCHATOLOGY TO CONFESSIONAL POLEMICS

The second half of the sixteenth century represented a second stage of development in this Reformation discourse of monsters. Two characteristics were prominent: first, the language of monstrosities became more complex as it acquired more signs, a profusion of signs, in other words; but, simultaneously, the specific meaning of these signs, and hence, the meaning of the discourse as a whole, became less clear. This paradox was equally manifest in Protestant and Catholic discourses of monstrosities, although the Protestant discourse was more suffused with prophecy and the Catholic with confessional polemics.

The Catholic ambivalence on prodigies and prophecies reflected the suspicion of religious enthusiasm in general and of that inspired by eschatological expectations in particular. Georg Witzel, a Catholic opponent of Luther, wrote in 1536 that "Luther had fabricated the message that the Last Day is at hand, and that the Antichrist has come, in order to frighten the world and draw people to his teachings. . . . This man is remarkable for his stubbornness in defending these fantasies, arguing that there are many signs, such as the flooding of the Tiber River, or the fall of Ghent in Flanders, that point to the immediate return of Christ."[32] While the Catholics did not reject all prodigies, they were more cautious in accepting monstrosities as signs of God's will, especially after the initial fervor of religious polemic in the 1520s and 1530s in the Empire. After the Council of Trent (1547–62), this caution was even more pronounced. The bishop of Bologna, Gabriele Paleoti, who played an important role in the last sessions of the council, wrote in his 1582 work, *Discorso intorno alle imagini sacre et profane,* perhaps the most important theoretical work on Counter-Reformation art, that painters should exercise extreme caution in representing monsters and prodigies because many have been led astray by false prophets. The occasional use of monsters as prodigies of Protestant heresy, such as the 1570 work *Tractatus de monstris* by Arnaud Sorbin, the bishop of Nevers, proved to be an exception rather than the rule.[33] Or take the epigram by the French physician Antoine Valet, who described the numerous monstrous offspring of Luther:

> *A witness, a witness, will be for us Germany*
> *When she opposed Christ with fraudulent Lutheran perjury,*
> *Stuffed with innumerable monstrous offspring*
> *Saxony suffered and felt the just wrath of Divinity.*[34]

The reference here was to Luther's constipation, a well-known motif that turned the metaphor of monstrous birth into a scatological reference to the reformer's own scatology.

The clearest example of the polemical use of monstrosities by Counter-Reformation authors was the 1569 broadsheet published in Ingolstadt by Alexander Weissenhorn. The site of the Bavarian university, Ingolstadt became a bulwark of the Counter-Reformation after the settlement of the Jesuits. This broadsheet of 399 verses with an accompanying woodcut, however, was composed by a friar, Johannes Nasus.[35] Entitled *Ecclesia Militans,* the image depicts, in the middle strip, the storming and the desecration of the Church by a host of monsters (figure 13). Numbered captions explain the action in the complex series of images. Numbers 20 to 34 depict a procession of monsters and monstrous animals lined up to enter and desecrate the Church. All of these creatures purportedly referred to actual monstrous births: the 1545 Saxon child with elongated head and torn skin (number 20)—"On zweifel es den krieg bedeüt" ("There is no doubt it signifies war," that is, the coming war between Charles V and the Protestant princes); a porcupine wearing a Saxon hat (number 21), "Darbei wirdt yederman bekandt" ("So will every man be known," meaning Luther); the 1553 two-headed infant of Meissen (number 22); the 1554 headless infant of Meissen (number 23); a horrid-looking creature born in 1568 (number 24); a child born in 1547 to Hans Eisleben and his wife near Mansfeld and Sangershausen, whose head alone grew to an abnormal size, signifying that everyone wanted to be king and prince and disobedient (number 25); the 1503 Hessian infant born looking like a magister (number 26); the 1519 Zürich child, born without eyes, ears, and nose, a hermaphrodite to boot (number 27); the 1546 black monk-fish (number 28); the famous 1523 monk-calf of Freyberg in Saxony, who "warned people to beware of Luther's calf-like courage, who led a cow's life, as Cochlaeus has shown" (number 29); the 1536 pig with the head of a priest, born in Hall, Saxony, signifying the Jew-loving Luther (number 30); a fox holding the flag with the words "*Dic Lux*" ("Speak the Light")—"even if it was from the Antichrist," remarked the author—and the man with two faces "who goes around in Germany to women, men, young and old, with many heads, mouths, and tongues, meaning to us Lutheranism" (numbers 31 and 32); the 1553 toad with a long tail born in Thüringen, signifying Anabaptists and Calvinists (number 33); and finally, the 1554 stillborn child in Stettin, born with an arm in place of an ear (number 34).

As the title of *Ecclesia Militans* indicates, this polemical broadsheet was "a wondrous counterattack on the Evangelical Exemplar." Notice too that all monsters depicted in the woodcut were taken from purported reports of monstrous births in Protestant territories: Saxony, Hessen, etc. No example of

Figure 13. Storming of church by monsters, *Ecclesia Militans* (1569). By permission of The British Library. Shelfmark 1870.d.1 (271).

monstrosities came from Catholic lands. Standing the monsters on their heads, as it were, Johann Nasus contested the Protestant interpretation of monstrosities: these prodigies signified not the corruption of the Roman Church and the Second Coming of Christ but the depravity and deformity of the new learning, brought forth in all its ugliness by Luther and his teaching, and spreading to Anabaptism and Calvinism. The language of monsters in this Counter-Reformation broadsheet was not one of prophecy but confessional polemic; the emotion it evoked was above all repugnance for heresy.

With the Lutherans, the story was very different. Even after the passing of Luther, the Protestant churches retained a very strong eschatological expectation.[36] With the opening of the floodgates of divine intervention in 1517, the Protestant divines experienced a continuous stream of signs and portents that heralded the sinfulness of the world and the impending Last Judgment. A language of monstrosity was very much alive. The profusion of monstrous births in the pamphlets of the second half of the sixteenth century was mostly of Lutheran provenance. The mechanism of the diffusion of this discourse points to the importance of Church superintendents, the clergy, and the government. These secular and ecclesiastical authorities in Protestant territorial states and cities were the ones who publicly displayed monstrous births. The language of monstrosities revealed God's warning, but not his specific design, and admonished the people to repentance and godly living. Several births of conjoined twins in the 1560s and 1570s illustrate this process.

A broadsheet published in Strasbourg in 1563 (figure 14) documented the birth of conjoined twins.[37] An honorable Strasbourg citizen was traveling on business and came to the village of Bischem three miles from the city, where he heard that a child had been born "of such a miraculous and frightening shape . . . and when he asked to see this birth, this miraculous handiwork of God Almighty, which he was allowed to see, and not only him, but all the inhabitants of the place, he saw that it was a shocking and miraculous child, born to the honorable and upstanding Jacob Schumacher and his spouse Jacobe." The description of the baby follows in the broadsheet: the birth occurred on 5 March at seven at night and the child was stillborn. The author

Warhafftige vnd Eigentliche Contrafactur einer

Wunderbarlichen geburt/so zů Bischen bei Roßen/in dem Elsaß gelegen/
geschehen/vnnd ist dise geburt den fünfften tag des
Mertzens geschehen/im Jar/
M. D. LXIII.

ALs man zalt nach der geburt vnsers Herren vnd Heiland Je
su Christi/M. D. Lxiij. Jar/da hat es sich begeben/Das ein Ersamer Burger
von Strasburg vber land gezogen ist/von wegen seiner geschefften/hat jhn der weg
biß gen Bischen im Elsaß getragen/drei meil wegs von Strasburg gelegen/Alda
gehört/wie das ein Kind geboren seye worden/einer solchen Wunderbarlichen vnd erschröckli,
chen gestalt (das ja gewißlich erschröcklich sein můß) als er nůn nach solcher geburt nachfra,
gens gethon/vnd solches wunderwerck Gottes Allmechtigen auch begert zůsehen/welches dañ
jhm zůgelassen worden/nit allein jhm/sondern allem Volck so daselbst worhafft ist/vnnd
ist solch erschröckliche vnd wunderbarliche geburt/Des Erbaren vnd fürnemen Jacob Schů,
machers Burger daselbst/vnnd seiner Ehlichen haußfrawen Jacobe genant/bürtig von Ra,
statt/jetzund wonhafft zů Bischen bei Roßen gelegen/an die welt bracht worden/vnnd in sol,
cher form vnnd gestalt/wie dann dise figur oben anzeige/Erstlich hat dises Kind eine breiten
Kopff/einen hals/zwei Angesicht/vier ohren/vier händ/vier füß/zwen füß seind vberstich dem
rücken zůgethon gewesen/zwen leib/vnd zwei hinder/seind beide leib knäblin gewesen/vnd ist di,
se geburt geschehen den 5.tag des Mertzens/vmb vij.vhren in der nacht/vnnd tod an die wele
kommen/Was aber Gott der Allmechtig mit disem wunderwerck/auch andern wûderzeichẽ/
so wir täglich hören vnd sehen/deüter/ist jm allein wissend. Derhalben so laßt vns Gott den
Allmechtigen vor augen haben/vnd jn freündtlich bitten/das er vns vor solchen vnerhörten ge
burten Vätterlich behüten wölle/durch Jesum Christum vnsern Herren/A M E N.

Getruckt zů Strasburg bei Peter Hug in S. Barbel gassen.

Figure 14. 1563 Strasbourg broadsheet, conjoined twins. Courtesy of Zentralbibliothek, Zurich.

concludes that "What God Almighty signifies with this miracle [*wunder-werck*] and other miraculous signs [*wunderzeichen*], which we hear and see daily, is only known to Him."[38]

Another pair of twins, joined at mid-body, was born on 10 June, 1569, in Berna in the Margravate of Brandenburg to the peasant Hans Strebels and his wife Barbara.[39] As a broadsheet published on the occurrence (figure 15) explained, one of the twins was stillborn; the other lived just under an hour after birth: "Such a miraculous, supernatural, and shocking birth was witnessed not only by the servants of the Church and the Village Headman of the said place, but also by almost the entire community plus nearby villages, some hundred people in all. But what such a rare and supernatural birth signifies and portends, we cannot really know, although it is highly probable, because other shocking signs in heaven and other elements in this year '69 have occurred, that we will not escape misfortune and punishment. May the Lord God admonish us to repentance with such signs."[40]

The authorities and the Protestant clergy usually put the monstrous dead infants on display as a warning; sermons and publications often followed, spreading this portent of God's admonition. The preachers Peter Rinovius and Peter Victorius, for example, preached on a monstrous birth in Havelsberg in 1581 at the request of their flock;[41] the language, however, did not carry the same interpretative self-confidence as in the earlier decades of the sixteenth century. Likewise, the Rostock superintendent Simon Pauli was aware that his interpretation of a monstrous birth at Grevesmuhl would be criticized. Tract after tract stressed the unknowable will of God; all that Christians could know was that monstrous births were signs from God to admonish the people to reform their sinful ways. From a function of prediction, monstrous births and the language of monstrosities increasingly took on a function of moral and social discipline; and one sign might have scores of meanings. As a 1578 Strasbourg broadsheet put it, monsters were portents of the many disorders in the natural and social order: unrest, uprisings, wars, bloodletting, repressions, hangings, mutinies, false teachings, the war cry of invading hordes, the plundering of cities; unusual diseases and plagues, the death of leaders,

Figure 15. 1569 set of conjoined twins. Courtesy of Zentralbibliothek, Zurich.

storms, thunder, flooding, crop failures, and the all-around falsehood and suspicion among people; un-Christian behavior, cheating, selling for profit, all kinds of shames and blasphemies, God's Word despised and turned around, the mocking of pious warnings, disobedience to the laws; in short, the cooling of all love.[42] Mocking this profusion of signs of monstrosities in the Lutheran Church, the Catholic cleric Johann Oldecop noted in his chronicle: "For some years now the rabbis and bell-ringers of the Lutheran sect have published many books and broadsheets with miraculous figures and news. . . . These figures are printed in such a way and read aloud to gatherings of poor, blind Lutherans, and interpreted in such a way, that the people, who until now have been living without fear and shame, and indulge in all sorts of wickedness, may repent and become obedient."[43]

CONCLUSION

By the last quarter of the sixteenth century, one can discern uncertainty in Reformation polemics on monstrosities. Let us contrast the pamphlet by Sebastian Brant (1495) on conjoined twins with the examples I have cited above from the 1560s and 1570s. For Brant, there existed an exact correspondence between the shape of the twins and the political events in the Empire this sign was meant to signify. The monster of 1495 represented a text that could be read precisely, for it used the specific grammar of the anthropomorphic language of prophecy. All created things were linked in this world of microcosms and macrocosms to the one Creator; and by locating the specific place of the given sign, one could find its corresponding meaning in the larger chain of signs. After a half-century of polemics, the profusion of signs (monstrous and otherwise) overwhelmed the interpretative capacity of prophecy: details such as whether twins were joined at the head, or the hip, or the body had no significance in and of themselves. The monster represented merely one kind of sign among the numerous portents demonstrating God's wrath; and the individual meaning of the specific monster was lost in the larger field of reference, one pointing to increasing sinfulness, disorder, and chaos in the created order.

The slippage of language in the discourse of monstrosities, first manifest in the Protestant-Catholic polemics of the 1520s and 1530s, intensified within Protestant discourse itself by the second half of the century. Portents, warnings, admonitions, and monstrous births failed to instill enough fear to make disciplined Christians in the new Protestant churches. For that the princes and magistrates of Protestant Germany established church synods, visitations, and marriage courts to police the morality and piety of their subjects. Enforcing church attendance, exacting tithes, demanding conformity, the authorities executed grievous sexual offenders, banished repeat moral offenders, and used fines and prison to shape the godly folk.[44] The ultimate design of God was no longer uncertain once the godly regimes were in place. With impiety and immorality banished by the princes' edicts, the monstrous lost its meaning in a theologico-political economy that nestled firmly in the natural right and divine sanction of princely rule.

4

"THE ANTICHRIST, THE BABILON, THE GREAT DRAGON"

Oliver Cromwell, Andrew Marvell, and the Apocalyptic Monstrous

LAURA LUNGER KNOPPERS

In an elaborate 1658 engraving, published shortly before his death, Oliver Cromwell, Lord Protector of England, stands over a complex but largely peaceful scene of conquest. *The Embleme of Englands Distractions. As also of her attained, and further expected Freedome, & Happines* (figure 16) depicts Cromwell as a martial heroic figure who has brought England through her civil wars to peace and prosperity.[1] The engraving shows a full-length Cromwell in cuirassier armor, an image based on earlier portraits by Robert Walker and Peter Lely, which in turn derived from the Caroline court portraiture of Sir Anthony Van Dyck and, ultimately, from Rubens and the Italian Renaissance.[2] But this illustrious iconographic heritage is here appropriated for polemical and rhetorical purposes, as Cromwell is placed in a highly allegorical and symbolic scene in which his military conquests and political achievements are interpreted in part through the images of monstrous apocalyptic, drawn from the biblical book of Revelation.

Hence, Cromwell stands with one foot on the sprawling dragon of Error (sectarianism), evoking the image of the archangel Michael who defeats the Great Dragon in Revelation 12. Cromwell's other foot rests between the bare breasts of a beautiful woman, whose label "Babylon" identifies her as the

93

Figure 16. William Faithorne, engraving of Oliver Cromwell between two pillars, *The Embleme of Englands Distractions* (1658). © Copyright The British Museum.

Great Whore who in Revelation 17 sits upon a seven-headed, ten-horned beast, dressed in scarlet and holding a golden cup "full of abominations and filthiness of her fornications." Here, marking the Whore as specifically popish (a common linkage in Protestant propaganda since the Reformation) is her rosary, stretched on the ground beside her head, and the writing on her cup: "Papa / Poculum aureum / plenum Abomnatio" (The pope: The golden cup when full is an abomination).[3] A crown has also tumbled to the ground. With the defeat of the papist threat on the one hand (or foot), and of sectarian error and faction on the other, the crises of the Protectorate are past: spears have become pruning hooks, swords have become plows, and bees are making their hive in a helmet. As the figure of Fame standing to his left no doubt proclaims, Oliver brings the olive of peace to the land.

This engraving—coming in the final year of Cromwell's rule as Lord Protector—thus uses monstrous bodies to represent the political and religious aberrations of his opponents. In its depiction of the defeat of the Whore of Babylon, this engraving constructs the military and masculine heroism of Cromwell in opposition to the deceptively beautiful feminine and the bestial. The defeat of the Whore and the Dragon bring peace and prosperity to England; national and individual identity rest literally and metaphorically upon the defeated and displayed body of the transgressive woman and her serpentine counterpart.

But if in this engraving bestial and gendered bodies serve to construct Cromwellian heroism, the preceding history of print and propaganda tells a much more complex story. From the mid-1640s through the years of civil war, regicide, and republic, the resonant figures of the apocalyptic monstrous—drawn largely from Daniel and Revelation and shaped by the visual and printed polemic of the Reformation—were variously deployed not only to support but violently to attack the controversial figure of Oliver Cromwell. In the early 1650s, Fifth Monarchists attack Cromwell as himself the "Antichrist, the [whore of] Babilon, the great dragon"; Andrew Marvell in turn praises the Lord Protector as "Angelique *Cromwell* who outwings the wind," chasing the Whore of Babylon to her Roman cave; and a 1656 Dutch tract again figures

Cromwell not as hero, but as Beast and Whore. Thus, while the late protectoral engraving, *The Embleme of Englands Distractions,* seeks to fix the allegorical references in a heroic and laudatory framework, further investigation reveals the problems in controlling and arresting meaning, as allegory moves
into history and bestial and grotesque apocalyptic bodies are used to figure
(variously defined) deformities in the body politic.

OLIVER CROMWELL, THE FIFTH MONARCHISTS, AND PROTESTANT CRUSADE

With the execution of Charles I in January 1649 and an imminent crusade
against Catholic forces in Ireland, the English republic seemed to its small minority of remaining supporters to be on the verge of ushering in the millennial
rule of the saints and the return of Christ himself on earth. The hopes for this
apocalyptic future were increasingly placed in the Lord General Oliver
Cromwell, who led military campaigns both to Ireland and to Scotland.
Cromwell was widely lauded as a hero of the new republic, constructed as a
military hero in print and in image (figure 17). A fervent antipapist, Cromwell
understood his Irish campaign as war against the popish Antichrist, drawing
upon the grotesque alimentary language of Revelation 12: "You are part of the
Antichrist, whose Kingdom the Scripture so expressly speaks should be laid in
blood; yea in the blood of the saints. You have shed great store of that already;
and ere it be long, you must all of you have blood to drink; even the dregs of
the cup of the fury and the wrath of God, which will be poured out unto
you!"[4]

Such eschatological expectations—without the violent antipapal rhetoric—continued to echo in the campaign against Scotland, which Cromwell
again led. In September 1650, Sidrach Simpson wrote Cromwell in the language of Revelation that "The Lord is . . . powring out his vial on the sun;
that is, on kings . . . you are throwing down what God is throwing down."[5]
Mr. William Hickman similarly assured Cromwell that "God hath designed
your Excellency to drive Ante-Christ out of all his forms."[6] A *Declaration of
the English Army* issued from Scotland under Cromwell's name was permeated

96

Figure 17. Engraving of Oliver Cromwell after Robert Walker, in Payne Fisher, *Irenodia Gratulatoria* (1652). Courtesy of Rare Books Division, Department of Rare Books and Special Collections. Princeton University Library.

with fervent millenarianism, as the soldiers sought "the destruction of Antichrist, the advancement of the Kingdom of Jesus Christ," having engaged against the late King and his Monarchy, as "one of the ten horns of the Beast spoken of, *Rev.* 17," guilty of the blood of the saints.[7] "Why should not *Scotland*," they asked, "as well as *England*, rejoyce to see the Horns of the Beast cut off, that we may joyn together to hate the Whore, and to *burn her flesh with fire?*"[8]

Likewise, radical sectarians saw the war that in 1652 broke out with the Dutch not as an end in itself but as a springboard for a march of conquest against the Catholic powers of Europe, ending in papal Rome. While war with a republican, Protestant nation might seem an anomaly—or to be stemming from economic and commercial rivalry—Steve Pincus has compellingly shown that this too was motivated by a religious consideration: punishment of the backsliding Dutch for their support of the Houses of Orange and Stuart and their failure to adhere to a Protestant vision.[9] With the outbreak of the war, radical preachers fulminated with visions of world conquest, in battle against foes figured in terms of the apocalyptic monstrous.

With Cromwell's dissolution of the increasingly conservative Long Parliament in April 1653, and with the convening in July 1653 of a nominated Parliament in which the radicals had a strong albeit minority voice, millenarian hopes reached fever pitch. Cromwell's own speech opening the Parliament on 4 July was notably apocalyptic: "I say, you are called with a high call; and why should we be afraid to say or think, that this way may be the door to usher in things that God hath promised; which have been prophesied of; which He has set the hearts of His people to wait for and expect? We know who they are that shall war with the Lamb, against his enemies; they shall be a people called, and chosen, and faithful."[10] Radical sectarian John Rogers wrote to Cromwell, "*Be of good chear!* for we will *ingage with you*—i.e. for *Christ,* in the quarrel against *Antichrist,* and the *bloody Beast.*"[11] Rogers exhorted Cromwell to "Stand on *Mount Sion* with the *Lamb* amongst the 144,000! *Revel.* 14.1. Help the *Woman* (the *Churches!*) *Revel.*12.16. And *hate* the Whore till you make her *desolate!* And *naked!* And *burn* her with *fire! Revel.* 17.16."[12]

Yet in the shifting and complex politics of mid-seventeenth-century England, such monstrous polemics—compelling to Cromwell at a time of civil war and in the early republic—could be turned against him. John Rogers was part of a loosely coordinated group of radical millenarians, primarily drawn from the ranks of Baptists and Congregationalists, who came to be known as "Fifth Monarchists" after the world-ruling fifth kingdom that followed the four Beasts or kingdoms envisioned in the prophecies of the book of Daniel.[13] While millenarian hopes were widespread at a time of civil war and regicide, the Fifth Monarchists emerged largely as an oppositional force after the disappointment of those hopes.[14] Initially they supported Cromwell, but his handling of the Dutch war and his taking upon himself power as Lord Protector eventually caused them to turn their rhetorical arsenal of apocalyptic monsters directly against him.

Fifth Monarchists fervently supported the war with the Dutch as part of a Protestant crusade that began with the English civil wars. According to a later source, Christopher Feake's Blackfriars sermon on 11 September 1653 abounded with fevered visions: "Thou gav'st a Cup into the hand of England, and we drank of it. Then thou carried'st it to Scotland and Ireland, and they drank of it. Now thou has carried it to Holland, and they are drinking of it. Lord carry it also to France, to Spain, to Rome, and let it never be out of some or other of their hands, till they drink and be drunk, and spew, and fall, and never rise any more."[15] In October, the Fifth Monarchist preachers explicitly opposed peace with the Dutch, exclaiming in violent terms that "God's vengeance would follow upon such a heathenish peace; for where should they have a landing place, when they went to do the great work of the Lord, and tear the Whore of Babylon out of her chair, if they gave back by making a peace with them, a people and a land, which the Lord had as good as given wholly up into their hands."[16]

Yet while the Blackfriars preachers were heating up their rhetoric of the Dutch war as the first step in an apocalyptic crusade against the Whore of Babylon, Cromwell himself was seeking peace. Hence, the same observer comments that "I fear for all our big words, we shall rather than have no olive branch, accept of a shitten one; for upon my word we are as weary of the war as the Holland dogs."[17] He goes on to point to "two violent factions," the "one great affectors of the peace, and the other greater loathers of it"; in this writer's view, the gaining of any kind of peace with the Dutch "so very much . . . concerns Cromwell in particular, and this state's safety and settlement in general . . . that I apprehend it much."[18]

Cromwell's reluctance to continue the godly crusade against the apostate Dutch caused the Fifth Monarchists to turn against him, even before the inception of the Protectorate. Late in November, one contemporary reported that "Harrison and his party do rail and preach every day against the General and the peace with Holland."[19] In early December, at the Monday lecture at Blackfriars, "three or four of the Anabaptisticall ministers preach constantly with very great bitternes against the present government, but especially against his excellency, calling him the man of sin, the old dragon, and many other scripture ill names."[20]

Cromwell's complicity in the disbanding of the nominated Parliament (whose radical attacks on tithes, law, and seemingly property had caused considerable alarm) and his taking on sole power under the Instrument of Government transformed him, in radical eyes, from great crusader to apocalyptic monster. The Instrument of Government, England's only written constitution, in fact provided for a system of checks and balances, with Cromwell and the Parliament sharing legislative power and Cromwell and the Council functioning as the executive.[21] But for radical sectarians, King Oliver had now—illicitly and outrageously—taken the place of King Jesus.

Visions of the apocalyptic destruction of the monstrous mark, for example, the works of Fifth Monarchist prophetess Anna Trapnel. *Strange and Wonderful Newes from White-Hall*, published in March 1654, tells of Trapnel's "many Visions and Revelations touching the Government of the Nation," after she had fallen into a twelve-day trance at Whitehall.[22] In Trapnel's culminating vision, monstrous bodies represent the political monstrosity of a Protectorate that had usurped the reign of King Jesus: "she saw as it were great darkness on the earth; and . . . at a little distance a great company of cattel, some like Buls, some like Oxen, and some lesser cattel, their faces and heads like men, having on either side their heads a horn: for the foremost, his countenance was perfectly like unto [Cromwell']s and on a sudden there was a great shout of those that followed him, he being singled out alone, and the foremost, and he looking back, they bowed themselves unto him."[23] The Cromwell-headed bull, worshiped like the Beast and false prophet in Revelation, threatens the saints, who nonetheless receive divine succor: "and immediatly they fawning upon him, he seemed to run at her; and as he was neer to her breast with his horn an hand and arm grasped her round, and a voice said to her, I will be thy safety; and then he run at many precious Saints that stood in his way, and that durst look boldly in his face."[24]

John Rogers's frenetic writings and speech—in sharp contrast to his earlier support of Cromwell—soon landed him in prison, which he used as a platform to continue his rhetorical opposition. According to the (admittedly hostile) report of his jail keeper, an unbowed Rogers aimed "at the destruction of this Government," encouraging his audience "a handfull of Scum, the very raf of Billingsgate, Redriffe, Ratcliffe, Wappen, &c . . . not in any misticall expressions, but in plaine words, viz:—That 'twill bee all their owne very shortly, and the greate man at Whitehall must suddenly be confounded and destroyed . . . that they are the saints that must shortly injoy and possesse the glory of the earth, and all men being either saints or devills, whosoever is not of their mind are devills, they being the saints."[25] In particular, Rogers drew upon the resonant language of the apocalyptic monstrous to urge that "the Antichrist, the Babilon, the great dragon, or the man of sin, *Oliver Cromwell* at Whitehall, must be puld downe."[26]

Yet the rhetorical deployment of monstrous bodies was not left to opposing voices in the early years of the Protectorate. While one Cromwellian moderate dismissed the Fifth Monarchists as having "ill made brains and disturbed fancies, strongly tinctured with an hypocondriak melancholy,"[27] and another scoffed, particularly with reference to Vavasor Powell, that their "chief work . . . to preach and advance Christ's *Personal Reign* here on *Earth* [was] the Ancient Errour and Fopperie of the *Chiliasts* or *Millenaries,* huffed and exploded out of the *Church of Christ* in the very *Infancy* thereof,"[28] Andrew Marvell envisions Cromwell in precisely the kind of Protestant crusade against the Whore that the radicals championed.

"ANGELIQUE *CROMWELL* WHO OUTWINGS THE WIND": MARVELL, CROMWELL, AND THE WHORE OF BABYLON

If the fifth monarchists tap into a tradition of apocalyptic monstrous bodies to attack Cromwell as Lord Protector, Andrew Marvell's poem, *The First Anniversary of the Government under O.C.,* published anonymously in *Mercurius Politicus* in early 1655, deftly reverses the terms.[29] While the *First Anniversary* is most often read in terms of domestic politics, re-viewing the poem in the context of an international Protestant crusade both explains otherwise puzzling features and shows its timeliness and its highly specific relevance for Cromwellian foreign policy.[30] Marvell's Cromwell, rather than being "the Antichrist, the Babilon, the great dragon" who attempts to destroy and must be destroyed by the saints, is the "great Captain" (l. 321) who—like the archangel Michael in Revelation—continues to lead the fight against the apocalyptic beasts.

Marvell's wide-ranging poem meditates on both Protector and state at the first anniversary of the Instrument of Government. The poem as a whole draws on multiple languages and narratives: classical, biblical, natural, and historical. The nature and force of the apocalyptic elements have been debated, with some scholars arguing that the millenarianism is highly conditional, even deliberately undercut, and other countering that nonapocalyptic elements in fact build up to the seemingly isolated apocalyptic core.[31] Scholars have not, however, placed the poem in relation to debate on Cromwellian foreign rather than domestic policy, current ideas of Protestant Crusade, or Reformation iterations of the Whore of Babylon, the Great Beast, or the kings by whom they are falsely worshiped. Such a context allows us to see both the force of the apocalyptic monstrous in shaping the message of the poem and its ongoing potency for representing and conceiving of Cromwellian foreign policy.[32] But we also see that Marvell stresses the opacity of apocalyptic signs and the difficulty of seeing and understanding the fraught events and figures of the end times.

Opening the poem is a vision of Cromwell in action: running, springing, contracting the force of scattered time, tuning the ruling Instrument. In this he is contrasted to the "heavy Monarchs" (l. 15) of Europe, who watch him with fear and misunderstanding:

> While by his Beams observing Princes steer,
> And wisely court the Influence they fear;
> O would they rather by his Pattern won
> Kiss the approaching, nor yet angry Son.
> (ll. 103–06)

Marvell's Cromwell presents apocalyptic opportunities: "How might they under such a Captain raise / The great Designes kept for the latter Dayes!" (ll. 109–10). But the Catholic powers of Europe, "ignorantly bred, / By Malice some, by Errour more misled" (ll. 117–18), refuse to join Cromwell's Protestant Crusade. Even worse, they comply with the popish powers of the Antichrist: "Hence still they sing Hosanna to the Whore, / And her whom they should Massacre adore" (ll. 113–14).

In realigning the Whore of Babylon with the Roman Catholic Church, Marvell both rebuts Fifth Monarchist attacks on Cromwell and draws upon a long and powerful iconographical and polemical tradition, as indeed did the Fifth Monarchists themselves, however violently and idiosyncratically. The notoriously difficult text of Revelation—replete with visions, symbolic language, numerology, armed horsemen, vials, candlesticks, trumpets, plagues, wars, and demonic and celestial forces—had been variously interpreted, since the time of Augustine, in moral, spiritual, present, or future terms.[33] While traditional Catholic exegetes read the various persecuting Beasts and the Great Whore herself as figuring pagan Rome with its cult of emperor worship, the Reformers seized upon these monsters to legitimate their own religious and political struggle, situating present-day events within a narrative of apocalyptic history.[34] Both Luther and Calvin appropriated the figures of Revelation for immediate polemical purposes, linking Antichrist, the great Beast from the sea, the Great Dragon, and the Whore of Babylon with the papacy.[35]

Reformation polemic was accompanied by visual illustration. The German artist Albrecht Dürer's woodcuts in his 1498 *Apocalypse* became the precedent for most post-Reformation illustrations of Revelation. Dürer's representation of the Whore of Babylon (figure 18) inscribes political and religious differences in and through particular bodies: female, monstrous, angelic, heroic. The body of the Whore is itself an allegorical text to be deciphered and read.[36] Her lavish clothing, jewelry, and gem-encrusted crown mark her as a prostitute, one who has enriched herself on the trade and exchange of others: the elaborate chalice that she holds aloft conceals the wine of her (economic) fornication.[37] The true monstrousness of the seemingly beautiful woman is revealed by the beast upon which she rides, with its grotesque heads of goats, asses, and birds, its monstrously scaly skin, its distended claw-feet, and its twisting tail.

In the Dürer engraving, female and bestial bodies emblematize the corruption of pagan Rome, which—in its literal form as a city—burns in the upper right-hand corner of the engraving.[38] Dürer also depicts the angelic forces that are arrayed against evil. The deceptively beautiful woman and the seven-headed, ten-horned beast upon which she rides are counterpoised in the upper left hand of the engraving by the heroic figures of the heavenly army, following the rider Faithful and True. But the foreground of the engraving belongs to the monstrous and the aberrant: the harlot, the false prophet (with a turban), and the gaping crowd that appears foolishly susceptible to the harlot's wiles.

In Reformation polemic, from the early wars in Germany to the later political and religious struggles in England, monstrous bodies are the site of political struggle and resistance.[39] Luther and other Reformers pulled the figures of Revelation from past history—or moral allegory—into present day political and religious critique, enhancing their message through print and visual

Figure 18. Albrecht Dürer, Whore of Babylon, from *Apocalypse* (1498). © Copyright The British Museum.

image.[40] Although based on Dürer, the twenty-one designs for the Book of Revelation or the Apocalypse in Luther's *Das Newe Testament Deutzsch* (September 1522) done by the workshop of Lucas Cranach the Elder showed the force of Reformation polemic and a new eschatological understanding. Three woodcuts, including one of the Whore of Babylon (figure 19), introduced papal tiaras that identified the various beasts or monsters of Revelation with the pope. Although, after objections, the tiaras were removed from the December 1522 edition of *Das Newe Testament,* they were reproduced in some later German Reformation Bibles.[41]

In sixteenth- and seventeenth-century England, political appropriations of the monstrous apocalyptic, including the Whore of Babylon and the Great Beast, became even more fraught and fragmented, as contemporary identifications moved beyond the papacy. Visual representations of the Whore of Babylon in both the Tyndale (figure 20) and Coverdale (figure 21) New Testaments derive from the Dürer and Luther prints, although the papal tiara is no longer present.[42] Coverdale's writings elsewhere, however, and printed glosses in the 1560 Geneva Bible explicitly link Babylon with the Papacy: "The beast signifieth ancient Rome and the woman that sitteth thereon, the newe Rome, which is the Papistrie, whose crueltie and bloodshedding is declared by skarlat." But this identification also moved beyond Protestant-Catholic polemics. At the time of the English civil war, even those perceived to be lukewarm in the fight against Rome—including Charles I himself—began to be identified with the Great Beasts of Revelation. In the 1650s, as we have seen, Cromwell himself was transformed in radical eyes into a monstrous conflation of the "Antichrist, the [Whore of] Babilon, the great dragon."

Writing to shape as well as to defend the new Protectorate, Andrew Marvell, in turn, boldly reinscribes Cromwell as the Great Captain and his foes as the monsters to be defeated in the apocalypse. Yet throughout the poem he also calls attention to the problems of misprision. The kings—as we saw earlier—far from combating, fall to worshiping the Whore. Until the kings read properly the signs of the last times, awakened from their "regal sloth and long

Figure 19. Lucas Cranach the Elder, Whore of Babylon, from Luther, *Das Newe Testament Deutzsch* (Wittenberg, September 1522). By permission of The British Library. Shelfmark C. 36.g.7.

107

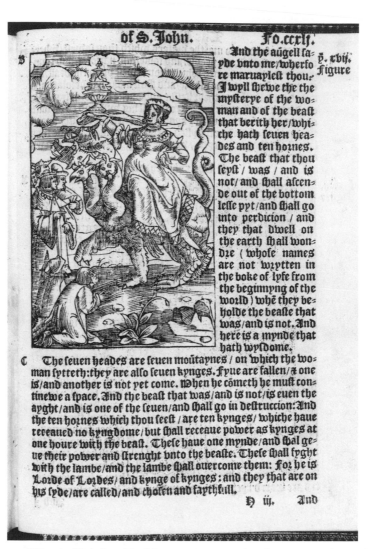

And thé augell sayde vnto me/wherfore maruaylest thou: I wyll shewe the the mysterye of the woman and of the beast that berith her/whiche hath seuen heades and ten hoznes. The beast that thou seyst / was / and is not/ and shall ascende out of the bottomlesse pyt/and shall go vnto perdicion / and they that dwell on the earth shall wondze (whose names are not wzytten in the boke of lyfe from the begimnyng of the wozld) whé they beholde the beaste that was/and is not. And here is a mynde that hath wysdome.

The seuen heades are seuen moūtaynes / on which the woman sytteth:they are also seuen kynges. Fyue are fallen/ꝣ one is/and another is not yet come. Whē he cōmeth he must continewe a space. And the beast that was/and is not/is euen the aypght/and is one of the seuen/and shall go in destruccion:And the ten hoznes which thou seest / are ten kynges/ whiche haue receaued no kyngdome/ but shall receaue power as kynges at one houre with the beast. These haue one mynde/and shal geue their power and strenght vnto the beaste. These shall fyght with the lambe/and the lambe shall ouercome them: Foz he is Lozde of Lozdes/ and kynge of kynges : and they that are on his syde/are called/and chosen and faythfull.

H iij.   And

Figure 20. Whore of Babylon, Tyndale New Testament (1536). Courtesy of Scheide Library, Princeton, N.J.

Figure 21. Whore of Babylon, Coverdale New Testament (Antwerp, 1538). Courtesy of Scheide Library, Princeton, N.J.

slumbers" by the shrill horn of Marvell's own poetry, the poet will strive to keep pace with the heroic Cromwell alone:

> *Till then my Muse shall hollow far behind*
> *Angelique* Cromwell *who outwings the wind;*
> *And in dark Nights, and in cold Dayes alone*

> *Pursues the Monster thorough every Throne:*
> *Which shrinking to her* Roman *Den impure,*
> *Gnashes her Goary teeth; nor there secure.*
> *(ll. 125–30)*

Marvell envisions Cromwell as pursuing the harlot/monster to her den at Rome: precisely the kind of crusade for which the radicals had been clamoring. As in early Reformation polemic, he links the Whore of Babylon with the Roman Catholic Church, conflating the Whore with the beast upon which she rides and adding in the graphic detail that her teeth are gory, presumably with the blood of the saints.

In less graphic and visual language, moving away from the monstrous papacy to be defeated, Marvell also elaborates on a vision of the end times:

> *Hence oft I think, if in some happy Hour*
> *High Grace should meet in one with highest Pow'r,*
> *And then a seasonable People still*
> *Should bend to his, as he to Heavens will,*
> *What we might hope, what wonderful Effect*
> *From such a wish'd Conjuncture might reflect.*
> *(ll. 131–36)*

While the signs of the end times cannot be clearly read—"But a Thick Cloud about that Morning lyes, / And intercepts the Beams of Mortal eyes" (ll. 141–42)—Marvell nonetheless makes clear Cromwell's central role in the final apocalyptic moments: "That 'tis the most which we determine can, / If these the Times, then this must be the Man" (ll. 143–44).

This vision, pointing to the revelation of the future, contrasts sharply with the malice and blindness of Cromwell's foes in *The First Anniversary,* figured in a series of increasingly pointed anecdotes about faulty vision that leads up to a direct attack on the Fifth Monarchists themselves. Marvell has already, as we have seen, set up the failure of vision in the European kings who misconstrue both the Whore (the Catholic Church) and the hero (Cromwell). Another failure of sight marks the center of the poem: the mistaken mourning—and gloating by the Fifth Monarchists—over Cromwell's riding accident in Hyde Park in October 1654.

Chastising the radical saints "Who watch'd thy halting, and thy Fall deride, / Rejoycing when thy Foot had slipt aside; / That their new King might the fifth Scepter shake, / And make the World, by his Example, Quake" (ll. 295–98), Marvell further corrects contemporary applications of the monsters of Revelation to current politics. The Fifth Monarchists themselves are now given a crucial place in the book of Revelation as "Accursed Locusts, whom your King does spit / Out of the Center of th' unbottomed Pit" (ll. 311–12). They are agents not of the millennial fifth kingdom that comes after the four beasts / kingdoms of Daniel, but of the fifth trumpet of wrath in Revelation 9.[43] Marvell hence depicts Cromwell's radical opponents as the grotesque locusts that emerge from the bottomless pit in Revelation: in doing so, he both indicates their infernal origin and intimates their pending destruction.

In Marvell's vision, Cromwell serves as an apocalyptic agent against the forces of evil, held back from the glorious events of the end time not only by opposition from the European princes—who worship rather than massacre the Whore—but by the intransigence of his own people, including his own illegitimate offspring, the Fifth Monarchists. Nonetheless Marvell points toward ongoing Protestant Crusade in a more immediate context than literary scholars, focused on the domestic English scene, have recognized. As Marvell composed the poem for publication, London was abuzz with speculation about two fleets that had been outfitted at great expense and effort. One, commanded by Admiral Blake, was prepared for naval battle only and left England in October to head to the Mediterranean. The other, led by General Venables, and including land forces as well as naval, left Portsmouth in late December. Although its destination was unknown, speculation was rife as to whether the second fleet was directed against Spain, long viewed as arch-protector of papists.[44]

Cromwell's recovery and return in *The First Anniversary,* then, is watched not only by the Fifth Monarchists, but by awestruck foreign princes. The poem ends with yet another scene of viewing and wondering: foreign princes puzzling over the rigging of a navy and rebuilding of a state: "Is this, saith one, the Nation that we read / Spent with both Wars, under a Captain dead? / Yet rig a Navy while we dress us late; / And ere we Dine, rase and rebuild their State" (ll. 349–52). The princes specifically focus on the power of the Cromwellian navy:

> *What Oaken Forrests, and what golden Mines!*
> *What Mints of Men, what Union of Designes!*
> *Unless their Ships, do, as their Fowle proceed*
> *Of shedding Leaves, that with their Ocean breed.*
> *Theirs are not Ships, but rather Arks of War,*
> *And beaked Promontories sail'd from far;*
> *Of floting Islands a new Hatched Nest;*
> *A Fleet of Worlds, of other Worlds in quest.*
> *(ll. 353–60)*

Although Marvell would likely have heard of the Caribbean destination only among other rumors, the fleet in fact had set out on what came to be known as the Western Design against Spanish possessions—source of much wealth and power—in the New World.[45] Following peace with the Dutch in spring 1654, the Council of State had almost immediately turned to thoughts of new war: with either Spain or France. Unusually detailed minutes of a Council meeting in summer 1654 record a debate between those who cautioned against the expense and uncertainty of an expedition against the Spanish colonies in the New World and those who urged it on grounds both of religion—a strike against popery—and material gain.[46] In a subsequent meeting, Cromwell was recorded as saying that "God has not brought us hither where wee are but to consider the worke that wee may doe in the world as well as at home."[47] Although historians debate whether the ensuing war was defensive—to stop the universal empire of the Spanish crown—or an Elizabeth-style crusade to eviscerate the allies of the Whore of Babylon,[48] Cromwell clearly saw the conflict as furthering both national interest and Protestant Crusade.

To attack Spain in the New World was for Cromwell a continuation of the cause of Christ against Antichrist and the Great Whore. Samuel Sewall later recounted that John Cotton, correspondent with Cromwell in the New World, advised him that "to take from the Spainard in America would be to dry up Euphrates; which was one thing put Him upon his Expedition to Hispaniola."[49] Cromwell himself later wrote to Vice-Admiral Goodson at Jamaica: "You are left there; and I pray you set up your banners in the name of Christ; for undoubtedly it is His Cause. . . . The Lord Himself hath a controversy with your enemies; even with that Roman Babylon, of which the Spaniard is the great underpropper. In that respect we fight the Lord's battles; and in this the scriptures are most plain."[50] While Marvell depicts the wondering foreign princes as seeing Cromwell without understanding, his final commendation of Cromwell may thus pointedly refer to the building and launching of the fleets and the much-anticipated crusade against popery: "And as the *Angel* of our Commonweal, / Troubling the Waters, yearly mak'st them Heal" (401–2).

In January 1655, there was no way of predicting that the invincible English forces—including the navy here admired as "wood-Leviathans / Arm'd with three Tire of brazen Hurricans" (361–62)—would, in fact, be humiliated and thoroughly routed in their initial attempt to take San Domingo.[51] Poorly equipped forces, the ravages of tropical heat and disease, and inconsistent leadership all played a role in a defeat and humiliation that would cause Cromwell to question his most cherished notions of serving as instrument of providence.[52] The ancillary conquest of Jamaica, later an important sugar plantation for the British, did little to alleviate the sting of defeat. And British interference with Spanish colonies in the New World led to war with Spain on the mainland, despite Cromwell's initial confidence that it would not. Writing to Vice-Admiral Goodson in Jamaica, we recall, Cromwell invoked scriptural grounding as "most plain." But in the dark days that followed the defeat in Hispaniola, God's intent was not so obvious. Nor were the binaries of the Revelation text, once brought into the turmoil of seventeenth-century European politics, stable, unchanging, or uncontested.

A DUTCH CATHOLIC RESPONSE: "CROM-GHEWELT" AS THE WHORE OF BABYLON

If Andrew Marvell breaks down monsters and heroes (with the exception of the Fifth Monarchists) along a Catholic/Protestant divide, others viewed England's situation in Europe in 1655–56 as considerably more complex. Our final, Dutch text shows the use of monstrous bodies from Revelation to place Cromwell's actions and the English republic in a narrative of the end times. But if Marvell's Cromwell is an angelic figure pursuing the gory harlot/monster to its Roman den, in the view of this Dutch, Catholic writer, Cromwell is not the hero but the Whore.

Cromwell's own pronouncements on foreign affairs often showed an enthusiasm for Protestant Crusade. But Cromwellian foreign policy and political alignments were not so clear-cut. In breaking with Spain, Cromwell forged closer links with a rising Catholic power, France. The Western Design helped to push England into an alliance with France that had long been sought by the French ambassador, Antoine de Bourdeaux, on behalf of Cardinal Mazarin and the French king Louis XIV.[53] In November 1655, a treaty between England and France signed at Westminster regularized commercial relations between the two countries, including the cessation of reprisals and the taking of ships at sea; reparations for losses already sustained; and agreement that neither nation should aid the rebels or enemies of the other. Although largely a commercial treaty, the Westminster agreement nonetheless firmly aligned England and France. A more broad-based treaty would be signed in Paris in March 1657.[54]

Cromwell was sharply criticized in the early Restoration for a blinkered foreign policy that operated on an outdated Protestant ideology: combating Spain as the traditional papist power, while neglecting or failing to recognize the true threats from the growing mercantile power of the Dutch, the dominance of France, and the aggressive policies of the new Swedish king, Charles X, which threatened the balance of power in the Baltic.[55] But to ally with a strong power against a weaker seemed to Cromwell to bring together religious and national interests. Cromwell also feared a rapprochement between Bourbon France and Habsburg Spain, which was rumored to be being undertaken by the pope himself. Aligning with the power of France brought promise—however specious—of better treatment for the French Huguenots; Mazarin had responded, however belatedly, to Cromwell's outrage and demand that he crack down on the duke of Savoy after his massacre of Protestant Vaudois in the Piedmont in summer 1655. The treaty with France also served to maintain a strong power against the potential threat of the (Catholic) Austrian Habsburgs, in particular the Holy Roman Emperor Ferdinand III. Conveniently, the treaty contained secret clauses expelling some of the Stuarts from France and hence forestalled French support for restoring the Stuarts by force or intrigue.[56]

The Dutch, however, had little reason to be pleased with the new alliance between England and France. Tensions between England and the United Provinces had continued since the conclusion of peace after the war of 1652–54. The terms of peace were resented by many of the Dutch and secret clauses barring the House of Orange from power in the province of Holland brought considerable backlash against the Grand Pensionary of Holland, John deWitt. Shipping and fishing rivalries continued to exacerbate tensions. The Dutch also feared that France and England might combine to carve up the newly independent United Provinces.[57] Cromwell's close relations with the aggressive Charles X, whose expansionist foreign policy had endangered the Dutch shipping trade to the North Sea, were a further source of anxiety and tension.[58]

Published in Cologne in 1656, a rare Dutch tract, *Kort Beworp vande dry Teghenwoordighe aenmerckens-weerdighe Wonderheden des Wereldts* (Brief Sketch of Three Contemporary Notable Wonders of the World)[59] depicts Cromwell as the "seven-hoofdigh, thien-hoornigh beest" of Revelation who has also taken on the roles of Antichrist and of Whore. The author's sympathies lie both with the (largely Protestant) Dutch republic and with Catholic doctrine. Set in the form of a "new Dutch chat," conducted on the night-boat from Amsterdam to Rotterdam, among Master Robert from London, Pieter Janssens from Amsterdam, and Jan van den Bosch and Samuel Jacobs from Zeeland, the tract situates current European events within (highly contested) apocalyptic history. The wonders are read as signs of the end times, revealing, in particular, Cromwell's moral monstrosity. Bestial and grotesque bodies are used to point readers away from Cromwell and his apostate ally, Cardinal Mazarin, and to prompt their support for the Habsburg Catholic stalwarts, Philip IV of Spain and Ferdinand III, Holy Roman Emperor.

The title page of *Kort Beworp* lays out the basic outline of the long tract to follow:

> First, it will be proved likely from God's Word that we live at the end of the last times of the world and walk in that time. Second, that Crom-ghewelt [literally, "crooked violence"] has come at the proper time, that is, to show himself to the world as the real Antichrist, and also has begun to play the part of the Antichrist very cleverly, with the king of Sweden and Mas-ruin—as no one in the world before them has ever played the part. Third, it will be shown that God has placed on the stage of the world the godly conversion [to Catholicism] of the illustrious Christina Alexandria Maria, Queen of Sweden, as a convincing mortification of the covenant-breaking king of Sweden, Crom-ghewelt, with Mas-ruin, and all the ungodly of the world in this time.[60]

The text hence uses revealed knowledge of cosmic struggle to show that the time of oppression is short: Cromwell's very successes in relation to other European nations adumbrate his impending fall and destruction.

A frontispiece engraving to *Kort Beworp* (figure 22) inscribes national and religious differences in and across bestial, masculine and heroic, regal, and gendered bodies. Cromwell, his hair strikingly dressed as a woman's (although he retains the armor of earlier portraiture), rides the seven-headed Beast of Revelation. He holds in one hand the feminine symbol of the Whore's Cup of Abominations: in the other, a martial and masculine flaming sword. Above Cromwell's head are the words *Crom Gewelt* or "crooked violence," a play on his name that continues throughout the pamphlet.

Guided by its rider, the seven-headed, ten-horned Beast of Revelation spews fire and drives before him three unarmed figures representing the States of Holland. Hence the caption on the left reads: "The States of Holland are frightened of Crom gewelt, / Because he now, as tyrant, tortures the whole world."[61] The tract draws on a compendium of Dutch resentments against England: not only the humiliations of defeat and the current threat to Dutch trade, but (from an Orangist point of view) the regicide and the treatment of the Scots and Irish. *Kort Beworp* rewrites these events in terms of the apocalyptic monstrous, bringing the biblical narrative to bear on judgment and condemnation of Cromwell and his allies.

Hence, the tract represents Cromwell's threats to the Dutch as continuing his nefarious activities from the British civil wars and evincing his identity as a creature of the Antichrist: "But the people who know and fear the Lord shall admonish each other, and the wise among the people shall teach many others, and therefore they shall perish through fire, sword, and prison, and will be robbed and plundered by the underlings of the Antichrist—just as Crom-ghewelt has done to the English, Scots, and Irish, and also to the Hollanders, Frisians, and Zeelanders, and still seeks to do every day."[62] In particular, *Kort Beworp* depicts Cromwell as a threat to the true, Catholic church and its sacraments: "And is it not Cromwell, as it is written of the Antichrist, who seeks (through his underlings) to take away

Figure 22. Oliver Cromwell as the Whore of Babylon riding on seven-headed beast, from *Kort Beworp vande dry Teghenwoordighe aenmerckens-weerdighe Wonderheden des Wereldts* (Cologne, 1656). By permission of The British Library. Shelfmark E 879(4).

the Holy daily Sacrifice of the Mass throughout the world?"[63] And indeed, underneath its clawing foot, the Beast upon which Cromwell rides is about to trample upon a miter, crucifix, chalice with the Host spilled upon the ground, a crown, and a scepter.

The joint condemnation of Cromwell and Cardinal Mazarin, in the engraving and in the printed text that follows, reflects Dutch animosity toward the French and the fears surrounding the recent Anglo-French treaty. The frontispiece shows Mazarin twisting the tail of the Beast upon which Cromwell rides, inspired by the devil who blows with a bellows into his ear. A caption over Mazarin's head reads:

"The Antichrist, the Babilon, the great dragon"

See how Masruin twists that tail full of evil venom
It's Mazarin who says, it should be more crooked
Before I can turn the true Church upside down
The States of Holland must learn to dance to French pipes.[64]

In the text itself of *Kort Beworp,* Cromwell and Mazarin are described as the Great Beast from the Sea, upon which the Whore rides, and the Second Beast that comes to its aid. The text alleges that, as the Beast demands worship, so does Cromwell:

And does he not also elevate himself as God when he makes himself to be honored and worshiped as a God on earth by all princes and potentates? No ambassador is so brave as to appear for an audience before "Oil-in-the-fire Cromtwel" without thrice bending the knee and bowing the head toward the ground. And when they bid farewell, they must walk backwards, with their face turned toward the Crooked Beast, again bowing to the ground three times for this seven-headed, ten-horned beast.[65]

Such worship is also visually represented in the lower right of the engraving, as the kings and other figures bow down before Cromwell on the Beast. While in the text itself, Cromwell is identified as the Beast and not as the Whore, he is represented—like the Whore—as falsely deceptive, with "beautiful" (*schoone*) words: "And is it not the seven-headed, ten-horned Beast of England who is able to stupefy and bewitch all the apostates from the Roman Church with beautiful words and promises and threats, in order to bring them under his tyrannical Antichristian power?"[66]

Mazarin, in turn, is depicted as the Second Beast: "Even though [Mazarin] bears the title of Cardinal, he is thereby not a priest of God. But he is like the seven-headed, ten-horned 'krom-gheweldigh' beast, a fearsome, grotesque, monstrous beast in England, which causes Christendom in our terrible time to shudder and tremble."[67] If Cromwell is the first beast from the sea, drawn from Revelation, Cardinal "Mas-ruin" is the grotesque monstrous beast ("wonderlijck monstreus dier") which comes to its aid: "This is the second beast, which bears horns like the lamb, but speaks like the dragon, and it carries all the power of the first beast, and causes all the earth and all who live therein to worship the beast, whose deadly wound was healed."[68]

Kort Beworp also reflects the tensions raised by Cromwell's close affiliation with the new Swedish king, Charles X, possibly shown as the kneeling crowned figure in the lower right of the engraving. Cromwell had a sentimental affection for Charles as heir to the Protestant Crusade of his heroic uncle, Gustavus Adolphus. He spoke to the Swedish ambassador of the united front of their two Protestant nations as a bulwark against Catholicism. And he seemed studiously oblivious to the threat that Charles's expansionist ambitions posed to the balance of power in the Baltic, wondering aloud to the Swedish ambassador why the Dutch would send in a fleet after the invasion of Poland and the threat to the major Baltic port, Danzig (guarded by a Dutch garrison), since their trade was not actually prohibited. But, in the event, Cromwell avoided any substantial aid to Sweden, as well as any treaty—offensive or defensive—that excluded the Dutch. If his heart was with the political rhetoric of Protestant crusading, either Cromwell himself—or his council—was shrewd enough to consider economic factors and political, not strictly religious, affiliations.[69]

Nonetheless, the Dutch viewed Swedish incursions in the Baltic—and English negotiations with both the Swedes and the French—with a wary and increasingly hostile eye. Hence, *Kort Beworp* interprets the 1655 invasion of Poland by the king of Sweden through the beasts of Daniel and Revelation: "And has that crooked Beast not been able to get the covenant-breaking king of Sweden on his side, with his clever tricks, with the intent of completely destroying the Kingdom of Poland, yes, even the Roman Empire, as he has already begun to do?"[70]

Citing the domination and corruption of the Antichristian powers of England and France, the author of *Kort Beworp* calls for his countrymen to align with the Habsburg powers of Spain and Austria, whose Catholic rulers, Philip

IV and Ferdinand III, refuse to worship the Beast. In the engraving, Ferdinand and Philip stand beneath the image of the Woman Clothed with the Sun from Revelation, traditionally interpreted by Catholic exegetes as a figure for the Virgin Mary and for the true, Catholic Church. Unlike the other kings and figures, they do not kneel in worship of the Beast. In contrast to the apostate Mazarin, then, these two rulers represent the true faith and the true Church—linked with the Woman in the Sun in the Book of Revelation, who stands as a binary opposite to the monstrous Whore upon her Beast.

England was, of course, directly at war with Spain by 1656, when *Kort Beworp* was published. But her intentions toward Austria were also perceived as unfriendly. Cromwell's alliance with Sweden was, indeed, aimed in part at what he perceived as the threat of Habsburg power: "Look but how the House of Austria, on both sides of Christendom, are armed and prepared to make themselves able to destroy the whole Protestant interest. . . . Who is there that holdeth up his head to oppose this great design? A poor Prince! Indeed poor; but a man in his person as gallant, and truly I think I may say as good, as any these last ages have brought forth; a man that hath adventured his all against the Popish interest in Poland [and] made his acquisition still good for the Protestant religion."[71] Although in the end Cromwell's assistance to Sweden did not go beyond what was necessary to maintain English commercial interests in the Baltic region, his predilection for the Protestant state and his propensity to fear a Habsburg behind every tree evoked animosity: from erstwhile friend and foe alike.

Kort Beworp thus deploys both the heroes and the monsters of Revelation in a powerful indictment of Oliver Cromwell and in firm adherence to the cause of the Roman Catholic Church. The display of monstrous bodies serves a polemical and disciplinary function, warning readers against alignment with the abject worshipers of the Whore on the beast and serving to shape political allegiance and action. The unusual positioning of the author—Dutch, Catholic, and royalist—reminds us that Catholic as well as Protestant uses of monstrous polemic remained a force in contesting as well as defending Cromwellian foreign policy in the 1650s.

RE-VIEWING MONSTROUS BODIES

The move away from future prophetic or past allegorical interpretation to read the Book of Revelation as applicable to immediate political circumstances brought not stability but newly labile and shifting meaning. The 1658 Faithorne engraving with which we began provides a counter-statement—albeit not in direct response—to the sentiments of the 1656 Dutch tract. From the point of view of his English supporters, Cromwell had tracked down and defeated the threats of popery and sectarianism: the Whore and the Dragon of Revelation. The engraving itself does not disclose the violent polemic contest over the monstrous bodies of the Book of Revelation: rather, other female figures show how Ireland, England, and Scotland move from past distractions to attained freedom, with further freedom and happiness to be expected.

Yet in the engraving the relative vitality of the vanquished Whore—her beauty, her seemingly lively gaze, the fact that she still grips her chalice of abomination—shows that the conquest is, in some ways, still ongoing. While broader European affairs are kept outside of the frame of reference, the animation of the Whore of Babylon shows that Cromwell, as in Marvell's *Horatian Ode,* must continue to act, to "keep his sword erect."[72] In this adaptation of Revelation, the whore is not stripped, burned, and eaten: she remains beautiful and lifelike. Although monstrosity is usually defined by the grotesque, the ugly, the bestial, the horrifying, we see finally that in this engraving—as in the Book of Revelation—the most dangerous monster is the morally and sexually transgressive woman who allures rather than horrifies, seduces rather than disgusts.

Similarly, while the Dutch tract *Kort Beworp* exclaims at length against Cromwell as the Great Beast, matched by the grotesque Beast Mazarin, a striking disjunction between the printed description and the visual text indicates that appearance alone fails to disclose inner monstrosity. Hence, while the printed text describes Cromwell and Mazarin as beasts the image shows them, rather, in heroic armor. While Cromwell's cross-dressed hair alerts the reader as does the Beast upon which he rides, his true monstrosity must be decoded and unveiled through the lens of the allegorical text of Revelation. The trappings of the Whore with which Cromwell is decked out both recall a long polemical tradition and provide guidance for the monstrosity that does not manifest itself in the flesh, that is more dangerous and unnatural because of the incongruity between attractive surface and underlying aberration.

Andrew Marvell's anxieties and recriminations about a failure to see, then, reverberate in the later visual texts, as well as link back to the altering perspectives and disappointment in Cromwell shown by the Fifth Monarchists. In the 1658 Faithorne engraving of Cromwell, the Whore of Babylon is beautiful, deceptive, alluring, dangerous, even in her fallen state. But, as we have seen, those opposed to the Protectorate both within and outside of England assert that Cromwell's own appearance masks a monstrosity within, that his martial heroism is as false and dangerous as the beauty of the Whore of Babylon.

Such texts make clear that apocalyptic language continued to impinge upon Protectoral domestic and foreign relations, that the Book of Revelation continued to resonate richly in early modern Europe. Yet in the move from allegory to history, the use of monstrous bodies to denounce current political monstrosities also brought ambiguity, multivalence, and instability. While in the biblical apocalypse, binaries hold and the world is structured in terms of absolute good and evil, in seventeenth-century polemics, monsters threaten not only to defeat, but to merge with or become indistinguishable from heroes. In Revelation, the saints war against the Whore and the various beasts. But in real life, discerning who were the saints and who were the beasts was in itself a monstrously difficult task.

PART 3

MEDICAL KNOWLEDGE, GROTESQUE ANATOMIES, AND THE BODY POLITIC

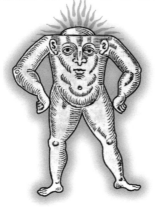

5

MONSTROUS MEDICINE

MARIE-HÉLÈNE HUET

In the preface to his 1573 *Des Monstres et prodiges,* Ambroise Paré gave this familiar definition of monsters: "Monsters are things that appear beyond the course of Nature (and are most often signs of some future calamity) such as a child born with a single arm, another with two heads, and other members beyond the ordinary. Prodigies are things that happen entirely against Nature, such as a woman giving birth to a snake, or a dog, or something else entirely against Nature."[1] With these words, Paré stressed the fact that every creature and every phenomenon should be ordered in terms of its relationship to a specific understanding of Nature; and, consequently, that the study of these extraordinary creatures, although they challenged the general rules of Nature, properly belonged to the field of medical science. This was not just because the physician's art was tested by the enigma surrounding extraordinary births, but also because the Renaissance practice of identifying and curing diseases itself straddled the boundaries of Nature, fitting almost exactly in the area defined by Paré as *beyond* the course of nature, and/or *against* nature.

As Nancy G. Siraisi described it: "Basic constituents of the human body, like deadly sins and cardinal virtues, formed part of a conventional set. This was the list of 'things natural,' which were, in turn, one of a group of three categories: the natural, the non-natural, and the contra-naturals. As the explanation of the three categories in the elementary book of medicine known as the *Isagoge* of Johannitius made clear, the contra-naturals, or things against nature, were pathological conditions of all kinds."[2]

In this sense, medicine was itself contaminated, as it were, by the monstrous, and intimately linked with the mysteries that surrounded the Creation. One of the reasons that monsters fascinated surgeons may lie in the fact that monstrous creatures were directly related to a field of knowledge deeply involved with the effects of a prodigious world. Since Galen, the world of the philosopher and that of the physician had been closely intertwined.[3] The art of diagnosis and the search for cures did not limit themselves to practical observations, but constantly sought to decipher secrets and riddles, interpreting the relationship between diseases and remedies in much the same way they sought to interpret the obscure origins and meanings of monstrous births. My purpose here is not to diminish in any way the irreducible character of monstrosity, but rather to discuss those elements in medical knowledge that were themselves imbued, as it were, with the concept of the monstrous: constantly interrogating the limits of the natural world, and eager to reclaim a long-lost mastery over it.

GOD'S PHYSICIAN

It could be said that two major battles embroiled the field of medicine at the time of the Renaissance. The first one opposed the Galenic physicians, trained in universities, to the vast number of clerics, "empirics," and other practitioners who claimed a knowledge inherited from folk tradition, religious beliefs, or mystical insights, and whose practice expanded considerably, reinforced by the undeniable success of Paracelsus's work. Alison Klairmont Lingo has described in great detail the different aspects of this battle in and around the city of Lyons.[4] As she notes, the physicians "did not acknowledge that certain folk healing techniques were efficacious or that some of their own healing techniques might have originated from folk beliefs. In their desire to obtain the trust of the public, they set up a dichotomy more imaginary than real between folk healing techniques and their own."[5] The second battle opposed the faculty physicians to the surgeons, with the physicians strongly opposing medical publications that did not emanate from their own group, or did not use Latin. In 1575, Ambroise Paré, the king of France's own surgeon, had to defend his work vigorously when the faculty of the University of Paris, joined by other institutions, sought to forbid the publication of his *Oeuvres*.[6] These two debates were fraught with religious passion, as Lingo points out, with "many Protestants being pro-Paracelsians and many Catholics being anti-Paracelsians."[7] Thus, even as corporations battled each other for prestige and authority, one observes a blurring of traditions and belief when it comes to medical knowledge and practices. I will concentrate here on some of the authors who were the most influential and the most debated at the time.

The first chapter of Paré's *Des Monstres et prodiges* listed the thirteen causes of monstrosity:

> The first [cause] is God's glory. The second is God's wrath. The third, too great a quantity of semen. The fourth, too small a quantity. The fifth, imagination. The sixth, narrowness or smallness of the womb. The seventh, the mother's indecent sitting position when, being pregnant, she sat for too long with her thighs crossed, or pressed against her belly. The eighth, falls or blows on the mother's belly when she is pregnant with child. The ninth, hereditary or accidental diseases. The tenth, rotten or corrupted semen. The eleventh, through compounding or mixing semens. The twelfth, through the artifice of evil beggars; the thirteenth, through Demons and Devils.[8]

This list of the causes of monstrous births included all the causes usually listed in medical works for common and rare diseases, with additional details associated with the question of generation (semen, pregnant women). Monsters resulted first from God's ire and glory. Similarly it had always been thought that the primary cause of the plague was God's will.[9] No doubt, the addition of evil beggars as the twelfth cause of monstrous births was meant to allow devils to occupy the fateful thirteenth and final position. Both this understanding of monstrosities and that of diseases involved religion and human physical and moral deficiencies, as well as poor habits.

Moreover, Paré's list duplicated the causes generally invoked at the time in natural philosophy. When, in his *Initia doctrinae physicae* (published in 1549), Phillip Melanchthon listed the causes that accounted for generation, corruption, as well as events that seem beyond human understanding, he similarly included the instability of matter or human behavior as well as planetary influences, God's will and evil doings.

During the Renaissance, the field of medicine thus seemed to encompass the entire creation: man, the microcosm, had to be understood in term of the macrocosm, the universe. A complex set of relations and correspondences between the two was thought to regulate human health. Sachiko Kusukawa has shown the importance of Melanchthon for Lutheran medics, particularly when it came to acknowledging the role of astrology in the development and cure of diseases. Kusukawa notes that in Italian as well as northern European universities, "medics actively used medical astrology . . . [The knowledge] that celestial bodies had influence on terrestrial bodies had also become part of scholastic Aristotelian philosophy."[10] The medical world was physical, cosmic, and metaphysical; nothing escaped its scope. In spite of the rigorous hierarchy that separated the various health practitioners—from university graduates and skilled medical practitioners to barbers and surgeons[11]—when called upon to identify a disease, establish its cause, and set a course for healing, the physician displayed a knowledge as varied as the Creation itself. In this perspective, monstrous births no doubt retained their specificity as rare and marvelous occurrences, producing a unique form of anxiety. Still they continued to haunt a medical domain that itself constantly interrogated the hidden causes of all physical alterations. Like monstrous births, illnesses could be attributed to God, the devil, the stars, and human frailties. If medical knowledge was particularly tested by monstrous occurrences, they, in turn, threw light, albeit emblematic or metaphorical, on the physician's role and beliefs.

But if disease was an accident, contrary to the recognizable course of a pre-ordained nature yet authorized by God, was not the physician usurping God in his attempt to correct it? I have tried to show elsewhere how the maternal imagination was thought to have the power to produce monstrous births, usurping the role of the legitimate father in the shaping of progeny.[12] Similarly, medicine's own practices were embedded in, or relied upon, a knowledge always tempted to usurp that of the Father of Creation. The physician's role was divine and doomed at the same time, called upon to discuss religious matters and miracles, as well as physical deformities, fevers, and poisons.

Some of the most famous cases of monstrous progenies were construed as messages sent by God to express His anger at the sins of men. As we know, this interpretation became particularly important at the time of the Reformation.[13] Luther used the birth of monstrous creatures publicly to denounce the sins of the Church. More discreetly, Ambroise Paré expressed his view of the excesses of Catholic wealth when he published the image of a "marine monster, resembling a bishop dressed in his pontifical garb" (figure 23).[14] No doubt, one of the most famous examples of monsters as bearers of divine warnings was that of the Ravenna monster (figure 24) first reported by Joannes Multivallis, then mentioned by Jacques Rueff, Conrad Lycosthenes, Caspar Hedio, Pierre Boaistuau, Fortunii Liceti, and by Paré who wrote: "At the time Pope Julius II caused great misery in Italy and led a war against King Louis XII, which resulted in a bloody battle near Ravenna: soon after that a monster was born in the same city with a horn on his head, two wings, and one foot similar to that of a bird of prey: he had an eye at the knee joint and was both male and female."[15] This monster was directly sent by God, but if its ultimate cause was known, its physiology required an interpretation, an exegesis. A specific meaning was thus attributed to each part of the wonderful body: the horn was seen as expressing pride and ambition; the wings revealed fickleness; the clawed foot represented usury and avariciousness; the eye in the knee signified excessive taste for earthly things, and the combination of the two sexes served as a denunciation of sodomy.[16] This interpretation also provided the precise reasons for God's ire: namely, the many human sins that flourished in the greedy and bloody war. But if the account of the Ravenna

LIVRE

Figure d'vn monſtre marin, reſſemblant à vn Eueſque,
veſtu de ſes habits pontificaux.

Figure 23. Marine monster, resembling a bishop dressed in his pontifical garb, in Ambroise Paré, *Les Oeuvres. Avec les figures & portraicts tant de l'anatomie que des instruments de chirurgerie, & de plusieurs monstres* (Paris: G. Buon, 1575). Courtesy of the Special Collections Research Center, University of Chicago Library.

132

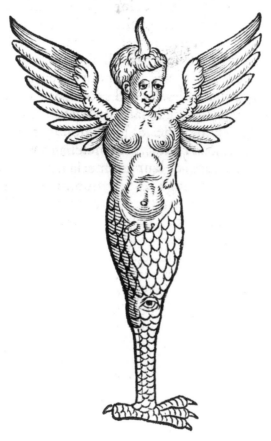

*Figure d'vn monstre ayant face humai-
ne, & vn pied de griffon, estant her-
mafrodite, ayant des aisles d'oiseau,
& vne corne à la teste.*

Figure 24. Ravenna monster, in Ambroise Paré, *Les Oeuvres. Avec les figures & portraicts tant de l'anatomie que des instruments de chirurgerie, & de plusieurs monstres* (Paris: G. Buon, 1575). Courtesy of the Special Collections Research Center, University of Chicago Library.

monster belonged to the literature of prodigies, its interpretation strangely duplicated the art of diagnosis and cure. For all practical purposes, the physician was first and foremost a reader of signs, which were part of a general, cosmic system of correspondences and signatures.

Moreover the physical differences between the monsters specifically sent by God and those resulting from more human sources, such as bestiality, imagination, or defects in the semen, were not always clearly defined. There was an unbroken continuity in the range of unusual deformities, so that, although it was possible to determine by observation what caused a specific progeny to appear monstrous, the great variety of its origins did not produce radically different categories of deformities, or separate studies: the same causes could produce a monstrous birth or an illness. And this was because nothing could happen in nature that God had not permitted from the beginning, including monsters thought to have been produced by copulation with an incubus, the subject of much debate in the Middle Ages and during the Renaissance. Divine and demonic monsters, or prodigious creatures, thus cohabited with progeny exhibiting less extraordinary physical deformities. They all occupied a place in the infinite scale of possibilities and were all subjected to the medical gaze. Thus medicine itself partook of the natural and the divine, and was both a physics and a metaphysics. "The mysteries of the Great and the Little World are distinguished only by the form in which they manifest themselves; for they are only *one* thing, *one* being," stated Paracelsus.[17] From the beginning, medicine was called upon to fulfill a sacred mission that led the physician to explore secrets, undo fateful spells, but most of all to understand the mysterious ways in which the natural world echoed the struggle between the forces of Good and Evil.

In order to understand the nature and goal of medicine, we are told, one had to go back to the Creation and its aftermath. In the beginning, plants were given the power to cure illnesses. In his *Introduction à la chirurgie,* Paré argued that God created plants "of almost incomprehensible size, color, taste, and shape," that were "endowed with virtues as excellent as they were divine."[18] God Himself revealed to Adam the precious properties of plants, but this knowledge, Paré lamented, was buried with our ancestor. It was one of the most disastrous effects of the loss of Eden that the Fall, which caused the diseases and pains that plagued all creatures, also deprived men of the knowledge to cure themselves. Left to itself, the human species would have had no hope of recovering the lost understanding of the virtues of plants, were it not for God's revelations. Since the Fall, Paré explained, "God has imparted this knowledge to certain men, who have been called to administer Medicine, and whose mission has been to deliver and prescribe [remedies] to whose who would be in need of them."[19]

The divine origin of medicine, Paré noted, was also recognized by the Greeks, who credited Apollo with its invention. Paré was quick to point out that the Greek myth could be understood metaphorically—"By Apollo, they meant the Sun, a planet that vivifies everything and gives virtues to plants with its benign and temperate heat"—or more directly, as describing the divinely inspired man who became the first to teach and practice the use of herbs. Adam, created in God's image, would have been familiar with all the intricacies of medical knowledge, and at least part of the knowledge he had forsaken was retrieved, and continued to expand. If this science was of divine origin, was not the man who possessed it also acting in God's name? Paré quoted Herophilus, an "ancient philosopher," as having seen in the physician the hand of the gods: "For man with his hands rescues a fallen man; thus the Physician and Surgeon knowledgeable in his art, cures and bans diseases from the human body, restoring it in its initial health, as if divinely."[20] The controversial Paracelsus was even more direct:

The physician was created by God, not by man . . . he must act like God, his Lord, who appointed him . . . God took away the disease of the Great World, and that is why every year the flowers grow, every year the snow falls, and so on. All these things would have died if God Himself had not been their physician and had not taken away the disease of the winter. To take away disease of the Little World, those of man, he ordained the physician. If the physician is thus a god of the Little World, appointed as God's deputy, on what foundation should he build, and from Whom shall he learn if not from the oldest physician, from God.[21]

Each cure could be considered a victory over death, over winter as it were, a distant but recognizable echo of God's power over the universe. "Truly," said Paré, "the origin of Medicine will always be divine and celestial."[22]

THE SERPENT'S EYE

But a knowledge so powerful that it evoked the divine right to rid the body of all evil was necessarily fraught with dangers and temptations. Even as Adam acquired in Eden the knowledge of all creatures and the remedies for all diseases, some argued, the instructor was none other than the serpent. It is significant that a large body of medical literature was devoted to snakes. Multiple treatises on this subject were published from the Middle Ages to the late eighteenth century. They advocated slightly different methods for curing bites, but expressed a similar fascination for the most mythical of deadly animals. In a *Treatise on Venoms,* variously attributed to Pietro d'Abano or Paracelsus,[23] the author claimed that medicine was contaminated from the start by the powers of evil: "[Adam and Eve] were thrown out of Paradise, and God threatened the serpent. . . . Such is the path that led Adam and Eve to the knowledge of nature, and the serpent, by God's permission, was their guide and doctor."[24] Thus empowered—or permitted—by God, the serpent became both the teacher and the tempter.

This interpretation of the Bible may not be unrelated to Greek mythology, which attributed miraculous healing powers to Asclepius, son of Apollo. Asclepius was said to have learned medical science from Chiron the centaur. According to some accounts, he was even capable of restoring life to the dead, thanks to his knowledge of a plant with miraculous properties, and this precious knowledge had been given to him by a snake. As Nancy G. Siraisi remarks, "[t]he god was believed to appear in dreams to supplicants who slept the night in the shrine precincts and to heal either with miraculous directness or by means of medical advice often resembling that given by human physicians."[25] Asclepius himself, one notes, came to be sometimes represented as a serpent.

For its part, the *Treatise on Venoms* did not comment directly on the loss of knowledge that deprived Adam of the power to heal, as Paré would do, but Pietro d'Abano endowed the serpent with sublime qualities. Because of the serpent's role in Eden, and ever since, he wrote, "snakes—and mostly those of Germany—have retained and still have great properties and virtues denied by idiots, similar to supernatural virtues." And because the serpent's power came directly from God, "after him, all other serpents until the end of the world, by God's same will and achievement of nature, have and hide in them great and admirable mysteries: one should not marvel that the first man's sin came through the serpent, or that in his creation God the Almighty gave the serpent more mysteries and of a higher nature than all his other creatures."[26] This is perhaps why poisons, no doubt emblematic of the serpent's venom, can have excellent effects not to be ignored by physicians. "Is not a mystery of nature concealed even in poison?" asked Paracelsus, "He who despises poison does not know what is hidden in it; for the arcanum that is contained in the poison is so blessed that the poison can neither detract from it nor harm it. In all things there is a poison. It depends only upon the dose whether a poison is poison or not."[27] Nor is it surprising, in Paracelsus's religious view, that the Devil chose the serpent and that God allowed a contract between the two.

This interpretation of the serpent's role in medicine may serve to explain why the treatises on snakes and venoms often took on added importance: their subject matter brought together the divine origin of medicine, the power to kill or save, as well as the right to judge. When Paré explained the reasons why he had decided to dedicate an entire book to venoms and poisonous bites, he warned at the beginning: "I wish that those who invent poisons had been aborted in their mothers' womb." Moreover, venoms had a unique potency that subsumed and transcended all other sources of diseases: "Venoms that operate through their specific qualities, do not do so because they are hot, cold, dry or excessively humid: but because they have this specific natural character of celestial influences *contrary to human nature.* This is why venoms taken in very small quantities are nevertheless of a strength so malignant and cruel, that they kill in an hour or less."[28] These words, "natural character of celestial influences contrary to human nature," perfectly summarize the range of the medical field. They stress the complexity of elements that were thought of as against human nature, yet themselves participated in the natural world created and permitted by God. In this way, nature was not just a wide and complex set of rules, but rather an infinite struggle in which one element battled the other. In this unrelenting struggle between contrary influences, the physician was called upon to observe, identify, and possibly tip the balance so that human nature, privileged because of its relationship with God, would ultimately prevail.[29] Perhaps it could also be read as a sign of this religious struggle that one of the most useful plants in medicine was the *Carduus benedictus,* or "blessed thistle," which could counteract venoms. It was mentioned in a list of remedies as late as 1753, when Claude-François Passerat de la Chapelle included it in his *Recueil de drogues simples ou matière médicinale.*[30]

Venomous creatures were thought to be so powerful that they could destroy by the sole power of their gaze. Paré noted: "These animals kill not only with their stings or bites or scratches, but also with their spittle, breath, foam, gaze, cry and hissing, with their eyes and with their excrements." Such was the basilisk, medieval avatar of Medusa, who "with his gaze alone, and with his cry makes men die."[31] Jean Clair quotes a Renaissance description of the basilisk given by Bruno Lattini in his *Thesaurus:* "The basilisk is so full of venom that it perspires outside his body and shines on his skin; even his eyes and the odor he exhales are loaded with venom that spreads near and far: he corrupts the air and kills trees; his smell kills flying birds; and the basilisk is such that with his gaze he kills men who are looking at him."[32] As Paré noted, in the case of the basilisk, "the venom of females is more dangerous than that of males."[33]

The medieval tradition had already suggested that during their menses women have a venomous gaze,[34] making clearer the association between the power of the serpent and the knowledge of sexuality. The *Great Albert* warned of this danger: "Old women who still have their menses, and others who do not have them regularly, if they look at children in their cribs, communicate venom through their gaze."[35] In Jean Clair's view, the organ of sight is from the beginning associated with sexuality. In Genesis, he notes, it is only when the serpent offers Adam and Eve forbidden knowledge that "their eyes open." Clair adds the following comment: "Let us recall from the biblical verse that the opening of the eyes is a consequence of evil, and that the power of seeing introduces knowledge in the heart of beings, i.e. the knowledge of sexual difference."[36]

No doubt, the knowledge of sexuality and generation occupied a primordial place in the development of medicine. It was its most sacred part, in that it was related to the Creation itself. In fact, from this knowledge all other forms derived. As late as 1771, the *Dictionnaire des gens du monde* made the following statement under its entry on "Generation": "Antoinette Bourignon says that original sin disfigured the work of God in men, and that, instead of the men they should be, they have become monsters in nature, divided into two imperfect sexes, incapable of reproducing alone, as do trees and plants, which from this point of view show a greater perfection than men and women."[37] Although Antoinette Bourignon, a mystic highly suspicious to ecclesiastical authorities, could hardly be said to have played a role in the history of medicine, her formulation was nonetheless suggestive in that it further associated the study of theology, sexuality, and monsters.

The most interesting examples of diseases associated, if only metaphorically, with the powers of the snake were those communicated by a poisonous air. Paré called a corrupted atmosphere "venomous air." The word "venomous" came to describe a wide category of impalpable contagion: the breath of a plague victim, the smell of rotten flesh, or unpleasant perfumes. "Venom acts as well through the air that accompanies thunder and lightning strikes," noted Paré, adding that those who eat an animal killed by lightning will become rabid and die. A poisoned atmosphere is all the more pernicious as air is essential to life: "Without [air] we cannot live. We draw it by the attraction coming from our lungs and other pectoral parts dedicated to breathing, and by the nose and brain ventricles . . . for this reason, if air is venomous, it alters our mind, corrupts our humors, and transforms them into its venomous quality; it infects all the noble parts, and principally the heart: and then follows a struggle between venom and Nature. If Nature is stronger, it will chase away the venoms through its expulsive virtue . . . Conversely, if venom is stronger, Nature is vanquished and death follows."[38]

For his part, Antonio Benivieni of Florence described the 1491 death of Philippo Strozzi, the famous Florentine who was "carried off by pestilent fever," with these words in his highly respected and influential 1507 *De Abditis Nonnullis Ac Mirandis Morborum Et Sanationum Causis:*

> Of the physicians . . . some believed the matter was being distilled from the head and engendering a putrescent fever. But I, when I came to consider this disease after a more careful examination, decided it was pestilent. This opinion was ridiculed by the other physicians, as they thought the fever had already abated (for the snake was lurking in the grass) and they resigned the cure to the family doctor. But on the seventh day the patient, who had seemed to be convalescing, was suddenly seized by relaxation of the sinews and a burning fever . . . and in a few days death followed.[39]

Venoms directly acted against nature, sometimes winning and killing, sometimes losing and sparing the life of the patient. When it came to fighting the effects of venomous bites, the physician brought into play the secret strength of nature: herbal remedies. Some herbs (dictamus, centaurea minor, prassium, arugula) were capable of saving those bitten by a venomous creature, but none was more valuable than the *Viperie.* Paré wrote that "The wild *bugloss,* among all herbs has the strength to fight all snake bites, and has been named *Viperie* for two reasons: one because it produces a seed similar to a viper's head; and the other because it cures its bite when either crushed and applied externally, or taken internally with wine."[40]

The venomous creature itself could be of use in curing diseases. Passerat mentioned that the grass snake's liver, heart, and flesh could be used to cleanse blood, and the deadly Viper was itself endlessly useful: "One uses the flesh, the heart, the lung and the liver of the Viper, after they have been dried and powdered" to mix in sudorific potions and cordial heart tonics. "One also uses fresh Viper, skinned, cleansed and diced, for broths capable of correcting blood, calming it, as in old galls, scrofulous tumors, or other cutaneous diseases, rheumatic pains"[41] William Cullen would mention in the last preface of his *Physics* (1796)—and with considerable skepticism, it may be added—Dr. Lieutaud's observation that the powder of toads given in wine might relieve dropsy.[42] But another approach consisted in using what had caused the bite as its remedy. "The Viper's bite is deadly if one does not act promptly," wrote Passerat, "it is a very coagulating venom, the course of which can only be interrupted by ligatures, scarification, and by putting the crushed head of the Viper that bit, or that of another Viper, on the bite."[43]

READING NATURE

Paracelsus may have produced the most complete treatise on the art of deciphering the natural world, the physician's complete and privileged mission. Although his work was not recognized at universities, and he himself endlessly challenged the limited teachings provided in medical schools, he acquired an important following, particularly in Protestant countries, and among the Huguenots living in France. As Charles Webster noted: "Paracelsus had shaken the authority of classical medicine, and Paracelsianism remained a vigorous force for more than a century. As a self-conscious movement of reform Paracelsianism constituted one of the vital ingredients of the so-called Scientific Revolution."[44]

One of the most crucial aspects of Paracelsus's work may be his theory of signs and signatures. Nature is covered with signs, which men have the task of discovering: "Even if [God] did conceal some things, He left nothing unmarked, but provided all things with outward, visible marks, with special traits—just as a man who has a buried treasure marks the spot in order he may find it again. We, men, discover everything that lies hidden in the mountain by external signs and correspondences, and thus also do we find all the properties of herbs and everything that is in the stones."[45]

Michel Foucault has described the four figures essential to the system of resemblances that articulated knowledge in the sixteenth century as *convenientia, aemulatio, analogy,* and the vital *sympathy/antipathy* couple. The same figures, but with a displacement, he added, also served as signatures enabling a correct interpretation of resemblances.[46] We should add that Paracelsus gave perhaps the most detailed example of the deciphering of signs for medical purposes:

> Behold the *Satyrion* root, is it not formed like the male privy parts? No one can deny this. Accordingly magic discovered it and revealed that it can restore a man's virility and passion. And then we have the thistle; do not its leaves prickle like needles? Thanks to this sign, the art of magic discovered that there is no better herb against internal prickling. The *Siegwurz* root is wrapped in an envelope like armor; and this is a magic sign showing that like armor it gives protection against weapons. And the *Syderica* bears the image and the form of a snake on each of its leaves, and thus, according to magic, it gives protection against any kind of poisoning.[47]

Signs revealed not only hidden medicinal virtues of plants, but when properly read, they also disclosed the best way to use them: "The chicory stands under a special influence of the sun; this is seen in its leaves, which always bend towards the sun as though they wanted to show it gratitude. Hence it is most effective while the sun is in the sky. As soon as the sun sets, the power of chicory dwindles."[48]

But man was also a signatory, and in the *De Natura Rerum,* Paracelsus wrote: "Now, in order that we may explain all the signs as correctly and as briefly as possible, it is above all else necessary that we put forward those whereof man is the signatory."[49] Should we wonder that Paracelsus's first list of men's signatures consisted of monstrosities?

Many men come to light deformed with monstrous signs. One man has a finger too many, another a finger too few . . . another brings with him from the
womb a distorted foot, arm, back, or other member; another has a weak or
hunched back. So also there are born hermaphrodites, androgyni, men, that is
to say, possessing both pudenda, male as well as female, and sometimes lacking
both. Of monstrous signs like this I have noted many, both in males and females, all of which are to be regarded as monstrous signs of secret sins in parents. . . . Just as the hangman brands his sons with degrading signs, so also
wicked parents mark their offspring with mischievous supernatural signs.[50]

Paracelsus was not alone in attributing the birth of monstrous progeny to the
moral sins of the parents,[51] but although the monstrous signs are called supernatural—i.e. above and beyond nature—for him, a similar process of signing
marks all the elements of the natural world, be they stars or men.

GOD'S WILL AND THE PHYSICIAN

In spite of the privileged position of medical knowledge and its divine origin,
the physician's powers remained limited by God's ultimate will. In Calvinist
England, David Harley notes, "Medicine was the means ordained for use in
sickness by God, who usually acted through second causes." By the same
token, "God's afflictions were sent to purge out corruptions, as the doctor
purged peccant humours." God's will also affected the power of the physician
to cure: "Since healing was in the gift of God, he might choose to cloud the
physician's judgement . . . God might also suspend the action of medicine if
he saw fit." Just as monstrous births were thought to be a warning and a punishment, epidemics such as the plague "were obviously sent to warn the whole
nation to repent from their sins."[52]

Paracelsus also made it clear that the power of the physician was limited by
God: "Health and sickness are granted by God. . . . You should divide the diseases of men . . . into those which arise in a natural way, and those which
come upon us as God's scourges. For take good note of it: God has sent us

some diseases as punishment, as a warning, as a sign by which we know that all our affairs are naught, that our knowledge rests upon no firm foundation, and that the truth is not known to us, but that we are inadequate and fragmentary in all ways, and that no ability of knowledge is ours."[53] Paracelsus's formulation was particularly suggestive in that it presented illness as the ultimate sign that canceled all other signs, as the very sign that reminded us of our inability to decipher the world. This great disease came from the Fall itself, which gave us this ultimate knowledge that we *do not* know.

Diseases could, as noted, be sent by evils, and those stood in fact a better chance of being cured, although they too tested the physician's knowledge. Antonio Benivieni contributed the following observation:

> A new and extraordinary disease is nowadays rife, and though I have seen and treated it, I scarcely dare to describe it. A girl in her sixteenth year was seized with pain in the lowest part of her belly and kept on trying to pluck it away with her hands. Then she broke into terrible screaming and her belly all swelled up at the spot, so that it looked as if she were eight months pregnant. When her voice failed, she flung herself from side to side on her bed, and, sometimes touching her neck with the soles of her feet, would spring to her feet, then again falling prostrate and again springing up. She would repeat these actions in exactly the same manner until she gradually came to herself and was somehow restored. When asked, she hardly knew what had happened.

"I employed suitable medicines," continued Benivieni, but when all failed, "I decided that she was possessed by an evil spirit who blinded the eyes of the spectators while he was doing this. She was handed to a physician of the soul."[54]

In his fight against a basilisk-like evil, Benivieni was careful not to request the aid of religion too promptly, nor to claim that a miracle cured his patient. In a case of "flux cured by prayer alone," he noted, "though I knew that God, to whom all things are possible, could have affected this [cure] with the utmost ease, yet I feared that the woman was mistaken in her assurance that she had now got what she was praying for, and that this same disease might return within a short while, even worse than before. But when three years had passed since the flux was suppressed, and meanwhile no sign of relapse had appeared, I frankly admitted and declared that this had been done by God's will alone."[55]

The physician's tasks were numerous and one of his most important responsibilities lay in his recognition of God's hand. Diseases, epidemics, natural remedies, proper diagnoses and cures all demonstrated the complexity of a world in which the marvels of nature, the sins of men, the influence of stars, and the Creator Himself produced an infinity of signs.

If the same causes applied to monstrous births and to disease, and if the physician well versed in his art could identify these causes by a careful observation that took into account the patient, the macrocosm, and the Maker of all things, in what way did the study of monsters differ from the study of diseases? Did not Paré define disease as "an affection against nature"?[56] If all fevers and sickness arose from elements disturbing the course of nature so as to produce effects that went beyond or against the ordinary human nature, in what way could Paré—following a rich tradition—separate monstrous progeny from ailments that could similarly be attributed to usual or extraordinary factors?

We know that the development of medicine had a twofold effect on the study of monstrous births. First, medical science slowly divested itself of religious beliefs. Not that religious questions would not continue to be an important factor until the end of the eighteenth century, as Jacques Roger has shown,[57] but medicine would be refocused on the workings of the human body, taking as its point of departure the functions and dysfunctions of the system rather than the remote influences that had been thought to allow for disruptions in the first place. Second, as it would increasingly privilege direct observation, medicine would integrate monstrous births into its empirical knowledge of the body, divesting monstrous births of their supernatural components. In this way, monsters as bearers of supernatural signs were excluded from the medical field, while at the same time monstrous deformities were being completely integrated as simply unusual occurrences.

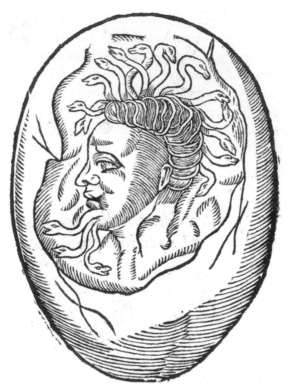

Figure 25. Man found in an egg, with a head covered by serpents, *Les oeuvres d'Ambroise Paré* 12th Edition (Lyon: Jean Gregoire, 1664). Courtesy of the Special Collections Research Center, University of Chicago Library.

But at the time Paré published his *Des Monstres et prodiges,* the most remarkable element of all the cases he listed and commented upon lay in what could be called the "miscreation" factor. Diseases only occurred, one could say, but monsters were born. Monstrous progeny was all the more disquieting as it reproduced an act of creation gone awry. Certainly the causes of monstrous births and their examination by physicians did not include any factor that was not already considered in the study of diseases, but because monsters were associated with human reproduction, a distant and imperfect echo of God's creation, their existence was necessarily endowed with a greater significance. It was not so much that monsters and prodigies were beyond or against nature, but that the human act of generation could never be but a disfiguration of the act of creation. Whether monsters reminded humans of their sins or of God's power, they always reminded humans that the knowledge of sexuality and its shame came after the Fall.

There may be no better illustration of the troubling relationship between monstrosity, medicine, and the loss of Eden than the strange case related by Paré of a man found in an egg, with a head covered by serpents—a male Medusa, as it were.[58] The extraordinary illustration (figure 25) provided in Paré's work could be said to represent the endless power of Nature to astound and "merveilleusement épouvanter," as well as an image of the universe with man as its center, divine but doomed by the power of the serpent. Finally, one could see in this remarkable figure a symbol, the portrait of the Renaissance physician, Asclepius's heir, the reader of secret signs, himself intimately connected to the endless prodigies of nature and the monstrous, supernatural, character of medical knowledge.

6

REVOLUTIONARY ANATOMIES

JOAN B. LANDES

As early as 1789, before the adoption of the guillotine as the privileged instrument of revolutionary justice, the Revolution was becoming associated in the eyes of defenders and opponents alike with the detached body part. The 1789 print *This Is How We Take Revenge on Traitors* (figure 26) underscores this association. The revolutionary crowd is shown holding aloft on pikes the impaled heads of its earliest victims: the governor of the Bastille, the marquis Delaunay, and the prévot des marchands, Jacques de Fleselles, who were killed in the assault on the Bastille, 14 July 1789. From across the political spectrum, severed heads and other body parts were no less emphasized. In one popular motif, the revolutionary was portrayed as a cold-hearted patriotic calculator of his victim's skulls, reckoning the heads already paid and those still due.[1] By the time of the Terror, the severed head had become perhaps the most frequently exploited synecdoche for the Revolution as a whole, exploited for opposing ends by revolutionaries and counterrevolutionaries alike. In this escalating language of dismemberment, the Revolution was associated with monstrosity—whether as monstrous and repellent act or as awesome and excessive instrument of justice—and corporeal anatomies became a common fixture in the rhetoric of revolution and counterrevolution.

Figure 26. Anon. *This Is How We Take Revenge on Traitors* (1789). Courtesy of the Library of Congress.

LIGAMENTS

It is certainly not only within the political discourse of the 1790s that one discovers bodily parts, dismembered bodies, and monstrosities. Taken as actual scientific specimens, bodies (normal and abnormal) and bodily parts also constituted an established field of anatomical objects that were being redistributed, under revolutionary auspices, within the newly organized institutions of medical and veterinary science.[2] Focusing on a marvelous series of life-size écorchés (flayed specimens), anatomical works composed by the anatomist Honoré Fragonard (1732–99) from preserved human and animal cadavers, this essay poses the question of what happened to the science of anatomy in the revolutionary context—a period in which monstrous bodies appeared not just in science but in the discourse of politics as well.[3] Fragonard's preparations were part of the anatomical collection of the Veterinary School of Alfort, the revolutionary successor to the Royal Veterinary School on the outskirts of Paris.[4] According to a 1795 inventory, drawn up by Fragonard and his colleagues for the temporary Commission of the Arts established by the republican government, there were originally 3,033 pieces, of which about 2,000 (some dried, some preserved in liquid, some stuffed) were anatomical and pathological specimens.[5] In addition to the écorchés, the collection comprised monstrous specimens, nineteenth-century examples of which are still on display at Alfort today, including: a two-headed cow, an animal cyclops, a four-legged chicken, a ram with four horns, and a human fetus labeled "sirenonome," after the mermaids of Western legend, because its joined legs resemble a fishtail.

Despite the well-acknowledged place of anatomy in republican science and medicine, criticisms leveled at the Alfort collection point to a similarly ambivalent relationship between the anatomical and the monstrous, not unlike that which one finds in revolutionary political discourse. In 1790, during a period of lively debate over the future organization of the nation's veterinary schools, a former adjunct anatomist of the Royal Academy of Science named Brousonnet complained that the cabinet of anatomy is "one of the most costly parts of the School at Alfort, and the most useless." Excessive sums were spent to form it, and the majority of its specimens were deemed inappropriate for veterinary art. "One sees there above all a lot of very bulky fish which cost considerable sums. The luxury is pushed so far that one finds there bones and stones discovered in animal bodies and preserved in spirits."[6] Chaussart, a former employee of Alfort, further claimed that the anatomical specimens "have no other use than to throw dust in the eyes of those who judge the knowledge of men by their library."[7]

Gentle doubts were also raised about the anatomical contributions of the anatomist Fragonard. For example, the influential Directory physician and first director of the Paris School of Health Michel-Augustin Thouret observed in his 1799 eulogy for the anatomist: "Throughout his anatomical work, [Fragonard] conceived and invented specimens that he strongly desired others would come to see; but he didn't write anything, and we could have said of him, as used to be said of [Frederik] Ruysch that he spoke to the eyes; also, he replied to those who spoke to him about his cabinet: come and see."[8] In other words, Thouret judged Fragonard's achievement to be less scientific than artistic. He regarded his colleague's anatomical methods as anachronistic, possibly even falling short of the standard advocated by late eighteenth-century reformers like the anatomist Jean-Joseph Süe (1710–92), for whom anatomy involved the union of theory and practice. By failing to produce any scholarship in the field of anatomy, Thouret implied, Fragonard had not achieved a scientific reputation.[9] What he did do was to demonstrate—that is, *démontrer* or *faire une démonstration*—not in the mathematical or logical sense of giving a proof, but rather in the visual sense of showing (*monstrare* in Latin, *montrer* in French), from which we also derive the word *monstre* or monster.[10]

The connection between the anatomical demonstration and the exhibition of monstrosity was long-standing. Because of their scarcity, monsters were especially prized objects in the anatomical collections comprising early modern *Wunderkammer*. As the historian Michael Hagner notes, "The rarity of monsters and their diverting appearance bore practical consequences. They were dissected, but whenever possible, they were anatomically prepared, preserved in spirits, and presented in public."[11] The influential Dutch anatomist Frederik Ruysch (1638–1731), to whom Thouret links Fragonard, included many monstrous specimens in his illustrious anatomical cabinet, as well as in the copperplates of his eleven-volume *Thesaurus anatomicus.*

As a practitioner of "natural" anatomy, Fragonard followed Ruysch's technique of dissecting, injecting, and preserving fresh cadavers. "Artificial" anatomy, the period's contrasting method, involved making a representation of the body from other materials: typically wax but also papier-mâché; or, as was the case with Fragonard's contemporary Marie-Catherine Bihéron (1719–86), silk, wool, threads, and wax-coated feathers.[12] Fragonard's procedure involved injecting the arteries with alcohol and aromatic spices in order to prevent putrefaction, following which the skin was removed, the body fixed in a frame in the desired position, and the dissection carried out, leaving the muscles and sometimes the nerves and the vessels, which were then injected with colored wax. Instead of treating a single organ or a limb, like Ruysch and others, Fragonard excelled in the handling of the whole body, and even more remarkably, bodies in relation to one another. It is of some interest, however, that while Ruysch customarily presented unusual bodily parts as single objects, this was not the case with monstrous specimens. Rather than dissecting monsters, he exhibited them in their entirety, a presentation strategy resembling that of Fragonard's most striking works.

Another result of natural anatomy's injection techniques was the spirited expression it produced in the specimens.[13] Exploiting this "liveliness" of expression, Ruysch in 1696 announced the dissection of bodies "which appear still to be alive but which have been dead for about two years."[14] Indeed, according to the French academician Fontenelle, Peter the Great was said to have been so moved by one of Ruysch's preparations that "he tenderly kissed the body of a still lovable small child who seemed to smile at him."[15] In the case of Fragonard's preparations, the audience's response to such "liveliness" might have been intensified by the widespread popularity of theories of sensibility. In addition, in contrast to the more accurate proportions of a freshly dissected cadaver that could be achieved in artificial anatomy, Fragonard's "injection of the resin into the blood vessels unnaturally enlarged them, giving an effect of swelling that is not found in the wax models"—a point to which we shall return.[16]

Ruysch is perhaps most famous for his dramatic, teasingly lifelike presentation of anatomical subjects. From this Fragonard learned as well, though he did not go so far as Ruysch, who dolled up his anatomized fetuses with scarves and embroidered baby hats.[17] By animating the specimen in "Fetus Dancing the Gigue" (figure 27) in a deliberately irreverent pose, Fragonard calls attention to the liminal status of the anatomical subject, not alive but also not wholly dead. It is here that the anatomized subject exceeds its purpose as an object of demonstration in the context of veterinary or medical instruction. This "surplus" effect or artifice in Fragonard's work produced in onlookers both admiration and discomfort. For some, the anatomist was a brilliant technician, a consummate artist, whose artistry preserved the cadaver against its inevitable decomposition. But for critics, far from being truthful, such affectations amounted to a trivial addition or a playful ruse, at odds with the developing protocols of serious science. What is at stake here is the place of the "natural" in the practice of anatomical modeling, as well as the physical status of dead matter. The fact that these issues were being sorted out in the context of a revolution in which the goals of human transformation and political renewal were tied to acts of death and execution, in which revolutionaries and counterrevolutionaries alike leveled accusations of monstrosity, is of more than passing interest. In the political sphere, attributions of monstrosity could be lethal, anticipating or even prompting death. Similarly, in the process of dissecting, preserving, and categorizing the deceased remains of once living humans and animals, the "natural" anatomist could not fail to confront the abject and potentially monstrous impact of dead matter.

MONSTROSITY

If the question "What is a monster?" has produced countless replies in different historical circumstances, there is one constant running through all these

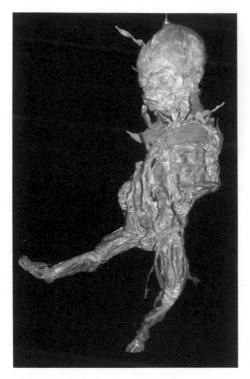

Figure 27. Honoré Fragonard, Fetus Dancing the Gigue (eighteenth century). Courtesy of the Musée Fragonard, France. Photo: C. Degueurce.

responses: whatever a monster is, it is not one of us.[18] Monsters violate the borders between man and beast or human and divine, but they are also a way of talking about the rejected or repulsive Other. Monsters disturb a shared sense of decorum, order, and taste. They are grotesque, distorted, ugly, bestial, and horrifying. They fascinate and repel. They are said to link bodily deformity to moral or political evils. And, above all, monsters offer a way of thinking about the world. So when a known social universe abruptly changes, as happened in France during the 1790s, it is not surprising that figures of monstrosity were everywhere to be found in visual and verbal imagery.

Revolutionaries made abundant use of the hydra of conspiracy, a many-headed beast signaling the threat of aristocracy, monarchy, and counterrevolution. Whereas to its supporters the Republic possessed one ideal body, its enemies—aristocrats, federalists, conspirators, and counterfeiters—were thought to possess many bodies. A print from 1789, *Hunting the Great Beast* (figure 28), depicts the events of 14 July 1789 at the Bastille as an allegory of the armed citizenry defeating the Revolution's enemies in the figure of a many-headed hydra of despotism.[19] The hydra is a distinctive, regenerating sort of monster, which grows a new head if one is severed. In terms suggested by the literary critic Mikhail Bakhtin, the hydra is a figure of death and growth.[20]

One certain measure of the king's fall from public grace—particularly after his capture by republicans at Varennes in June 1791 following his abortive flight to join with counterrevolutionary armies on France's eastern frontier—is the manner in which caricaturists portrayed the monarch: as a pig, swine, ox, cat, tiger, or a giant stomach, whose disorder and gluttony put the health of the nation (the body politic) at risk. In *The Ci-Devant Great Family Feast of the Modern Gargantua* (c. 1791) (figure 29), an image that takes its inspiration directly from Rabelais, Louis XVI appears as the gluttonous giant, about to eat an entire pig as his subjects struggle to satisfy his voracious appetite with the nation's produce and game. The marquis de Bouillé—identified in the print's caption as the "Butcher of Nancy" for his role in the violent repression of the mutiny that occurred in that city in 1790, and represented here as stabbing a young soldier in the neck—is asked by the king if there is enough to fill his gullet for a year. Marie Antoinette interrupts, wondering if the blood filling her glass will not also serve as her bath, eerily anticipating the violent downfall of the royal bloodsuckers.[21] According to the revolutionary journalist Prudhomme, the queen was a carnivorous female tiger, ravenous for her people's blood. As he stated, "once she catches the sight of blood . . . [she] can no longer be satisfied."[22] Indeed, it was the queen who inspired many of the most venomous political attacks leveled by revolutionaries against the monarchy, the clergy, and the aristocracy. One of her defenders, the Abbé Barruel, makes this same point in recounting the "horrible" events of 10 August 1792, which

Figure 28. Roze Le Noir, *Hunting the Great Beast* (1789). Courtesy of the Library of Congress.

Figure 29. Anon., *The Ci-Devant Great Family Feast of the Modern Gargantua* (c. 1791). Courtesy of the Bibliothèque nationale de France.

set the stage for the trials and executions of the royal couple. As he stated, "It was against her above all that the Jacobins unleashed the people; it was most of all her head that their menacing cries demanded."[23] More familiar is the passionate defense of the queen in Edmund Burke's *Reflections on the Revolution in Paris,* where it is the heroines of October 1789, the market women who marched on Versailles, who are transmuted into monstrous harridans.[24]

The queen had already been a target of court libels before 1789, and now again, revolutionary attacks on her featured her monstrous body, said to be composed of disparate (mythological and real) animals—harpy, cat, eagle, pig, hyena, tiger, or panther—or of hermaphroditic male and female parts. In a particularly vicious slander, *The Austrian She-Panther, in Her Most Distant Posterity, Sworn to Contempt and Abomination for the French Nation* (c. 1792) (figure 30), she is the product of miscegenation and vile hybridization: "This dreadful Messalina, fruit of one of the most licentious and illicit couplings (concubinage), composed of heterogeneous matter, fabricated from several races, part Lorrainer, German, Austrian, Bohemian)."[25] In addition, the queen's fiery tresses are here related to those of Judas, her nose and cheek bloated and made purple by corrupt blood, and her mouth fetid and infected. From being a foreigner, suspected of betraying the nation, she has become a foreign body—not only in a cultural, but in a material sense. In *Fureurs utérines de Marie-Antoinette, femme de Louis XVI,* she is accused of unquenchable libidinal appetites—for both men and women.[26] Another pamphlet continued the themes of bestiality, incest, and licentiousness, maintaining that the queen's brother, Joseph II, "the most ambitious of rulers, the most immoral of men," was merely the first of her lovers [les prémices]. According to this version, "the introduction of the imperial phallus [priape] into the Austrian canal accumulated there, so to speak, the passion of incest, the filthiest pleasures, the hatred of France [rectius: des Français], the aversion for the duties of spouse and mother, in a word all that lowers humanity to the level of savage beasts."[27]

However, revolutionaries were not the only purveyors of the hyperbolic language of monstrosity. For royalists, émigrés, and foreign opponents, the

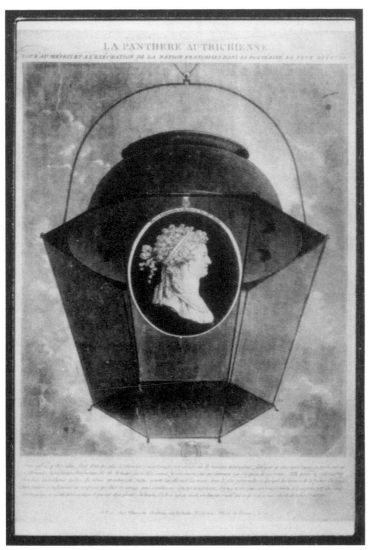

Figure 30. Anon., *The Austrian She-Panther, in Her Most Distant Posterity, Sworn to Contempt and Abomination for the French Nation* (c. 1792). Courtesy of the Uppsala University Library.

counter-principle reigned: in the rhetoric of massacre, as described above, it was the revolutionaries who performed monstrous, bestial acts, and, not surprisingly, acquired monstrous attributes. Thus, it was alleged that during the September massacres of 1792 the exhausted murderers refortified themselves by drinking spirits laced with gunpowder and eating small rolls drenched with blood from the wounds of "their palpitating victims." In one witness' words, "never did the cannibals show themselves to be so ferocious and barbarous."[28] Equally hyperbolic was the widely circulated, gruesome story of Mademoiselle de Sombreuil's effort to save her father's life by agreeing to his captor's demand that she drink a glass of blood drawn from his wounded head.[29] *Un petit souper, à la parisienne: or, A Family of Sans-Cullotts refreshing, after the fatigues of the day* (1792) (figure 31), a print by the British artist James Gillray, crystallized many of the most extreme accusations, depicting the Revolution as an act of murderous dissection or butchery. In a den of bloodsuckers, a *sans-culottes* family is shown devouring a cadaver. A *sans-culotte* is about to eat an eye, which he has just gouged out of a severed head. The other family members—including the smallest babies—feast voraciously on such human body parts as hearts, feet, eyes, and even testicles, while the wife is busy at the open hearth, basting a baby who is skewered on a pit.

ANATOMY: REVOLUTIONARY AFFILIATIONS

Gillray's image metaphorically anatomizes the Revolution. In a travesty of the mass, these monstrous cannibals indiscriminately feed on their own kind, indifferently consuming high and low body parts (hearts and testicles). This image disturbs by linking cannibalism to revolution, and both to dissection. Yet no matter how extreme, Gillray was not alone in deploying anatomical imagery. Two French prints from the period of the Terror, of contrasting politics, demonstrate the monstrous role played by the body part (the anatomical fragment) and dismemberment in both revolutionary and counterrevolutionary consciousness. In his Medusan image of the king's severed head dripping blood, raised up by a disarticulated hand (another bodily part), titled *Matter*

Figure 31. James Gillray, *Un petit souper, à la parisienne: or, A Family of Sans-Cullotts refreshing, after the fatigues of the day* (1792). © Copyright The British Museum.

for Reflection for All Crowned Jugglers / May an Impure Blood Run through Our Fields (1793) (figure 32), the revolutionary artist Villeneuve captured with horrible effect the grotesque reversal of the king's classical body, which in reality occurred at the guillotine on 21 January 1793.[30] By the time of his death, as Antoine de Baecque has noticed, the once weak and impotent monarch was transformed into a "monster-king": "Already, at the time of Louis XVI's trial, numerous deputies alluded to the blood of 'martyrs,' crying for vengeance at the expense of royal blood. Thus the king becomes, very legitimately in the mind of every Republican, an assassin, even a 'drinker of blood.'" Louis XVI,

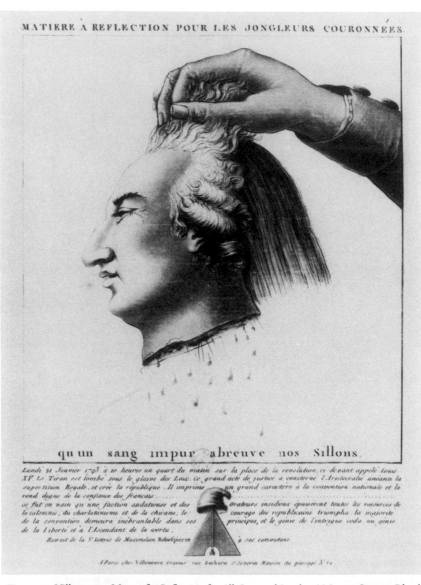

Figure 32. Villeneuve, *Matter for Reflection for All Crowned Jugglers / May an Impure Blood Run through Our Fields* (1793). Courtesy of the Bibliothèque nationale de France.

till then ridiculed by the grotesque association with the bestiary of comedy or by the rumors concerning the impotence of his "imbecile body," metamorphoses into a monster under the effects of this eloquence of blood. " 'I have seen this thirsty brigand drink in ruby-red cups the sweat and blood of a Frenchman, while that same Frenchman, a soldier crippled for the nation, begged for alms,' cries out Citizen Dorfeuille a few days after the execution of the king . . . Under the pressure of events, the image of the king turned upside down in revolutionary propaganda: his story is rewritten as the terrible role of a despot."[31]

For opponents, the most horrific aspects of the guillotine were thought to be its basis in reason—the rationalism of the *philosophes*—and its disquieting, machine-like repetitiveness.[32] Recalling the argument of early revolutionary imagery, the Thermidorian print *The Government of Robespierre, or the Executioner Guillotines Himself* (c. 1794) (figure 33) presented a bitter satire on the Terror. Having guillotined everyone else, the executioner has to guillotine himself. His awkwardly raised arm is shown grasping the cord that has released the blade.[33] But oddly, even among its victims, the severed head became a badge of pride. Marat's assassin, Charlotte Corday, is said to have asked that her head be paraded through Paris after her execution. In these prints, the range of emotions evoked by the guillotine—a more "rational" and equitable method of execution in the minds of its defenders, a barbarous machinery of death gone awry to its detractors—echoed the widespread ambivalence surrounding the practice of anatomy.

ANATOMY: THE ART AND SCIENCE OF THE ABJECT

In the ancient Galenic conception, anatomy is an "opening up in order to see deeper or hidden parts."[34] As the man credited with founding modern anatomy in the sixteenth-century, Vesalius (1514–1564) likewise appreciated that in order to describe and analyze the true structure of the human body it was necessary first to dissect it.[35] The art of anatomy stands apart from the other arts, not so much for its interest in and investigation of the body—for this became

(La Scène se passe sur la place de la Révolution)

Admirez de Samson Intelligence extrème ?,
Par le conteau fatal, il a tout fait perir ?,
Dans cet affreux etat que va t'il devenu ?,
Il se guillotine lui même.

Figure 33. Anon., *The Government of Robespierre, or the Executioner Guillotines Himself* (ca. 1794). Courtesy of Musée Carnavalet. Copyright Photothèque des musées de la ville de Paris.

the hallmark of Renaissance art and its successors—but for its direct, unmediated involvement with corporeal substance(s) and the materiality of the body.[36] In this respect, anatomy is more akin to science. Yet whichever classification we choose to adopt, anatomy was from the outset marked by its traffic with the dead, with body snatching and the unsavory trade in corpses, and with the handling of the decaying matter of human and animal corpses. Indeed the rhythm of anatomical investigation was dictated by the seasons, and not surprisingly, winter was the favorite time of year for its practitioners. The rapid decay of the corpse necessitated expert handling by dissectors. There was also growing concern across the eighteenth century with the health effects of human and animal waste, particularly in cities where cemetery practices were a matter of concern for public health officials. The 1804 suppression of burials in the cemeteries inside Paris additionally constrained anatomists to go farther to provision themselves with corpses.[37]

The prominent anatomist Félix Vicq d'Azyr captured as well as anyone the central paradox of the anatomical pursuit, the study of life by way of decaying matter. As he stated:

> Anatomy is perhaps the science whose advantages are most celebrated and which has been the least favored. It is perhaps also the one whose study offers the greatest difficulty. Its investigations are not only devoid of the charm that attracts, but in addition it is accompanied by circumstances that repulse: Torn and bloody members, infectious and unhealthy odors, the ghastly machinery of death are the objects that it presents to those who cultivate it. Altogether foreign to the average person, concentrated in the amphitheaters and hospitals, it has never received the homage that it needs in order to captivate by the elegance and mobility of its spectacle. Only by descending into the tombs and braving the laws of men, in order to discover those of nature, has the anatomist extended in a painful and dangerous way the foundations of useful knowledge. And, there is no point in the century where prejudices of various kinds have not placed the greatest obstacles in the way of its work.[38]

As a collector and technician of cadaver art/science, the anatomist thereby participated in the social processes that Mikhail Bakhtin has labeled the "grotesque" and Julia Kristeva "abjection." For Bakhtin, the grotesque body is not separated from the world, but "blended with the world, with animals, with objects." It is associated with the bodily lower stratum, with degradation, filth, death, and rebirth: a "pregnant death, a death that gives birth." Bakhtin describes the grotesque—open, secreting, multiple, irregular, changing—as those elements that are extruded from the bodily canon of classical aesthetics, with its transcendent, monumental, finished, closed, and self-contained body.[39] Whereas the grotesque is aligned with the lower orders, the classical body is associated with the higher social orders of the official Renaissance, and later with bourgeois rationalism and individualism. Accordingly, revolutionary caricaturists exploited the weapons of ridicule and critique, social rejection and repudiation, within the realm of grotesque exaggeration, to satirize and repulse the elevated claims, practices, or bodies of their opponents.

Supplementing Bakhtin's concerns, Kristeva explores the psychic implications of social abjection, or that which is expelled, cast out and away. She follows Freud's and Mary Douglas's explorations of boundary rituals, maintaining that the force of expulsion works to constitute the individual. On her account, the self only becomes social by expunging the elements that society deems impure, among which are excrement, menstrual blood, urine, and semen; though she holds that the goal of expulsion is never wholly achieved. Abjection is the process by which the impossibly rejected and fluid elements come to haunt the edges of the subject's identity, threatening the self with danger and dissolution. For Kristeva, "abjection is above all ambiguity."[40]

The dead corpse with which the anatomist must work incorporates ambivalence and ambiguity. It is a frustratingly intractable object, a constant challenge to the savant, as Vicq d'Azyr admonished:

A cold, inanimate body, deprived of life, offers only fibers without elasticity, slack and empty vessels. The art [of dissection], in truth, succeeded in filling them, but a foreign and coarse fluid leads the widest canals to become excessively distended. If, on the other hand, one uses a more refined fluid, it transpires through the pores like dewdrops, and teaches us nothing about the structures of the pathways through which it has passed. The nervous system that determined the strongest reactions, this pulp which was the focus of the most varied shaking, on which light itself imprinted images and left traces of its vibrations, is wholly insensible, wholly mute. The muscle no longer stiffens under the instrument that wounds it. The nerve is torn without excitement, trouble or sorrow. All connection, all sympathy is destroyed, and the bodies of animals in this state are a great enigma for those who dissect them.[41]

Anatomy was exceptional nevertheless for the public manner in which it confronted the risks of death, disease, and abjection. Not only did doctors and artists "visit" the insides of the body by attending a dissection, but throughout northern and western Europe, the institution of the anatomy theater afforded large numbers of people the opportunity also to take an "anatomy lesson."[42] As Michel Lemire notes, "These anatomical amphitheaters, sometimes installed in the church of a hospital, were particularly important in the period because dissections, in themselves, constituted a veritable theatrical spectacle. They lasted several days and attracted an immense crowd." The creation in 1635 of the Jardin Royal, the forerunner to the Jardin des Plantes, provided an important venue for anatomical demonstration. The most celebrated courses, for example, those of Pierre Dionis (1643–1718) and Joseph-Guichard Duverney (1648–1730), underwritten by the Crown, even became fashionable events. "Not only did students press around the dissection table, but all of high society came to assist in the spectacle mounted like a play. And they commented on the anatomy lesson even in the salons."[43] What the observer of eighteenth-century Paris Sébastien Mercier termed a "passion for anatomy" is said to have been "part of the indispensable equipment of every well-educated man."[44] Diderot, who authored the article on anatomy in the *Encyclopédie* with the help of the anatomist Pierre Tarin, had followed the courses of César Verdier, royal demonstrator at the College of Surgery, and he assisted in the demonstrations of Marie-Catherine Bihéron. When his own daughter was of marriageable age, he had her study anatomy with the help of Bihéron's models.[45] As for how to meet the demand for cadavers, savants like Diderot generally deemed the dissector's use of the bodies of criminals or paupers to be legitimate exercises in the advance of knowledge and the social good.[46]

However, the excesses of the bodily register, like the body's disturbing by-products, were not easily overcome. The goal of severing the utilitarian and rationalist side of anatomy from its unsettling association with death and the material reality of the corpse remained at best a goal, not an accomplishment. Suspicions lingered that anatomists were vivisectionists.[47] Moreover, as Philippe Ariés attests, "the almost fashionable success of anatomy cannot be attributed solely to scientific curiosity. . . . it corresponds to an attraction to certain ill-defined things at the outer limits of life and death, sexuality and pain."[48] In a series of four allegorical works, collectively known as *The Plague Figures,* the Italian wax artist Nicolas Zumbo (1656–1701), represented the stages of the body's decomposition, capturing their form and also the bilious colors of physical decay. As Georges Didi-Huberman observes, in these works, "the decomposition of the flesh is pushed so far that it is alternatively fascinating and revolting. Exact putrescence and baroque mortality: Zumbo produces artifacts of a raw, non-transposed anatomy, endlessly observed on real cadavers."[49]

An anecdote concerning the results of the first art competition held under the new Republic reveals a great deal about both the aesthetic and political resistances that a dead body could provoke. The subject of the contest was the death of Brutus. In January 1794, following a very public viewing and accompanied by a written justification of their decision, the jury chose to award first prize to the work of Harriet, student of Jacques-Louis David, rather than that of Pierre-Narcisse Guérin, student of Jean-Baptiste Regnault. Despite the latter's skill, virtuoso style, and more confident maturity, the jury "cried out in indignation against the appearance of Brutus's corpse." As Antoine de Baecque recounts, whereas Harriet's work took into account all the stereotypes of the representation of *la belle mort*—"vigorous and vast" corpse, "very colorful," "voluminous," even endowed with "too much freshness" and thus "not dead enough"—Guérin chose the opposite side: he painted a corpse where the marks of decomposition are already advanced, dislocated in parts (notably the shoulder), fixed in a contorted rigidity (the right hand), with an almost repulsive facial expression, and with an absolutely deathly complexion of a greenish hue. Guérin's canvas, in its composition, disposition, and play of colors, and in the appearance of most of the bodies, nonetheless conforms thoroughly to the canons of the classical revival. But to paint the central corpse, Guérin seems to have departed radically from the concept of ideal beauty, choosing grotesque expression rather than serenity, repulsive death as opposed to harmony, morbid realism against the ideal of virile flesh. "Thin and almost livid," "dislocated corpse," "unrecognizable hero": these are some of the verdicts that motivated the rejection of the painting, summarized by Lesueur's expression, "This was not the image I had formed of a free man who has just died for his country."[50]

The episode is revealing of the taboos that surrounded the corpse, a prohibition that accelerated in the years following the Terror. Beginning with the Directory, both public hygiene and good manners were invoked in a campaign to conceal the corpse from public view, by confining it to either the morgue or the family, and thereby rationalizing "the "body of Paris" (*corps de Paris*), controlling its impulses, whether morbid or sexual, political or social."[51] There is an interesting analogue to the subsequent confinement of the corpse in the manner in which anatomists and their teaching were enrolled within the newly organized medical and natural sciences of Directory and Napoleonic France.[52] Although the public taste for anatomy courses did not immediately abate, anatomy was well on its way to becoming a specialty of and for a scientific and medical elite, rather than the vocation of cultivated amateurs and the fashionable public. One might surmise that the anatomist's ability to please the crowds, as in former times, also carried with it a noxious taint of public execution, heightened not only in France but also throughout Europe by the recent experience of the Terror.

To contain the dead cadaver within the medical arena or the mortuary was to strive to put at bay the dreaded association between dissection and violence, a connection further charged in the case of veterinary medicine.[53] Upon its relocation to the Paris region in 1765, Alfort was the target of hostile demonstrations. The rioters threw animal cadavers at the gates, and attacked and pillaged the feed convoys, acting upon a deep-seated taboo against touching the corpse or entrails of an animal. The veterinarian remained for many an equivocal figure, assimilated to the animal slaughterer, who in turn was associated with the executioner, an affinity heightened by the fact that the same person often performed both tasks in old regime France.[54] Considered in this light, the act of dissection—the dismemberment of an already decaying corpse, the opening up to the gaze of what is inside and concealed, the cutting that is no longer curative but inquisitive—always carried with it the ambiguous effect about which Kristeva speaks. As Barbara M. Stafford notes, "as the dissector dug deeper into the corpse, he exposed a mutable organism at once unified and fragmented, simple and complex, ideal and grotesque."[55]

BODY PARTS AND STAGED ANATOMIES

Fragonard's two most remarkable *écorchés,* "Man with a Mandible" and "The Anatomized Cavalier," are a testament to his extraordinary skill. In "Man with a Mandible" (figure 34) the full human figure is displayed, stripped of its outer covering, not just of the garments of culture but of the body's own protective sheath, the skin. What is revealed is the material inner substance of the body, very much in the manner suggested by Descartes—who spent much time observing the slaughterhouses and gallows in Amsterdam—when he pronounced: "I consider myself first, as having a face, hands, arms, and whole of this machine composed of bones and flesh, such as it appears in a cadaver, which I designate by the name of body."[56]

Using a routine technique of the natural anatomist, Fragonard replaced the eyeballs with glass replicas. This simple artifice breathes a sort of life—sensible, irritable life—into the dried, injected body. According to Sylvie Hugues, this sensibility accorded well with the new more activist conception, which by mid-century was altering earlier materialist suppositions concerning inert matter. As she explains, "the body becomes a closed field where vital forces and forces of dissolution are opposed: 'life is the ensemble of functions which resist death'" In this context, "Man with a Mandible" offers a solution (artistic and scientific) to the problem within vitalist philosophy of how to represent the dead body.[57] In any event, Fragonard has certainly introduced a kind of turmoil in this figure—in the jumbled network of arteries and veins that lie below the surface, in his open stride, turned head, and raised arm, which

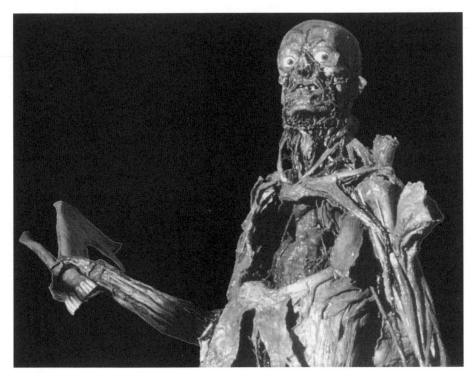

Figure 34. Honoré Fragonard, Man with a Mandible (eighteenth century). Courtesy of the Musée Fragonard, France. Photo: C. Degueurce.

holds the mandible as a potential weapon against a possible intruder. It is as if this man sees and hears something surprising and horrifying. Though dead, he appears to be stiffening against danger.[58] The injected veins and arteries on his skull and face further communicate horror.

If "Fetus Dancing the Gigue" gently mocks the conventions established in the Vanitas tradition, "Man with a Mandible" appears to be a response to the canonical tradition of baroque anatomical illustration in which the *écorché* evoked Christ's tormented journey. In such representations, the immaterial soul confronted the material body, with all its worthless flesh. The *écorché* is a two- (in the case of drawings) or three-dimensional (in the case of plaster or bronze casts) representation of the human body, in which the envelope of skin and fat has been removed; the artist's intention being to depict the surface muscles with anatomical correctness. As a modern physician comments, "The figure is usually shown in action, one leg before the other, one arm raised over the head. They were invariably carefully constructed and beautifully proportioned. For surgeons, écorchés were reminders of what they had dissected and guides to what they would be operating on. Artists used them as a standard to check the anatomical accuracy of their life drawings. . . . [Whereas the muscular structure is never completely observable in even the most revealing drawings], the écorché rendered the underlying structures clearly apparent."[59]

Intentionally lowering the figure's arm, and arming him with a nonhuman body part, which mimes his own forward thrusting jaw, Fragonard pointed not to man's transcendent nature, but to his material substance. Beyond that, it is important to remember that, as an anatomist first at Alfort and then at the Paris School of Health, Fragonard stood at the beginning of what would emerge by century's end as the new science of comparative anatomy in the remarkable group of natural philosophers around Buffon, Vicq d'Azyr, and others, which was institutionalized in the newly organized Museum of Natural History of 1793. Although there is no existing record of Fragonard's teaching, neither is there anything to suggest that he attached didactic descriptions to his anatomical pieces of the sort one finds in the anatomical wax models executed under the supervision of Felice Fontana, presently housed at La Specola Museum in Florence. Perhaps this is the reason that some of the scientific visitors to Alfort were less than enthusiastic about Fragonard's accomplishments. For example, the German surgeon Georg Ludwig Rumpelt, who visited at the end of 1779, remarked that while even the most difficult preparations were executed with a surprising facility, nonetheless a large number of the specimens seemed to have only a very modest practical or scientific utility. In Rumpelt's report, Fragonard appeared as less a man of science than something of a showman, interested in fabricating curious montages suitable for dazzling the public, not for the advancement of science.[60] What is more, Rumpelt insisted,

Figure 35. Honoré Fragonard, The Anatomized Cavalier (eighteenth century). Courtesy of the Musée Fragonard, France. Photo: C. Degueurce.

"No preparation, executed with the greatest care, has for me any value if it doesn't serve to demonstrate a new fact or to solve a contentious question."[61]

"The Anatomized Cavalier" (figure 35) is surely the most spectacular of all of Fragonard's surviving *écorchés*, testing the physical limits of natural anatomy by posing a human figure on a galloping horse. It is also the work that gave rise to the greatest speculation. Presumed by many to be modeled after one of the German artist Albrecht Dürer's *Four Horsemen of the Apocalypse*, it also inspired a macabre legend recounted by another of Alfort's foreign visitors. According to a travelogue read by the Swedish naturalist Karl Asmund

Rudolphi, the cavalier was Fragonard's deceased sweetheart, the daughter of a local grocer, who died from grief because of her father's opposition to a marriage with the anatomist. When questioned about this matter by Rudolphi, Fragonard remained silent but melancholy. However, the museum's guardian cleared up the matter: The "anatomized Amazon" was really a man, whose "virile attributes were a bit "shortened" in order not to disturb his seated position."[62] Rudolphi seems to have enjoyed the titillation the original tale produced in his own readers, for he chose to conclude his account by noting that the preparation was "tender enough" (*zart genug*) to be presented as a woman.[63]

Although Fragonard's anatomies were appreciated for their skillful fabrication, Rudolphi's account underscores the extent to which viewers were attracted to them as captivating spectacles.[64] Indeed, much like the animated statues so popular among Enlightenment artists and *philosophes,* the "Anatomized Cavalier" seemed to come to life, or better yet, rise from the dead.[65] For the gist of this anatomical romance turns on Fragonard's disinterment of his beloved in order to immortalize her as an anatomical work. In that sense, Fragonard was not playing Pygmalion to his Amazon on horseback. Once dead, she remains dead, but through the addition of varnish, wax, and spirits, he endeavors to make his statue of her eternal. Even as fable, Fragonard's Amazon captures something about the impulse behind the works as a whole. As Michel Ellenberger stresses, "Science furnished Fragonard the occasion for modeling sculptures in flesh . . . dissecting, injecting, anatomizing: manual activities that gave the tactile joy of materialized flesh and embodied matter, shared by the surgeon and the sculptor. By means of a biological diversion, a chemical disguise [*travestissement*] and a subtle surgery, he conferred on the cadavers the eternity of statues."[66]

Most recent examinations of Fragonard's work come up against the stubborn question of whether it qualifies as science; whether the motivation behind the works is scientific or voyeuristic, even perverse or monstrous, as Michel Lemire notes, in their "expressive morbidity, [in the] gestural rhetoric of these beings beyond the tomb, perishable bodies transformed into hallucinating statues."[67] In the estimation of many of his contemporaries, he was more the artist than the scientist. For example, in his 1798 report on the occasion of the Paris School of Health's third anniversary, Director Thouret, whose views we have already encountered, situated Fragonard as one of the school's three artists, along with André-Pierre Pinson and Anicet-Charles Lemonnier. The result of this simple classification was to diminish the anatomist's actual institutional position as the superior rather than the equal of his two colleagues.[68] There are further indications that Fragonard's position after 1795 was more titular than real, and that "sick, physically diminished, he was most likely relieved progressively of his responsibilities."[69]

In July 1792, just two months before the declaration of the Republic, Fragonard had addressed the Legislative Assembly to plead for the creation of a National Anatomical Cabinet, with himself as the director. He offered to make a personal donation of fifteen hundred anatomical samples in exchange for the nation's support of his proposal. This was anatomy in the service of the nation, or as Fragonard and two colleagues put it on this occasion, "the desire to unite ourselves with the public welfare."[70] The Assembly's attention, however, was elsewhere in the tempestuous summer months of 1792. Only toward the end of 1794 and in 1795 was a decision finally made, according to which the Alfort holdings were divided—and effectively disciplinized—between veterinary medicine, human health, and natural history in, respectively, the Veterinary School of Alfort, where the majority of Fragonard's surviving works still reside, the School of Health of Paris, and the Museum of Natural History.

Not only was Fragonard's grand project of a unified assemblage never to be realized, but also by this time the specimens were suffering from serious neglect. Earlier, in spring 1794, as members of the anatomy commission of the Temporary Commission of the Arts,[71] Fragonard and Vicq d'Azyr were charged with inspecting the collections at Alfort. The report of 15 Floréal Year II (14 May 1794) was "a cry of alarm" from the two anatomists. But it served even more as a stark reminder of the anatomist's struggle to wrest from its own ghastly putrefaction the earthly, perishable matter of which his work was fashioned: "parasites were attacking the precious preparations, which were ex-

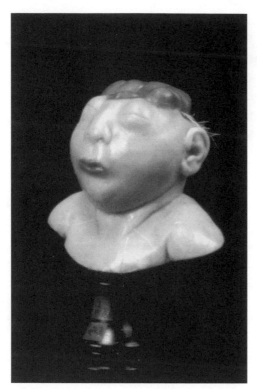

Figure 36. André-Pierre Pinson, Wax Bust of an Anencephalous Birth. Collection: Muséum national d'Histoire naturelle. Photo: B. Faye.

posed to the dust. Rain was leaking through the roof; the cabinets didn't close. Rats were running into the halls; the bottles used for preservation were not airtight."[72] In contrast to the smooth, clean lines of artificial anatomies, as in the wax representation of an otherwise monstrous or anencephalous birth executed by Pinson (figure 36), the didactic surfaces of Fragonard's écorchés are constantly disturbed by the jumbled, injected entrails of their flayed interiors. Normative yet somehow also monstrous, this collection straddles the borders of idealized expression and its grotesque reversal, a fitting testimonial to a revolution in which the ideals of unity were constantly betrayed by division and fragmentation.

PART 4

DISPLACING MONSTERS:
SIGN, ALLEGORY, AND MYTH

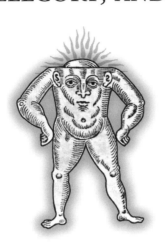

7

SIGNS OF MONSTROSITY

The Rhetoric of Description and the Limits of Allegory
in Rabelais and Montaigne

TIMOTHY HAMPTON

*Monsters are nothing more than mysterious hieroglyphs and images figured forth by
Nature, either in scorn of men, or as a record of their actions.*
—Emanuele Tesauro, *Cannochiale Aristotelico* (1654)[1]

ALLEGORY AND SIMILITUDE

Pierre Boaistuau's *Histoires prodigieuses* (1560) was one of the most popular of
the many collections of material on monsters to be published in sixteenth-
century France. Like many other books in this genre, it is a hodge-podge of
descriptions of monsters (both classical and modern), moralizing commentary about their meaning, and retellings of literary anecdotes about monstrosity, from the Bible to Pliny. The book closes with a description of the so-called
Monster of Ravenna, which was born in Italy early in the century and was one
of the most famous monsters of the period. Boaistuau presents the monster as
follows: "There was born in Ravenna a monster with a horn on the head, two
wings, and a foot like that of a bird of prey and an eye in the knee."[2] A few
lines later we are told that the wisest men in the country puzzled over the

meaning of this creature and interpreted it as a commentary on the sins of Italy: "by the horn were figured pride and ambition; by the wings, frivolity and inconstancy; by the lack of arms, the lack of good works; by the foot of a bird of prey, rapine, usury and avarice."[3] Of interest here are the descriptive strategies deployed by the author to depict the monster. In the description of the creature we are told that the monster's foot is "like" that of a bird of prey ("semblable à celuy d'un oyseau"). Yet in the interpretive gloss the foot has actually become that which it earlier only resembled. As it moves from description to interpretation Boaistuau's text transforms resemblance into corporeity.

In what follows, I want to pursue the implications of the detail I have just noted in Boaistuau—the seemingly innocuous slippage from a description characterized by word such as "like" or "similar to" (that is, through similitude) to a description involving a firm identification, in which the child "becomes" the figure to which he is initially only compared. This is a rhetorical displacement that one finds frequently in early modern writing dealing with monsters, from compendia such as Boaistuau's to history writing to more properly "literary" representations. My own analysis will deal principally with the literary description of the monster. I want to focus first on a series of encounters with monsters in a major literary text of the sixteenth century, the *Quart livre* or "Fourth Book" of the adventures of Pantagruel, written by François Rabelais in the 1540s. Then, in my conclusion, I will look briefly at a text by Montaigne, written some forty years later. In my reading of Rabelais I will argue that the slippage from similitude to identity has broad implications. For one thing it raises questions about how the figure of the monster is implicated in the rhetoric of description, in the problem of how the strange or the unnatural may be depicted in language. In a somewhat larger context, these details of style and rhetoric touch on important issues involving interpretive and rhetorical authority, issues germane both to the ideological struggles that mark sixteenth-century France, and to the emergence of the new forms of literary representation that characterize the period. The monster is, of course, through the very etymology of its name (*monstrum*) a sign, a portent or display of meaning. Or as the Italian baroque writer Tesauro puts it in the epigraph to this essay, monsters are hieroglyphs, signs put into nature by God. As such, it will be useful to think about how these signs in nature interact with signs in language, and in particular with the ornaments and tropes of rhetoric and style.

The modulation we saw in Boaistuau from description through similitude to firm identification with the monster's body part is, as I noted, a stylistic tic found in much Renaissance writing about monstrosity. But it also has a distant ancestor in one of the most important discussions of monstrosity in classical literature, Aristotle's treatise called *The Generation of Animals*. There, in the midst of a discussion of the resemblance of parents and children, Aristotle notes that the production of the embryo comes from the interaction of the hot elements coming from the male acting on the colder humors of the female. He goes on to suggest that one possible explanation for the creation of monsters comes from the fact that, on occasion, the movement of the two elements relapses "and the material is not controlled." When this happens, all that remains in the blending of the two parents is "what is most universal, that is to say the animal." From this comes a monster: "the offspring . . . appears finally to be not even a human being, but only some kind of animal, what is called a monstrosity. Then people say that the child has the head of a ram or a bull, and so on with other animals, as that a calf has the head of a child or a sheep that of an ox."[4] However, Aristotle goes on to reject the idea that a child might actually have the head of a ram or a bull. This is impossible, he comments a moment later, because different animals have different gestation periods. Instead, the irregularities in nature responsible for monstrosity produce simulations, body parts that merely look as if they came from other animals. As he goes on to observe, "All these monsters result from the causes stated above, but they are none of the things they are said to be; there is only some similarity, such as may arise even where there is no defect of growth. Hence often jesters compare someone who is not beautiful to a goat breathing fire, or again to a ram butting, and a certain physiognomist reduced all faces to those of two or three animals, and his arguments often prevailed on people."[5] Aristotle refers to the birth of monsters only to reject their existence.

Yet, as in the case of the Boaistuau passage quoted earlier, the unfolding and vocabulary of Aristotle's description are particularly interesting. The passage moves, in a few phrases, from a reflection on the causes of monstrosity to a consideration of how monstrous beings are described by onlookers ("then people say"). This shift from being to saying then gives way, through a comparison, to a discussion of fiction-making, emblematized in the figure of the jester who describes certain people in certain ways. And we end with an allusion to the physiognomist, who deludes the simple with his spurious arguments. In other words, no sooner has Aristotle begun speaking about what monsters *are,* than he finds himself speaking about how monsters *may be described,* and then about how monstrosity is used as a trope to describe the nonmonstrous. The last sections of the passage suggest that once one tries to describe the monstrous the actual distinction between the monstrous and the nonmonstrous becomes difficult to pin down.

The passages I have analyzed from Aristotle and Boaistuau suggest that a meditation on monstrosity must also, necessarily, be a meditation on the dynamics of resemblance. The notion of similitude, of one thing being "like" another, is, to be sure, one of the most obvious ways of relating things and writing about them. Classical and Renaissance writers on language consider the question of similitude both under the heading of invention—that is, of the relationships of ideas—and under the heading of tropes and figures—that is, of the ornamentation of language. Yet, as Heinrich Lausberg notes in his authoritative guide to rhetorical theory, the limits of similitude are vague and the relationships between similarity as an organizing principle of composition, on the one hand, and simile as a rhetorical trope, on the other, are often fluid. Indeed, similitude seems to lie at a midway point between allegory (an "extended simile") and metaphor (a "shortened" simile).[6] Classical and Renaissance discussions of rhetoric often acknowledge a lack of precision and even a certain productive vagueness in similitude. Thus, for example, Aristotle's *Rhetoric* juxtaposes the rhetorical trope of simile (*eikon*) with metaphor, from which, he says, it differs little. Yet he notes that metaphor is more precise, since with a metaphor the details of both halves of the comparison correspond exactly. Similes, by contrast, are metaphors "without the details."[7] The pseudo-Ciceronian *Rhetorica ad Herennium* stresses the importance of comparison through similitude for proving or disproving arguments in courts of law, but notes that the usefulness of the technique stems from the fact that all elements of the things compared need not correspond precisely: "the resemblance between the two things need not apply throughout, but must hold on the precise point of comparison."[8] In the *De Oratore,* Cicero includes simile under the heading of ornaments of speech, comparing it, again, to metaphor, but noting that metaphor is a "shorter form" of simile, which is then put in a place where it does not belong ("in alieno loco").[9] Quintilian offers a slightly less dismissive account when he notes that the advantage of simile over metaphor lies in the fact that a simile sets before our eyes simultaneously ("pariter ostendit") both halves of a comparison, enabling us to see the workings of the poet's or orator's mind.[10] In a Renaissance context, Erasmus makes a similar claim in his *De Copia,* noting that "A simile is a metaphor that is made explicit and specifically related to the subject."[11] And he goes on to contrast the simile with metaphor and allegory. With metaphor, he says, "a word is transferred away from its real and proper signification to one which lies outside its proper sphere," and allegory is "nothing more than a metaphor carried on beyond the bounds of a single word."[12] Thus similitude might be seen as a particularly transparent or pellucid strategy of figuration. It enables the viewer or reader to hold in mind both the thing compared and the comparison.

We shall see that the use of similitude in the description of monstrosity is intimately linked to the deployment of allegory. By allegory here I simply mean the imposition of a moralizing interpretive gloss that transforms the monster into some sort of sign of a larger purpose. I will suggest that monstrosity may be seen as a site at which allegory and similitude overlap and confront each other. Thus, to return again for a moment to Boaistuau's depiction of the Monster of Ravenna, the slide from similitude to identification marks the enabling condition of the author's own allegorical interpretation. If Boaistuau is to allegorize the monster and make it the sign of some larger moral meaning (in this case, the decadence of Italy), the monster must be identified as what it first only appeared to resemble. It cannot simply remain a human who "looks like" something else. It must actually become that other creature. Allegorical interpretation thus presumes a fixed identification of the object of scrutiny (in this case, the monster). Once the precise nature of the object has been defined through description, an allegorical meaning can be affixed to it that will reveal it to be a sign of some greater purpose. In this context one might suggest that the recognition of likeness, the establishment of similitude, poses a kind of threat to the establishment of allegorical interpretation. For if the child under scrutiny only "looks like" an animal, there is no need for alarm—or, at the very least, the "problem" that it raises may lie with the viewer, who cannot discern correctly, rather than with the nature of the monster. Indeed the establishment of similitude is such a common reflex for describing things—and, in particular, for rendering the unfamiliar familiar— that the evocation of likeness threatens to diffuse or undermine the solidity upon which allegorical interpretation depends. Similitude thus plays a double role in the language of monstrosity: as both a descriptive technique and a marker of arbitrary fictionality.[13]

In a collection of anecdotes such as Boaistuau's *Histoires prodigieuses*, the intersection of similitude and allegory helps to define the author's project; he is both compiler and interpreter, both describer and allegorist. In a more complicated text such as Rabelais's *Quart livre*, as we shall see, the intersection of allegorical representation with tropes of similitude produces a reflection on the political nature of language, as well as on the ways in which characters and communities distinguish the familiar and the strange.[14]

MONSTERS AND SIGNS

Rabelais's *Quart livre des faicts et dicts héroïques du bon Pantagruel* (1552), to which I now want to turn, is the account of a sea voyage. It is occasioned by the wish of Pantagruel's friend Panurge to start a family, and by his inability to decide upon marriage, since he is afraid that he will be cuckolded. Seeking help with this difficult decision, Pantagruel and his men undertake a journey to the Oracle of the Holy Bottle, which they hope will advise the unhappy Panurge. The trip recounted in the *Quart livre* follows, more or less, the route taken by the Portuguese to India. The narrative consists of a loose string of episodes in which the company puts in at different islands and meets strangers, both natural and unnatural. At the exact center of the book, in chapters 29 through 42, Pantagruel and his men encounter a series of monsters. The first of these monsters appears as Pantagruel and his men sail past an island called Tapinois, or the "Sneaky Island." As they draw near to the island, the pilot of the ship, whose name is Xenomanes ("lover of the strange"), identifies it as the demesne of the monster Quaresmeprenant—that is, the king of Lent. Pantagruel says that he has heard of this character and would like to meet him. Pantagruel's friend, the monk Frère Jean, who is noted for his bellicose nature, proposes that they fight the monster, since he is reputed to be an enemy of the (female) Sausages of Carnival. Xenomanes notes that it would be a costly detour to make an extra stop and Pantagruel cautions that war would be risky. Instead, Xenomanes volunteers to describe Quaresmeprenant, thereby saving time and money, and averting potential violence. A description will substitute for an adventure; we will get words instead of actions.

Xenomanes's description takes up several chapters, and paints in detail the anatomy of what Pantagruel calls this "Cas estrange," a strange case.[15] The description consists of an enormous list of similes: "His lobes like a gimlet. His vermiform excrescences like a tennis-racket. His membranes like a monk's cowl. His funnel like a mason's hod. The vault of his cranium like a patchwork bonnet. His pineal gland like a bagpipe."[16] In Pierre Jourda's edition of Rabelais, the most frequently used modern scholarly text, the list goes on for six pages. It is then followed by another list, this one detailing Quaresmeprenant's activities: "If he blinked his eyes, it was waffles and wafers. If he coughed, it was boxes of quince-jelly. If he made a speech, it was last year's snows."[17] It is one of the most exorbitant descriptions in a book by a writer noted for his exorbitant descriptions.

To be sure, it is possible to link some of these phrases to proverbial utterances about Lent, to the themes of plenitude and scarcity, or to conventional satire on the Church: "If he blew out, it was boxes for Indulgences."[18] This proverbial dimension would seem to be especially pertinent to the descriptions of Quaresmeprenant's various activities. Yet this description also asks us to think about the relationship between the "otherness" of the monster and the language through which that "otherness" is described. Quaresmeprenant, of course, is an allegorical figure, an emblematic representation. But he is a representation of a sacrament of the Church that all Catholics know only too well. In this regard he is perfectly familiar—and both the popular and learned culture of Rabelais's day featured many such allegories of Lent.[19] Thus Rabelais's text presents a familiar phenomenon as a monster requiring description, and then proceeds to use the "transparent" technique of similitude to describe it. What results, however, is anything but the type of fixing of meaning through allegorical interpretation that one saw in Boaistuau. Instead, the list of similitudes has the effect of fragmenting meaning, of sending the reader in dozens of different directions to try to figure out how, say, an earlobe can be like a gimlet. Rabelais deploys a rhetoric of similitude borrowed from conventional writing about monsters. Yet through his very description he succeeds in representing the familiar as unfamiliar, in making conventional allegory into something unreadable, a kind of monster made out of words. Rabelais pushes the overly familiar rhetorical strategy of similitude to its breaking point by doing precisely what the rhetorical manuals say he should do, by describing the strange through a reference to the familiar. The metonymic or horizontal slide from one part of Quaresmeprenant's body to the next produces precisely the strangeness that the more vertically oriented logic of simile seeks to mitigate. Rabelais gives us more similitude than we can handle. In the process, he renders the object of his description strange, instead of making it familiar.

This rhetorical distortion is not merely a question of literary pyrotechnics. It has theological and political resonances that link it to debates over the status of Lent in the middle years of the sixteenth century in France. Lent, of course, was one of the Catholic rituals most vociferously attacked by both Protestant reformers and more moderate Christian humanists such as Rabelais's friend and teacher Erasmus. What is striking about these attacks is that they tend to focus on Lent as a form of representation, as a kind of rhetorical excess. It is an exterior "ceremony" (Erasmus's word) which stands in for a missing interior piety. Calvin even argues that Lent constitutes a kind of rhetorical distortion of history—an allegorical violence done to the deeds of Christ. In the *Institutes of the Christian Religion* he attacks Lent as a crime against the *literal* meaning of Christ's sacrifice. When Christ fasted, says Calvin, he did so not "to set an example to others," but to demonstrate that his doctrine came from God, and not from men: "Nor does he fast after the manner of men, as he would have done had he meant to invite men to imitation; he rather gives an example, by which he may raise all to admire rather than study to imitate him."[20] When Catholics observe Lent, Calvin continues, they "substitute signs and external appearance for integrity of the heart."[21] In other words, Lent, as practiced by Calvin's contemporaries, is a kind of transformation of a sacred, singular act into a trope or figure; it makes into ritual deeds that should not be repeated.

The Protestant notion that Catholic ritual is a kind of semiotic distortion of history is consonant with the many debates over the meaning of signs (principally, of course, of the sign of the Eucharist) that mark the 1520s and 1530s in France. These debates connect up to the language of Rabelais's text in several ways. For one thing, the very notion of the Incarnation, of a God made man, suggested a monstrosity. And in one of his most virulent attacks on the distortions of the Church, a treatise entitled *Des Scandales* (1550), Calvin insists on the essential mystery of the Incarnation. It is not a humorous fable, he says ("une fable pour rire"), or a terrifying monster ("un monstre qu'on doive avoir en horreur"), but a mystery for us to adore ("un mystère pour adorer").[22] And the deeds of Christ are signs that show the truth of John the Baptist's assertion that he would do things worthy of the Son of God ("ses oeuvres ont monstrée clairement que Saint Jehan n'a pas dit en vain"). Yet our weakness leads us to forge wild imaginations ("des imaginations sauvages") instead of following what God has shown us with his word ("monstrée par sa parole").[23] The echo here between the French word for "monster" (*monstre*) and the verb *monstrer* (to show), to which it is etymologically linked, is no mere coincidence. Calvin's treatise is replete with appearances of these terms, as well as, especially, with the feminine noun "monstre" (a display or demonstration), which appears dozens of times, particularly in the phrase "faire monstre" (to make a show or a display). The problem with human beings, says Calvin, is that they are in love with appearances, they love to "se monstrer," and as such become victims of Satan, who counterfeits religion ("fait grande monstre de religion").[24] Christ, by contrast, is he who makes no display ("qui n'a nulle monstre"), but whose majesty is shown ("se monstre") through the simple language of the Gospels ("langage bas et de nulle monstre").[25] The deeds of Christ are signs, which show us how to live. Yet they are unique in that they are signs which make no show.

It is of course impossible to prove that Rabelais intends us to see the parallel between the monster Quaresmeprenant and the vocabulary of current discussions about Catholic excess and display. However, this language appears with such obsessive frequency in Calvin's writings (to mention only the most authoritative French figure in this context) that it would be virtually impossible to confront polemics around Lent without finding oneself in debate about signs and "monstres." When that debate is read in the context of traditional allegories of Lent, it becomes a debate about the relationship between monsters and signs.

This thematic emphasis on monsters as signs and signs as monsters is strengthened when we recall that the encounter with Quaresmeprenant is part of a very specific polemic against Calvin's text on scandals. In that text Calvin had attacked Rabelais personally in terms consonant with the themes and language I have been tracing. In his discussion of perversions of the Christian faith, Calvin attacked Rabelais and several of his humanist friends for having turned their backs on the Gospels after having tasted them. This, he says, is behavior worse than monstrous: "For if it is a monstrous thing for a man to be turned into a brutal beast, such people are to be deplored even more, since they are not even affected by their evil."[26] And he goes on to declare that God has singled out ("monstre du doigt") people like Rabelais as "mirrors" to remind us to follow His way, lest we meet a similar fate.[27]

Rabelais answers Calvin. At the conclusion of the pilot's description of Lent, Pantagruel notes that the monster reminds him of the story of Misharmony and Discord ("Amodunt et Discordance"). He goes on to recall the tale, which thus functions as an exact mirror or double to the description of Lent just provided by Xenomanes. He transmits a fable, which Rabelais borrowed from an Italian humanist named Celio Calcagnini. It tells of how Antinature (Antiphysie) copulated with the Roman god of the earth Tellumon and gave birth to Misharmony and Discord. These unappealing offspring had round heads ("like a balloon"), with long ears ("like the ears of an ass"), and protruding eyes ("like heels").[28] Nevertheless, Antinature found her children to be beautiful and put forth arguments to that effect, which actually "won the admiration of every brainless idiot, of everyone, indeed, who lacked sound judgment and common sense."[29] Since that time, notes Pantagruel, it is Antinature who has given birth to all types of "pious apes, holy hypocrites and popemongers; the maniacal nobodies, demoniacal Calvins and impostures of Geneva; the furious Puy-Herbaults . . . and other deformed monsters, misshapen in Nature's despite."[30] With characteristic narrative abruptness, the Rabelaisian text moves from the mighty allegory of Lent to a topical and very personal quarrel with two personal enemies, a monk named Gabriel de Puy-Herbaut (who attacked him from the perspective of Catholic orthodoxy) and Calvin. As should be clear by now, Rabelais's counterattack involves both a doctrinal-political debate and a meditation on the language of representation. Calvin's depiction of Rabelais as a monster comes in the middle of a vicious affirmation of doctrinal rigidity. By depicting Calvin himself as a monster—that is, by rhetorically doubling him, by making him a monstrous "mirror" of his own description of Rabelais and a structural double of the very Lent that Calvin attacks in his own writing—Rabelais suggests that doctrinal intolerance—belief without charity—is a kind of monstrosity. Moreover, by associating Calvin with the fools who mistake the monstrous for the beautiful, Rabelais underscores the subjective nature of interpretation, the sense that, as the description of Quaresmeprenant has already shown, the familiar and the unfamiliar are mediated by the figures we use to describe them.[31]

Rabelais's satire of Calvin thus has both a literary and an ideological dimension. On one level, it underscores the fictive nature of representations of the strange—and by extension, of Rabelais's own narrative. Ideologically, it serves a mediating function. As a moderate Catholic humanist, Rabelais would have found himself in some sympathy with Calvin's attacks on the traditional practices of both Lent and Carnival—as well as with his critique of the elaborate displays or "monstres" of piety and excess that accompanied them. (This makes Calvin a more interesting and difficult foe than Puy-Herbaut.) Yet at the same time, he would have had difficulty embracing Calvin's attack on Catholic orthodoxy and on the semiology of history as endorsed by Catholic thought. He thus finds himself in a kind of representational double bind, neither able to endorse the traditional representations of Lent, nor able to attack them in any way that might associate him with the positions of a Calvin. His satirical dismantling of the topos of Lent and his reflexive satire on dogmatism occur through an exaggeration of the very rhetoric of description traditionally applied to monsters. They suggest that one possible response to the rhetoric of political extremism is to unmask the linguistic procedures through which it is construed and represented.

ALLEGORIES AND THINGS

If the description of Quaresmeprenant raises issues about how language renders the unfamiliar familiar (and vice versa), the episode that follows it shifts those issues into a slightly different context. No sooner have Pantagruel and his men passed the island of the sneaks than they sight a whale, what the text calls a "Phystère." And if the evocation of Quaresmeprenant is exorbitant and diffuse, the description of the whale is remarkably straightforward and direct: "Pantagruel sighted in the distance a huge and monstrous spouting whale, making straight towards us. It was snorting and thundering, and so puffed up that it rode high on the waves, above the main-tops of our ships."[32] Panurge is terrified, and begins stuttering uncontrollably. Yet he soon rights himself and provides an explanation for the vision before him. He claims that what swims toward the ship is "the Leviathan described by the great prophet Moses in his life of that holy man Job."[33] A moment later he adds, "I think it's the same sea-monster that was sent in the old days to gobble up Andromeda"—an allusion to a tale in the fourth book of Ovid's *Metamorphoses.*[34] Whereas the narrator names the whale for what it is, the cowardly Panurge uses the discourse of typology. He lends legendary and metaphysical meaning to the beast by likening it to the two great sea-monsters of the Old Testament and classical mythology. Like Boaistuau discussing the Monster of Ravenna, he allegorizes and makes the natural object into a sign of something greater that itself. This is made clear yet again, a moment later, when he cries, "Oh, oh, Satan, Leviathan, you devil!"[35]

If Frère Jean wants to fight Quaresmeprenant, Panurge wants to run from the whale. Yet the contrast between the narrator's matter-of-fact description and Panurge's panic suggests that what is at issue here may be less the nature of the monster than the way it is perceived. Anything may be Leviathan if thinking makes it so. For it is precisely the supernatural or mythic dimensions of the beast that are demolished a moment later, as Pantagruel steps to the prow of the ship and kills the monster with a well-placed barrage of arrows. First he gouges its eyes and mouth with three arrows that form an equilateral triangle, then he sends three more, equally spaced, along its spine, and fifty into each flank, which give the whale the appearance of a galley. "Then, as it died, the spouter turned over on its back, like all dead fish; and lying on the water, with its beams beneath it, it looked like that scolopendra, or hundred-legged serpent, described by the ancient sage Nicander."[36]

The rapidity with which the text shifts figures in describing the whale underscores the tension between allegorical interpretation and descriptive similitude that I have suggested inhabits and structures discourses about monstrosity in Renaissance France. Upon its approach, the animal, which the narrator calls a "monstrous spouter" ("monstrueux Physetere"), becomes an allegory of evil. Once Pantagruel has wounded it fatally, the arrows in its head take on the appearance of horns ("trois cornes").[37] When he adds a supplement of a hundred extra arrows the beast turns—again, through similitude—into a ship:

"the spouter's body *resembled* the hull of a three-masted galleon."[38] After it has been killed, it becomes nothing but a dead fish. Then, as it rolls over, it takes on the appearance of a serpent from Nicander's classical book of anatomy. All of this happens in the space of a few sentences. And as if to stress the normalcy of the whole business, the men of the ship immediately set about cutting away its blubber, which they plan to sell. As for Pantagruel, we are told, not only is he not frightened of the whale, he's not even impressed: "For he had seen others like it, and even more enormous, in the Gallic Ocean."[39]

The natural marvel that is the whale turns out to be no marvel at all, and the juxtaposition of Panurge's terror with the metonymic mobility characterizing the description of the dead beast suggests that any attempt to fix its meaning may well be subjective illusion. The animal may *seem* to be Leviathan, but then it also *seems* to be a galleon and a serpent from the works of Nicander. No sooner does one think one knows what it is than the metamorphic energy of Rabelais's language assimilates it to something else. This is not to say that the monster—or the scene as a whole—may not be read allegorically (certainly, Pantagruel's courage in fighting the monster is unmistakable), only that whatever reading we impose on it is revealed to be provisional by the very movement of a text that immediately shows us the ways in which the monster changes identities before our very eyes. Indeed, the slide from figure to figure moves from a moment at which the culture of the past imposes itself on the present (through the typological references to Job and Ovid), through a moment at which the whale becomes that which would seem to be its adversary (a ship), and back to the classics and something like the type of monster Panurge associated it with at the outset (though now safely put away on the shelf, in the works of Nicander). No less than the evocation of Quaresmeprenant, this process affirms the subjective and fragile nature of interpretation, the problem of reading both monsters ("monstres") and signs ("monstres"). The narrator seems to reinforce this subjective dimension to the scene when he hints that we have passed from terror to pleasure, that the whale's appearance as a galleon was "a jolly sight to see."[40]

The juxtaposition of the encounter with the entirely "fictional" monster of

Lent and the "realistic" whale suggests the ways in which the rhetoric of monstrosity in Rabelais moves constantly between allegorical excess and the dismantling of allegory, between the signs that signify abstract truths and the contingency of the everyday world.

ALIEN SAUSAGES

In his initial description of Quaresmeprenant, Xenomanes tells Pantagruel that he is the ancestral enemy of the Sausage People, who live nearby. In other words, Carnival and Lent are always in opposition. On an earlier visit to the island, he reports, he himself tried to reconcile them, and succeeded in slightly appeasing their hostility. However, since that time, there has taken place the convocation of what Rabelais calls the Council of Chesil, that is, the Council of Fire (in Hebrew)—Rabelais's code word for the Council of Trent. And the Council of Chesil has issued a denunciation of the Sausages and a proclamation stating that Quaresmeprenant is to be reviled if he enters into any type of alliance with them. Through the allusion to the Council of Trent Rabelais condemns the so-called peacemakers of the Catholic Church. He suggests that those who are in charge of mending the rifts in the body of Christendom have, no less than Calvin, merely deepened them. This condemnation of the corruption of Catholic traditionalism is not, of course, unusual for Rabelais. However, what is interesting is the way in which he depicts the consequences of ecclesiastical hypocrisy and doctrinal extremism. No sooner have Pantagruel and his men landed on the fierce island and sat down in a grove for a quiet meal, than they are threatened by nearby Sausages. The reason for this attack, as Xenomanes tells Pantagruel, is that continual warfare against their ancient enemy has made them like Dido, in Virgil's *Aeneid,* constantly watchful over their coasts and borders. When Pantagruel assures his men that he will be able to make peace with the Sausages through parley, Xenomanes is dubious. The reason for their aggression, he suggests, is that, following the violent attack against the whale, they have become upset, and they have taken Pantagruel and his men for Quaresmeprenant, their mortal enemy, "even though you do not in the least resemble him."[41]

Coming on the heels of Rabelais's own rhetorical exorbitance in the preceding chapters, this evocation of monstrous misprision is important. The motif of resemblance, of similitude, evoked in Xenomanes's earlier description of Quaresmeprenant, is picked up again. Yet if the earlier scene mocked the problem of representing the monstrous, here we get a vision of political paranoia, a kind of failure to see the Other, based on misplaced identity and indifferent to similitude. Though they *in no way resemble* Quaresmeprenant, Pantagruel and his men will be mistaken for him and killed. The question of resemblance and difference and the dynamics of misprision were earlier allied with the description of the monster, with Antinature's faulty vision of her children, and with the metamorphoses of the whale. Now they are projected into the gaze of the monsters as they look upon the nonmonsters—that is, upon Pantagruel and his men—and see them as enemy monsters. Rabelais effectively turns the discourse of monstrosity against itself, as the "same" becomes the Other. The violence that has become habitual among European Christians has made it impossible to distinguish who is who, who is a monster and who is not.[42]

But this reversal has a literary dimension as well. For Rabelais then inscribes the problem of the vision of the Other into the very narration of the scene. The preparations for the battle against the Sausages are interrupted by a short chapter in which the narrator addresses the reader, asking him why he laughs at what he is reading, and pointing out that these Sausages are not, in fact, harmless. "I know well enough what I saw," he says, attesting to his authority as witness.[43] And he goes on to evoke the giants of old who, he says, tried to topple Mount Olympus and bring down the very gods. These giants, he says, were in fact Sausages, since part of their bodies was serpentine. This leads him, by association, to note that the serpent who tempted Eve in the Garden of Eden was a Sausage, and there follows a whole list of cagey, warlike, and alien figures who, says the narrator, were in fact Sausages. Thus, just as the Sausages mistake the narrator and his friends for Lent, and as Panurge takes the whale to be Satan, the narrator construes the Carnival creatures as snakes and ties them to the very pride that first led to the scattering of peoples across the face of the earth. In a series of episodes that feature repeated misapprehensions and distortions of the Other, the narrator shows himself to be as prey to rumor and free association as his most cowardly and blinkered characters. Our narrator may be no more trustworthy a reader of monsters than is Panurge.

Thus Rabelais invests his own narrative with the same epistemological and moral problems raised by the plot. When read in the context of the whole sequence of encounters I have been tracing, this self-referential turn underscores the ways in which any attempt to ascribe fixed identity or meaning to the monstrous Other runs the risk of a misprision which may degenerate into uncharitable calumny (Calvin) or even violence (the Sausage people). Rabelais's own response to the ethical and political problems that shape the representation of the Other seems to be to reconfigure them as problems of language, and to dramatize them at diverse levels of his text, from the rhetoric of description (Quaresmeprenant, the whale), to the thematics of collective identity (the Sausages) to the very problem of narration itself. In the increasingly shrill polemical atmosphere of the 1540s, this satirical enquiry into the relationship of language and power may have been the only option available to the moderate humanist Rabelais. At yet another level, the intervention of the narrator—limited in his perception as he shows himself to be—works to undermine the generic authority of traditional allegories of Lent and Carnival, as well as the traditions of travel narrative in which witnesses present encounters with spouting monsters from first-hand experience. Throughout the Rabelaisian episodes, literary subtext undermines empirical observation even as empirical observation undermines literary authority. These multiple failures of authority underscore those aspects of Rabelais's work that scholars have traditionally linked to the development of the novel as the characteristic literary form of modernity: problematic narrative authority, direct contact between the world of the narration and the matter to be narrated, an open-ended exploration of the phenomenal world, etc. What is important in this context is that the multiple figurations of the monster function as a mediation between political ideology and literary form. For it is through reflection on the representation of monstrosity that Rabelais undermines the ideological rigidity and epistemological authority of traditional genres, thereby making possible new forms of representation.[44]

MONTAIGNE AND THE RETREAT FROM ALLEGORY

The turn of the sixteenth century, as Lorraine Daston and Katharine Park have pointed out, was marked both by a proliferation of reports of monstrosity and by a shift in the nature of those reports. In contrast to the medieval tradition of the monstrous figure as exotic and distant, the onset of the Renaissance brings an emphasis on the monster as portent, and as a portent that is increasingly located at the center of European culture itself: in the next town, or just down the road.[45] Certainly, we may read Rabelais's interest in the topos as a response to the same vogue of monstrosity singled out by Daston and Park. Moreover, as is often the case with Rabelais, his vision seems to swallow and transcend any categories (medieval, late medieval, Renaissance, etc.) that we might try to apply to his text. Here he blends the exotic and the portentous, placing figures from beyond the horizon side by side with images at the center of current theological debate. Yet for Rabelais the question of monstrosity seems predominately individualized, limited in scope. His meditation on the rhetorical distortions surrounding the figure of the monster involves a kind of humanist moralism and an attack on the hypocrisy of faith without charity. This limited reach may have its roots in the moment at which Rabelais began his career, the moment of the first flowering of Protestantism and of attempts by Christian humanist moderates such as Erasmus to resolve theological conflict through debate and spiritual renovation. The *Quart livre* appears at the end of this moment of intellectual debate, at the very moment at which the Council of Trent was moving toward the reaffirmation of doctrinal rigidity, instead of turning toward the spiritual renovation and self-examination that moderates such as Rabelais and Erasmus had hoped for. Thus the *Quart livre* is contemporaneous with the moment at which theological schism shifts from being an intellectual disagreement to being a political rift grounded in institutions. The disorienting shifts in his text between personal polemic and mythic confrontation may reflect this double focus. In slightly later writers, by contrast, the relationship between political conflict and monstrous iconography will become much larger in scale and involve figuration of the fate of Europe itself.[46] In any event, Rabelais's sensitivity to the relationship between the description of monstrosity and the dangerous rhetoric of theological extremism provided a warning that was largely ignored in the three decades after his *Quart livre*. For during the long period of religious war that followed the death of Henri II in 1559 the trope of the monster, combined with the moralizing rhetoric of allegory, is repeated countless times in the propaganda exchanges between Protestants and Catholics. It is against this noisy background that we may turn, in a final moment, to a text that postdates Rabelais's by some forty years. This is the brief chapter from Montaigne's *Essais* (1580) entitled "Of a Monstrous Child" ("D'un enfant monstrueux").

"This tale will go simply," says Montaigne to introduce the chapter, "for I leave it to the doctors to discourse about it." He goes on to tell how two days earlier he had been shown a child by two men and a nurse who claimed to be its father, uncle, and aunt. They were seeking to make money by displaying it, "because of its strangeness" ("a cause de son estrangeté").[47] And he goes on to describe the child. Yet instead of beginning conventionally, through a description of what is "strange," Montaigne insists on what is normal about the child: "It was, for the most part, of a common form, and held itself up on its legs, walked and gurgled more or less like others of the same age."[48] He then notes its deformity objectively (part of another body seemingly attached to the chest, extra limbs, etc.), without recourse to the similitude which more conventional writers on the topic such as Boaistuau seem to require. The only detail about it that he notes as particularly striking is its voice: "Its cries did in fact have something particular."[49] He goes on to note that the figure of a child showing two bodies and a single head might well seem to the king of France a positive sign ("favorable prognostique") regarding the future of France, torn as it was between warring Protestants and Catholics.[50] However, says Montaigne, one had better resist such an interpretation: "for fear that the event may prove it wrong, it is better to let it pass by."[51]

My account of the essay so far is of the first version, published in 1580. Toward the end of his life Montaigne returned to his text and added a gloss. The gloss underscores the refusal of allegory set forth in the first version and generalizes it: "What we call monsters are not monsters to God, who sees in the immensity of his work the infinity of the forms that He has put there."[52] In fact, he concludes, a particular creature that astonishes us may only astonish us because we see it alone. It may, in fact, be one of a species, the rest of which are unknown to us. Whereas conventional writers on monstrosity describe the monster by likening it to something familiar, Montaigne simultaneously accepts and explains its strangeness by linking it to something unknown, but just like it. In this acceptance of the unknown his concluding gloss recalls the first line of the essay, where he decides to "leave it to the doctors" to discourse about the curiosity he recounts. These two moments make a frame for the essay. Taken together they turn both to the authority of the medical men and to the wisdom of God. In the process they set the monster beyond the politicized representations that define so much of the rhetoric of the period. At the same time this frame projects a discursive authority in which a kind of protoscientific investigation of Nature goes hand in hand with divine benevolence.

Montaigne's prudent acceptance of the variety of the world suggests that he is familiar with the dangers of the types of strong interpretation practiced by Boaistuau. His retreat from political allegory—which he both evokes and rejects—betrays a tacit awareness of the abuses to which any attempt to pin down the meaning of monstrosity may fall prey. We may also see the simplicity and brevity of his presentation as a kind of rejection of the extraordinary rhetorical overkill which an earlier writer like Rabelais had to deploy to try to question traditional descriptions and uses of the figure of the monster on their own terms. Rabelais undermines the authority of allegory by questioning the language through which monsters are described and defined. Montaigne takes the more prudent approach of simply backing away from allegory altogether. He chooses to decouple the monstrous figure from interpretation and, perhaps, from rhetorical description itself. His more modest course is to let both events and monsters go their own way.

8

MONSTROSITY AND MYTH IN MARY SHELLEY'S *FRANKENSTEIN*

DAVID ARMITAGE

The boundary between early modern and modern monstrosity has usually been drawn at the border between superstition and science. On one side of this boundary lies the monster as prodigy and portent; on the other, the monster as specimen and even species. As the preceding essays in this volume have shown, that boundary was more fluid than conventional teleological narratives of monstrosity would allow, not least because monsters could not be reduced to one single meaning, nor could they be captured within a single realm of signification. Monsters could never entirely escape the mythical, whether as objects of prodigious significance or as the subjects of skeptical scrutiny. Competing conceptions of monstrosity coexisted well into the nineteenth century, in science, literature, and myth. The connection between monstrosity and fiction-making was thus not only an early modern phenomenon but would remain a modern one, too.[1]

The subject of this essay is perhaps the most famous myth of monstrosity to emerge at the intersection of science and literature, Mary Shelley's *Frankenstein; or, The Modern Prometheus* (1818). That myth was, in part, the product of the political ruptures surrounding the French Revolution which are often taken to mark the advent of modernity itself.[2] It was also the offspring of literary and scientific models whose roots lay in early modern (and even pre-modern) models of myth, extending back through eighteenth-century mythography via late seventeenth-century deism to Milton and ultimately to Ovid's *Metamorphoses*. Modernity's most enduring myth of monstrosity thus had antecedents which marked it as at once the culmination of the traditions of early modern monstrosity and also the beginning of a recognizably modern attitude towards monstrosity.

Frankenstein has attained the status of myth—endlessly reproducible, promiscuously applicable, yet always recognizable—in part because it seems monstrous in itself. Modernity should be inhospitable to myth, that residue of primitive rationality; myths should dissolve at the approach of modernity's demystifications. Like Victor Frankenstein's creature, Shelley's *Frankenstein* is "an anomaly, a scandal . . . Such a thing simply should not exist."[3] Yet, of course, *Frankenstein* not only exists, but exists in multiple subsequent versions which testify to its resilience as a modern myth. The aim of this essay is to show how this came to be: that is, how this modern version of a classical myth emerged in the early nineteenth century, and why it should have seemed so anomalous in its own time, even though it appears to be quite natural, even inevitable, now.

Frankenstein arose, in part, from a convergence in conceptions of monstrosity and mythology in Shelley's own generation. That convergence made the construction of a modern myth possible, albeit not inevitable, because of Shelley's own interest in mythography and, through that, in monstrosity. Monstrosity, it has been argued, became "naturalized" over the course of the eighteenth century. In the seventeenth century, and before, monsters had been revealing but unclassifiable anomalies whose very existence challenged the natural order and demonstrated the limits to rational understanding. In the eighteenth century, monsters were increasingly perceived as evidence of primitive forms, the living and tangible fossils of earlier stages of development. They thus became less threatening because more readily assimilable to modern schemes of classification. They also became more revealing, precisely because they embodied the past: by their very existence they helped to locate contemporary creatures within temporal lineages. Horror retreated before curiosity as monsters were dissected, discarded, and depicted in textbooks of pathology and embryology. This process of "enlightening monsters" thus temporalized and aestheticized them even as it naturalized them.[4]

Mythology followed similar trajectories across the eighteenth century. Deists and skeptics naturalized classical mythology by explaining it anthropologically and psychologically. Myths were no longer supernatural or metaphysical, but rather the comprehensible products of human needs and fears. Such naturalism was not entirely distinct from a renovated version of classical euhemerism, the procedure that identified the pagan gods as magnified images of historical heroes. However, this version understood them instead as revelations of broad cultural trends, as in the foundational philosophical work of cultural anthropology, Giambattista Vico's *Scienza Nuova* (1725–44). Ancient euhemerism had traced mythic characters to flesh-and-blood heroes; modern allegory had derived them instead from the abstractions they embodied. Baroque imagery sustained such allegorical interpretations, at once keeping them alive and making them fair game for ridicule, as in Pope's *Rape of the Lock* (1712–14).[5] The process of enlightening mythology thus naturalized myth by historicizing and anthropologizing it, but while it was aestheticized it could also be satirized.

Eighteenth-century mythography, in all its various forms, enshrined two maxims that *Frankenstein* would successfully confront: that modernity and myth were, by definition, antithetical, and that the proper vehicle for myth was not prose but poetry. Johnson, Coleridge, and Wordsworth all pointedly counterposed myth and modernity. Johnson lampooned "the puerilities of mythology"; Wordsworth observed "the hacknied and lifeless use into which mythology fell towards the close of the seventeenth century"; and Coleridge condemned Thomas Gray's deployment of "an exploded mythology." Likewise, Johnson surmised that "[n]o modern monarch can be much exalted by hearing that, as Hercules had his *club*, he has his *navy*," and Wordsworth thought the flaccidity of mythological allusion "disgusted the general reader with all allusion to it in modern verse," just as Akenside had earlier judged it "but little interesting to a modern reader."[6] William Hazlitt politicized the death of the ancient mythology in the late eighteenth century by associating the origins of the "Lake School" with the aftermath of the French Revolution: "Nothing that was established was to be tolerated. All the common-place figures of poetry, tropes, allegories, personifications, with the whole heathen mythology, were instantly discarded . . . kings and queens were dethroned from their rank and station in legitimate tragedy or epic poetry as they were decapitated elsewhere."[7] However, in the years immediately following the end of the Napoleonic War, with republicanism on the retreat, mythological renovation and political counterrevolution accompanied one another, at least according to Hartley Coleridge, who discoursed "On the Poetical Use of the Heathen Mythology" in 1822: "The present is, doubtless, an æra of restorations and revivals, political and poetical. The Bourbons have returned to the throne of France, and the Gods and Goddesses of classic fame, with all the noblesse of Fauns and Satyrs, Dryads and Hamadryads, are beginning to reoccupy, with limited sway, their ancient places in poetry."[8] Mythology may have been exploded, but it could evidently be restored. Hartley Coleridge's judgment called in question the incompatibility of myth and modernity, but by confining his analysis to the specifically "poetical" use of the heathen mythology (in the work of Keats, Percy Shelley, Wordsworth, and "Barry Cornwall" [Bryan Waller Procter]), he confirmed the by then conventional association of myth and poetry.

The mythographers of the preceding century had pursued the natural history of mythology as a means to explain ancient poetry (particularly Homer) and as a window into what would later be called the "primitive mind."[9] In the *Scienza Nuova,* Vico characterized the primitive understanding of the world as *sapienza poetica* ("poetic wisdom") expressed in the *caratteri poetici* ("poetic characters") of myth. Vico's intellectual archaeology implied a continuing privilege for poetry as a mythopoetic medium. As he put it in his account of the "Discovery of the True Poetic Allegories": "the mythologists seem, rather, to have been poets, inventing so many different things on the basis of their fables, and the poets, who meant their fables to be the true narratives of the things of their own times, were the real mythologists."[10] Primitive humans were poets by nature, and thus myth-makers; the custodians of mythology in later ages should therefore be the poets. As Mary Shelley's father, William Godwin, writing under the pseudonym "Edward Baldwin," put it in 1806, "It is universally confessed that of all systems of mythology and religion that of the Greeks is the most admirably adapted to the purposes of poetry. . . . The multitude of the Gods of the Greeks, however it might be calculated to shock the reasoning faculty if regarded as an object of faith, suits wonderfully the demands of the composer in verse."[11] If myth had an intellectual home at all in a disenchanted modern age, that home was in poetry.

The association of mythology with poetry and "poetic wisdom" has tended to obscure the relation of mythology and prose in early nineteenth-century British literature. The decade after 1815 comprised the second great period of mythological literature in English as a belated counterpart to the late sixteenth-century Ovidian revival to which the young Romantics looked back nostalgically. Though much energy has been expended on the analysis of mythology and the Romantic tradition in English poetry (to appropriate the title of Douglas Bush's classic work), there has been much less attention to the place of myth in prose fiction before George Eliot.[12] "It seems quite clear . . . that Romantic Hellenism in England and France found its home mainly in poetry rather than prose," one scholar of myth and fiction has remarked, but perhaps not quite so clear as has usually been assumed.[13] The outstanding exception was, of course, *Frankenstein; or The Modern Prometheus,* whose peculiarly fertile combination of monstrosity and myth helped to generate two further prose fictions, John William Polidori's *Ernestus Berchtold; or the Modern Oedipus* (1819), and William Hazlitt's *Liber Amoris; or the New Pygmalion* (1823), with which this essay will compare it.

Hegel, in his *Lectures on Aesthetics,* called his era the age of prose, presided over by the genre of the novel, and distinguished it from the age of epic, in which myth was credible and poetry the dominant literary form.[14] He thereby captured a widespread perception among the European Romantics that they were latecomers, born into a disenchanted epoch. As Hölderlin, Hegel's fellow seminarian in Tübingen, lamented in 1801:

> *Aber Freund! wir kommen zu spät! Zwar leben die Götter,*
> *Aber über dem Haupt droben in anderer Welt.*
> *[But, my friend, we have come too late. Though the gods are living,*
> *Over our heads they live, up in a different world.]*[15]

As if in reply, Keats diffidently prefaced *Endymion* (1818) with the hope that "I have not in too late a day touched the beautiful mythology of Greece, and dulled its brightness."[16] He, like other young Romantics, looked back to the century before Cowley and Dryden as the golden age of mythological writing in English, before the cold-eyed epistemology of Locke and the reductive rationalism of Newton had driven the goblin from the hearth and robbed the rainbow of its mystery, as he complained in a review of Edmund Kean of 12 December 1817, and as he and his companions affirmed at Benjamin Robert Haydon's "immortal dinner" two weeks later when they toasted "Newton's health, and confusion to mathematics."[17] Keats may have come too late, but only by a matter of centuries rather than millennia. He and his contemporaries now faced the challenge of making myths new, to combat the contemptible familiarity into which they had fallen over the course of the eighteenth century. This often meant taking obscure variants from arcane sources or reviving little-known myths (as Keats did, when taking the story of Lamia from Burton's *Anatomy of Melancholy* [1621], for example). Only thus could poets avoid Johnson's damning epitaph, pronounced over the corpse of Nicholas Rowe's *Ulysses* (1706): "We have been too early acquainted with the poetical heroes to expect any pleasure from their revival; to show them as they have already been shown, is to disgust by repetition; to give them new qualities, or new adventures, is to offend by violating received notions."[18]

The gap between such "received notions" of classical mythology and postrevolutionary disenchantment was graphically exploited in the political and social satire of Gillray, Cruikshank, and their contemporaries. Mythology was, of course, only one weapon in the satirists' arsenal of deflating allusion, but it was a consistent one from the 1790s until at least the publication of *Frankenstein*. Its consistency lay in the literal modernization of myth. Between 1784 and 1819, the London print-shops displayed a "Modern Colossus" (Charles James Fox), "The Modern Circe," "The Modern Calypso" (Lady Hertford, seducing the Prince Regent), a "Modern Pegasus" (a velocipede rider), "The Modern Phæton," two "Modern Venus's," four "Modern Atlas's," and six "Modern Hercules's" (including "Hercules and Omphale, or Modern Mythology"). Most elaborately of all, Gillray's "New Pantheon of Democratic Mythology" (7 May 1799) unflatteringly portrayed Fox as Hercules, Walpole as Mars, the duke of Bedford as "The Affrighted Centaur," and various other minor characters as "Harpyes Defiling the Feast," "Cupid," and "The Twin Stars, Castor and Pollux."[19]

The ridiculous disparity between the modern subjects and the mythological objects in these prints served to emphasize the pettiness and vulgarity of the satirists' subjects but also demonstrated that classical myth could still yield aesthetic pleasure and political capital by the ironic juxtaposition of ancient and modern.[20] The greatest falling-off of the period was, of course, the defeat, exile, return, and defeat again of Napoleon. On both sides of the Channel, Napoleon appeared as the greatest mythological overreacher, brought low and punished eternally for his hubris, in prints by George Cruikshank and an anonymous French engraver: for the one, he represented "The Modern Prometheus, or Downfall of Tyranny" (July 1814?) (figure 37); for the other, he was simply "Le Prométhée de l'Isle de Ste. Héléne" (15 October 1815), the light of his glory extinguished as "un Vautour assidu," in the guise of the Imperial eagle, gnawed at his flanks (figure 38).[21] This "modern Prometheus" had become as unthreatening, even pathetic, as the dandified "Monstrosities" Cruikshank annually lampooned from 1816 to 1825 (in imitation of Gillray's "Monstrosities" of 1799) (figure 39).[22] On the eve of Shelley's composition of *Frankenstein,* monstrosity itself had been defanged and do-

Figure 37. George Cruikshank, *The Modern Prometheus, or Downfall of Tyranny* (1814). © Copyright The British Museum.

Figure 38. Anon., *Le Promethée de l'Isle de Ste. Hélène* (1815). © Copyright The British Museum.

mesticated while mythology had been naturalized, aestheticized, and politicized by being modernized.

Satirical representations of mythological characters are relevant to *Frankenstein* because they provided the most immediate precedents for the modernization of mythology in the decades after the French Revolution. The satirists had not been entirely alone earlier in the eighteenth century in their identification of modern Prometheanism: Shaftesbury, in his *Characteristics* (1711), had thought of "the manner of our modern Prometheuses, the mountebanks,

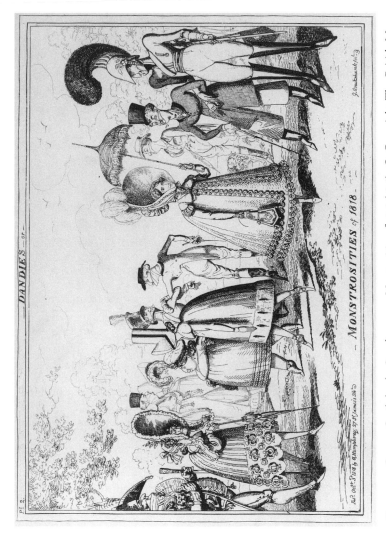

Figure 39. George Cruikshank, *Dandies—or—Monstrosities of 1818* (1818). © Copyright The British Museum.

who performed such wonders of many kinds here on our earthly stages," and Kant, in 1756, had hailed Benjamin Franklin as the "Prometheus der neuern Zeiten," the Prometheus of modern times.[23] Such references were sparse, however, and allusions to Prometheus in graphic satire balanced them exactly. Moreover, both sets of references outnumbered parallel constructions in the eighteenth-century novel. That genre, by definition, offers itself as a means of making new. Subtitles throughout the century frequently signaled that innovative capacity by announcing novel versions of previous narratives—as, most famously, Rousseau's *Julie, ou la Nouvelle Héloïse* (1761)—or variations on contemporary themes, such as William Godwin's *Fleetwood, or the New Man of Feeling* (1801), whose subtitle proclaimed it as a successor to, and perhaps even replacement for, Henry Mackenzie's novel of sensibility. Closer in time to Shelley's adoption of "the Modern Prometheus," such modernizations had become associated exclusively with women writers, as in Maria Edgeworth's *The Modern Griselda: A Tale* (1805), Selina Davenport's *The Hypocrite, or The Modern Janus* (1814), and Barbara Hofland's *Patience and Perseverance, or The Modern Griselda* (1816).

Shelley's mythological subtitle evoked a narrative rather than a single character, and hence the possibility of repeated correspondences between ancient and modern. The etymon of "myth" itself—*mythos,* a "story" or "plot"—implies a correspondence with narrative and hence with the novel. As Lévi-Strauss argued, in a formulation comforting to the appropriators of myth in an age of prose, "[p]oetry is a kind of speech which cannot be translated except at the cost of serious distortions; whereas the mythical value of the myth is preserved even through the worst translation. . . . Its substance does not lie in its style, its original music, or its syntax, but in the *story* it tells."[24] Classical mythology survived the historical and anthropological skepticism of the mythographers; it weathered its trivialization at the hands of poets; it even endured its employment as a vehicle of visual satire, not least because its characters inhabited resilient narratives of a kind that Shelley may have been the first to resurrect. The mythographers, poets, and caricaturists of the eighteenth century rendered the idea of a modern myth paradoxical, self-contradictory, and even monstrous. For this reason, *Frankenstein* has been taken as anomalous and monstrous in itself. Its status as a modern myth has also been traced to its appropriations and afterlife, rather than to its antecedents: "That series of adaptations, allusions, accretions, analogues, parodies, and plain misreadings which follows upon Mary Shelley's novel is not just a supplementary component of the myth," Chris Baldick has argued: "it *is* the myth."[25] The rest of this essay will deal, in part, with *Frankenstein*'s immediate afterlife in the mythological fiction of Polidori and Hazlitt, but mostly concerns the precedents for Shelley's innovation, and hence the possible sources for this monstrous modern myth.

Mary Shelley was a conspicuously grateful writer. In *Frankenstein,* she was scrupulous in acknowledging her literary debts, and punctilious in giving thanks for her personal obligations. Just as the reader of the fiction approaches the heart of the novel—the Monster's own narration—through the concentric rings of Walton's and Frankenstein's own narratives, so multiple thresholds of subtitle, epigraph, and dedication block the way to the novel itself. The 1818 title page supplied the keys to reading the work by announcing its relation to classical mythology (*"the Modern Prometheus"*), and to a heritage of allusion—to literature in general, and to Milton in particular—with an epigraph from *Paradise Lost,* 10.743–45 ("Did I request thee, Maker, from my clay / To mould me man? Did I solicit thee / From darkness to promote me?"), a passage the educated Monster himself recalls later in the book. Though these two sources, in mythology and literature, were central to the novel, and were vital to its immediate genesis, the dedication registered a more pervasive intellectual and familial debt: "To William Godwin, Author of Political Justice, Caleb Williams, &c., These Volumes Are respectfully inscribed by The Author." The motif of pursuit which animates the novel's plot was drawn from *Caleb Williams* (1794), just as the Monster's account of the evil bred into it by its loneliness and estrangement derived from Godwin's *Political Justice* (1793).[26] The coyly unspecific "&c." may also have hinted at more fundamental debts, because Shelley's debt to her father's writing derived immediately from her childhood as much as from her later, adult, reading. Godwin always tried out his works on his family before publication. Chief among his most popular works were the textbooks of mythology and fable he published specifically for children under the pseudonym "Edward Baldwin," *Fables Ancient and Modern Adapted for the Use of Children* (1805) and *The Pantheon: or Ancient History of the Gods of Greece and Rome* (1806).[27] In the latter, Shelley would have found a distinctive respect for classical mythology as the product of a religious sensibility that foreshadowed Christianity (a syncretism she was later skeptically to invert, as we shall see), as well as an appreciation of the continuing utility of myth against the allegorists and naturalists of the preceding century.[28] Godwin claimed that "[i]t was no part of my purpose . . . to strip the Grecian religion of its beautiful forms, and present it in the nakedness of metaphysical truth; it was rather incumbent on me to draw out those forms in their utmost solidity and permanence, and 'give to airy nothing a local habitation' and substantial character." He claimed his intent was not to risk "seducing one votary from the cross of Christ" (as he thought some eighteenth-century mythographers, like Andrew Tooke, the translator of the Jesuit Pomey's *Pantheum Mythicum* [1697], feared they might do), but rather to "improve [young persons'] taste" and to provide "perpetual models in the art of fine writing."[29] This he surely did for Shelley, and thereby later helped to inspire her modernization of classical myth in *Frankenstein*.

The version of the Prometheus myth found in Godwin's *Pantheon* can reasonably be assumed to be the earliest version that Shelley would have encountered. In Godwin's telling, the supremely cunning Prometheus was the enemy of Jupiter, condemned to live without fire but determined to avenge himself by creating a being to challenge his divine antagonist. He "formed a man of clay of such exquisite workmanship, that he wanted nothing but a living soul to cause him to be acknowledged the paragon of creation"; this Minerva supplied by leading Prometheus into heaven, where he stole celestial fire from the chariot of the sun: "with this he animated his image: and the man of Prometheus immediately moved, and thought, and spoke, and became every thing that the fondest wishes of his creator could ask."[30] This version was, of course, close enough in itself to be an analogue to Frankenstein's creation of the Monster. Prometheus was not culpably hubristic, merely curious and extraordinarily skilled; his creation was successful, but needed a spark to animate his workmanship. The cause of Jupiter's enmity, in Godwin's account, provided a further telling parallel. As Godwin retold the myth, Prometheus had volunteered to adjudicate a dispute over which parts of animals sacrificed to Jupiter should go to the god or to the worshipper:

> He killed two bulls, and skillfully divided the flesh, the fat, the offal and the bones: he sewed up the flesh very neatly in the skin of one of the bulls, and the bones enclosed in an envelop of fat, in the other: he then called upon Jupiter to look on the parcels, and to say which of them he chose for his own share: Jupiter, deceived by the fair appearance of the fat which peeped here and there through the apertures of the skin, chose that parcel, in preference to the other which contained all that was most wholesome and valuable of the two animals.[31]

"This is an ugly story," Godwin moralized; "and the part assigned in it to Jupiter is wholly unworthy of our idea of a God."[32] Be that as it may, Godwin's version contained all the elements that would be necessary for Shelley to fashion a modern Prometheus: the craftiness, the creativity, the animating spark, and even the charnelhouse rummaging among dismembered carcasses to create deceptively integrated creatures.

Out of such a myth, the Monster could easily have sprung, but not out of Godwin's telling alone. Shelley's interest in classical mythology was consistent and sustained in the period before and after the composition of *Frankenstein.* She construed Ovid's *Metamorphoses* almost daily throughout April and early May 1815 (in fact, probably for longer, since her journal from 14 May 1815 to 20 July 1816—that is, during the period of *Frankenstein*'s genesis—is missing, though the *Metamorphoses* is listed among her "Books read in 1815"). During the composition of *Frankenstein,* she also read the comtesse de Genlis's fashionable mythological drama *Pygmalion et Galatée:* as she noted in her journal for 24 July 1816, "We arrived wet to the skin. I read [Genlis's] 'Nouvelles Nouvelles' and write my story": that story, of course, being *Frankenstein.*[33] Genlis's play presented Galatée's first day as a human being, as she learns of love, death, and social injustice; in this sentimental education it marked an advance upon earlier versions of the Pygmalion myth, like Rousseau's "scène lyrique" *Pygmalion,* which Genlis's play was written to follow.[34] The first scholar to note Shelley's debt to Genlis suggested that it "helped to suggest the device of awakening and the actual injustices of society with which both naive intellects [Galatée's and the Monster's] become acquainted."[35] Just as importantly, Genlis's play confirmed what Shelley learned from Godwin's retelling of the Prometheus myth: that the construction of novel creatures was a piecemeal affair. As Eurinome tells Galatée, Pygmalion "was not content with just a single model for the rest of your figure, and took five or six for it: you have the feet of little Aglaure, the arms of young Cephise, and, surprisingly to you, you have my hands and my waist."[36] The play's dramatization of an asexual, nondivine creation, the awakening of Galatée through her sentimental education but, above all, the example of a modernized myth outside poetry may have strengthened Shelley's determination to modernize Prometheus in her novel.

Shelley's decision to modernize this myth could also have been propelled by the Romantic cult of the Titans which also produced Percy Shelley's *Prometheus Unbound* (1820) and Keats's *Hyperion* (1818–19), for example. The Prometheus myth can be located even more precisely as a topic of the discussion at the Villa Diodati in the summer of 1816—that is, in the time and place at which *Frankenstein* emerged from the famous ghost-story competition between Shelley, Percy Shelley, Byron, and Polidori. Percy Shelley translated Aeschylus's *Prometheus Bound* to Byron, and Byron thereafter composed his "Prometheus," a poem whose moral was close to that of Shelley's novel:

> *Thy godlike crime was to be kind . . .*
> *And strengthen Man with his own mind . . .*
> *Thou art a symbol and a sign*
> *To mortals of their fate and force (ll. 35, 38, 45–46).*[37]

However, though Byron's lines may point to one reading of *Frankenstein* as a fable of Victor Frankenstein's overreaching and hubris, it is by no means certain whom Shelley meant to be identified with "the modern Prometheus." Two years after *Frankenstein*'s publication, when she had reread Ovid's *Metamorphoses* in order to compose two brief mythological dramas, *Proserpine* and *Midas,* Shelley refused to judge between readings of the myth as "the doom / Of impious Prometheus" or "the tale which says / How great Prometheus from Apollo's car / Stole heaven's fire—a God-like gift for Man!"[38] She was prodigal with such Promethean motifs, and did not confine them to the title character of her novel. In manuscript additions to the original 1818 text which Shelley made in 1823, Frankenstein's friend Clerval became a noble soul inspired with the true Promethean fire, with the myth redirected to make the fire Apollo's rather than Jupiter's, and the power artistic rather than political: "His own mind was all the possession that he prized . . . —daring as the eagle and as free, common laws could not be applied to him; and while he gazed on him you felt his soul's spark was more divine—more truly stolen from Apollo's sacred fire, than the glimmering ember that animates other men."[39] This passage did not appear in the revised text of 1831, but did indicate Shelley's desire to mythologize her characters with a selective fragmentation and reordering of mythic elements.

Shelley's technique of mythological modernization was thus rather different from that now expected in a mythological novel like Joyce's *Ulysses* (1922), the device of "manipulating a continuous parallel between contemporaneity and antiquity" which T. S. Eliot hailed as having "the importance of a scientific discovery. No one else has built a novel on such a foundation before: it has never been necessary."[40] Shelley did not attempt such a "continuous" parallel but rather distributed elements of the myth among different characters in the novel—especially between Frankenstein and the Monster—not least to reinforce its central *Doppelgänger* theme. Frankenstein may be Promethean in his ambitions and his rebellious challenge to the divine prerogatives of creation, but the Monster who suffers at the hands of his creator (as Prometheus suffered at the hands of Jupiter) and discovers fire realized the more pathetic strain of the myth. Ovid's "Prometheus plasticator" and Aeschylus's *Prometheus Bound* were split between the two characters, just as Frankenstein and the Monster shared the roles of Adam, Satan, and God from *Paradise Lost,* as when the Monster commented: "I often referred the several situations [in *Paradise Lost*], as their similarity struck me, to my own. Like Adam, I was apparently united by no link to any other being in existence. . . . Many times I considered Satan as the fitter emblem of my condition; for often, like him, when I viewed the bliss of my protectors, the bitter gall of envy rose within me."[41] Just as Walton lost the heterocosmic "Paradise" of Romantic poetry he had created from himself, so the Monster lost Paradise after setting fire to the DeLaceys' cottage: "'And now, with the world before me, whither should I bend my steps?'"[42] he asked plaintively, quoting the concluding lines of *Paradise Lost,* and thereby adding *Frankenstein* to the peculiar Romantic genres of the wanderer-myth (exemplified by Byron's *Cain,* Coleridge's "The Ancient Mariner," and Charles Maturin's *Melmoth the Wanderer* [1820]) and of the postparadisal prose work, which also includes Hazlitt's *Liber Amoris* and Thomas De Quincey's *Confessions of an English Opium-Eater* (1821).[43]

Frankenstein was a syncretist novel, combining elements of classical mythology and Christian epic. It merged the ambiguous syncretism of the Prometheus myth with *Paradise Lost* to question the legitimacy of the pursuit of knowledge at all costs. The Promethean motifs occur from the very beginning of the novel as Shelley first composed it (that is, from the beginning of chapter 4 in the 1818 text, and of chapter 5 in the 1831 text), as Frankenstein recalled that he "collected the instruments of life around me, that I might infuse a spark of being into the lifeless thing that lay at my feet."[44] Both Prometheus and Milton's Satan were overreachers, seeking power through knowledge while challenging the established order, and both Walton and Frankenstein followed them in this pursuit. Prometheus and Satan both aspired to omnipotence, or at least equality with the Creator, and were cast out from heaven and from humanity by being chained, Prometheus to the frozen summit of Caucasus, Satan on the burning lake of hell, "In adamantine chains and penal fire" (*Paradise Lost,* 1.48). Milton here alluded to Aeschylus's *Prometheus*

Bound, and this connection was not lost on the Shelleys: as Percy Shelley noted, in the preface to *Prometheus Unbound,* "The only imaginary being resembling in any degree Prometheus is Satan; and Prometheus is, in my opinion, a more poetical character than Satan."[45] Shelley herself allowed for the ambiguous transference between the two characters in her 1831 preface to *Frankenstein,* when she defined the horror of her story in terms that could apply either to Satan's rebellion or to Prometheus's act of creation: "supremely frightful would be the effect on any human endeavor to mock the stupendous mechanism of the Creator of the world."[46] Frankenstein was Promethean in his act of creation but his consequent suffering is, one might say, Satanic: "All my speculation and hopes are nothing; and, like the archangel who aspired to omnipotence, I am chained in an eternal hell."[47] Shelley's syncretism depended on Milton's but her originality lay in transposing it into prose, and in threading the two myths through her modern narrative as a guide to its interpretation and a sign of the interpenetration of the creator and his Monster.

The novelty of Shelley's syncretism can be pointed up by comparing it with Percy Shelley's *Prometheus Unbound.* Though not completed until at least a year after the novel's first publication in 1818, the drama casts light back on *Frankenstein.* The play was a more conventional form of mythic renovation in that it combined a sequel to an established literary treatment of a myth (in this case, Aeschylus's) with arcane symbolism and a modernizing interpretation of the myth itself. Shelley invoked a traditional reason to reject tradition when he observed that Greek tragedy itself thrived on innovation: "The Greek tragic writers, in selecting as their subject any portion of their natural history or mythology, employed in their treatment of it a certain arbitrary discretion. They by no means conceived themselves as bound to adhere to the common interpretation or to imitate in story as in title their rivals and predecessors . . . I have presumed to employ a similar license."[48] Shelley's Prometheus can be seen as an apostle of imaginative freedom; the type of the creative artist; a Jesus-like leader of a revolt against autocracy ("The savior and strength of suffering man" [1.817]); or even as the ambivalent intellectuals of Shelley's own day recollecting the legacy of the French Revolution. That Prometheus could be all these at once arose in part from the adaptability and capaciousness of the myth itself and partly from Percy Shelley's own innovations. He made the myth new by superimposing a modern sensibility on ancient material, but did not attempt "a continuous parallel between contemporaneity and antiquity." Percy Shelley's play interpreted the myth; Mary Shelley's novel used the myth as a tool for interpretation.

Shelley's engagement with mythological syncretism continued in the years after *Frankenstein*'s publication. In 1821, she turned syncretism into outright skepticism in her fragmentary tract, "The Necessity of a Belief in the Heathen Mythology to a Christian." This tract arose immediately from a challenge thrown down to both Shelleys by Byron to refute Charles Leslie's defense of orthodoxy in his frequently reprinted *Short and Easie Method with the Deists* (1698). Percy Shelley replied with his "Essay on Miracles and Christian Doctrine" (*c.* 1821–22),[49] Mary Shelley with this devastating syllogism:

> If two facts are related not contradictory of equal probability & with equal evidence, if we believe one we must believe the other.
>
> 1st. There is as good proof of the Heathen Mythology as of the Christian religion.
>
> 2ly. that they [do] not contradict one another.
>
> Con[clusion]. If a man believes in one he must believe in both.[50]

Shelley then laid out a strategy for comparing the Christian revelation with the truth of the heathen mythology, by examining the reliability of their respective witnesses, the coherence of their texts, and the interpenetration—and hence the mutually reinforcing plausibility, or mutually disconfirming implausibility—of the two systems. Her conclusions were corrosive of Christian revelation, at least according to Leslie's criteria of proof: "The revelation of God as Jupiter to the Greeks—a more successful revelation than that as Jehovah to the Jews . . . prophesies of Christ by the heathens more incontrovertible than those of the Jews." Pagan and Christian epic had equal heuristic standing: "Vergil & Ovid not truth of the heathen Mythology, but the interpretation of a heathen—as Milton's Paradise Lost is the interpretation of a Christian religion of the Bible." The heathen mythology and the Christian revelation stood or fell together: "The coming of X. a confirmation of both religions. The cessation of oracles a proof of this." Further evidence came from the syncretism of Aeschylus and Christianity in the New Testament itself: "Prometheus desmotes quoted by Paul."[51]

Myth has been a plausible tool for the interpretation of *Frankenstein,* at least since Shelley herself used it. Thus, Leigh Hunt wrote to Shelley in March 1819, "Polyphemus . . . always appears to me a pathetic rather than a monstrous person, though his disappointed sympathies at last made him cruel. What do you think of this Polyphemic theory of mine?"[52] Shelley replied by adducing *Frankenstein,* a new mythological reading of the novel striking her while she wrote: "I have written a book in defence of Polypheme—have I not?"[53] Later, in 1837, a particularly able parody of the novel appeared in *Fraser's Magazine,* entitled "The New Frankenstein." It neatly caught the allusive spirit of Shelley's enterprise with a tissue of Miltonic and Romantic quotations and echoes, while describing the new Frankenstein's creation of a man with mental qualities extracted from the greatest thinkers of the day. At the moment of his creature's awakening, the narrator recalls "a picture in one of the exhibitions in Paris . . . the subject of which was Pygmalion and his statue. . . . My feelings were different but no less acute. Motionless as the sculptor, or almost turned to stone as one who had seen Medusa, I stood all eyes and ears fixed on my phenomenon."[54] Shelley would no doubt have relished the implicit mythological comparison at work here, not only as evidence that myth and prose remained compatible almost twenty years after she had published her pioneering effort of rapprochement, but also as a sign that her novel had become, in its transformations and afterlife, a modern myth of monstrosity.

The most immediate legatee of Shelley's renovation of classical mythology in the cause of monstrosity was John William Polidori. Polidori was present at the Villa Diodati in the summer of 1816, in his capacity as Byron's personal physician, and took part in the ghost-story competition which produced both *Frankenstein* and his germinal fragment *The Vampyre* (1819).[55] He candidly acknowledged his own insecurity as a writer: "A young author must in many cases be a plagiarist, his personal experience is limited—he must therefore copy the feelings of others, and his imagination must fill up the shading where the original has only been given the bold outline."[56] That insecurity may account for the alacrity with which he rode on the reputation of Shelley's novel by seizing her mythological method when composing his novel, *Ernestus Berchtold; or the Modern Oedipus* (1819), which, like Frankenstein, was partly set in Switzerland, deployed literary epigraphs (in Polidori's case, from Dryden's *Oedipus* and Byron's *The Giaour*), and, of course, possessed a modernized mythological subtitle.[57] In case any reader had missed the connection with Shelley's as yet anonymous novel, Polidori informed them that "[t]he tale presented is the one I began at Coligny where Frankenstein was planned."[58]

Despite the obvious and intended affinity with *Frankenstein,* however, Polidori's mythological method was radically different from Shelley's. "A myth introduced by a modern novelist into his work can prefigure and hence anticipate the plot in a number of ways," one scholar of the prosaic use of myth has written, and this seems to have been Polidori's intention in subtitling *Ernestus Berchtold* "the modern Oedipus."[59] Not until the final sentence of the book does it become clear just who is meant to be identified as "the modern Oedipus," though the subtitle does create suspense even as the reader wonders whether the novel will ever live up to its mythological promise. Until the final sentence, which completely overturns the plot in an almost comic peripeteia, the novel's only parallels with Oedipus were incidental and not signaled openly by allusion, as Shelley had done. Ernestus's mother had abandoned him as a child in a remote Swiss village; he became a legendary freedom fighter for Swiss independence in the aftermath of the Austro-Prussian war of the 1790s (much as Oedipus had been hailed as a deliverer by the Thebans), only to be seduced into vice in Italy by the aristocratic Olivieri Doni. Doni seduces Ernestus's sister, Julia, and Ernestus marries Doni's sister, Louisa;

Ernestus and his bride go to live with her father, the Count Filiberto Doni. In the closing pages of the novel, Ernestus and his wife, Louisa, have portraits of the count and Ernestus's dead mother made: upon seeing them, the count faints, "crying, 'It is too late, too late, the crime is consummated'."[60] Louisa dies of shock when it is revealed that she and Ernestus were children of the same mother, and had thus unwittingly committed incest. The novel concludes with the count's tangled confession: "Your mother's portrait was Matilda's. Olivieri had seduced, you married a daughter of Matilda, of Matilda's husband, and I was the murderer of her father."[61]

The coincidence of peripeteia and anagnorisis in this concluding scene perhaps made the novel a modern *Oedipus Tyrannus,* though Polidori of course handled the revelation with much less tact and cumulative horror than Sophocles. Polidori's subtitle promised prefiguration, but while Shelley's method of dispersed mythological correspondences implicated Frankenstein and the Monster in each other's fates, Polidori's use of the same device was strained and confusing. Both Ernestus Berchtold and Olivieri Doni had claims to be seen as Oedipus (because each was revealed to have committed incest with his own sister), as does the count, who killed his own father-in-law (albeit not his own father, as the myth would demand). Slight though Polidori's novel certainly was, it was evidence of the transferability of Shelley's mythological method, though not of her subtle syncretism. It was also evidence of Polidori's own mythological interests. Polidori committed suicide two years after the publication of *Ernestus Berchtold,* but not before he had supplied himself with an epitaph on the title page of his poetic collection, *Ximenes, The Wreath, and Other Poems* (1819):

Parce pias scelerare manus. Non me tibi Troia
Externum tulit . . .
Quòd Polydorus ego (Virgil, Aeneid, *3.42–43, 45).*[62]
[Spare me the pollution of your pious hands. Troy did not bear me so that I
should be a stranger to you. . . . For I am Polydorus.]

Like some Greek or Roman noble tracing his ancestry back to Zeus or Iulus, Polidori supplied himself (not just his fiction) with a mythical forebear: the sign of a mythological method comparable in activity though not in achievement to Mary Shelley's.

William Hazlitt's *Liber Amoris; or the New Pygmalion* (1823) was the last in this line of Romantic mythological prose, and was even more self-dramatizing in its use of myth than Polidori's proud assertion of epic ancestry. Hazlitt's confessional autobiography sprang, in part, from his admiring reading of *Frankenstein;*[63] it was also indebted to his long-standing interest in myth. Hazlitt had begun reading Ovid's *Metamorphoses* avidly at the age of ten, he was taught French by John de Lempriére, compiler of the *Bibliotheca Classica; or, a Classical Dictionary* (1788), and later in life he read William Godwin's mythographical works.[64] In the *Liber Amoris,* Hazlitt did not attempt a consistent renovation of the Pygmalion myth, and left it as only one structural metaphor among many rather than a controlling narrative. He attempted an interpretation of the amorous archetype which the myth itself interpreted. As he had written in a Chesterfieldian letter to his son in 1822, "We hunt the wind, we worship a statue, cry aloud to the desert" in pursuit of unrequited love.[65] The line was a quotation from *Don Quixote* (1.2.5), and thus exemplified the allusively literary habit of self-dramatizing that the *Liber Amoris* would stretch beyond most of his readers' endurance. Hazlitt called the work "a book of our conversations (I mean mine and the statue's) which I call LIBER AMORIS," referring to his landlord's daughter, Sarah Walker, the object of his clearly unwanted and invasive attentions.[66] His allusions to her as the statuesque Galatea to his imaginative Pygmalion were sparing and inexact: when he addressed her as, "Cruel girl! you look at this moment heavenly-soft, saint-like, or resemble some graceful marble statue, in the moon's pale ray," this referred less to the Pygmalion myth than to the quasi-Christian conventions of amorous idolatry.[67] That Hazlitt intended a critique of such conventions, rather than a whole-scale modernization of the myth, is confirmed by the novel's central symbol, a bronze bust of Napoleon, which Sarah identified with Hazlitt,[68] and which Hazlitt himself perceived to be the image of his most precious adoration, invested as it was with the character he most mythologized among his contemporaries.

Hazlitt's *Liber Amoris* was a palimpsest of Romantic mythologizing. For example, he combined the heathen and Miltonic mythologies, but without Shelley's purposiveness; his strategy was intuitive, rather than actually syncretic, and was the result of a tormented mind grasping literary motifs in a desperate and increasingly unsuccessful (and self-indulgent) attempt to communicate its descent into incoherence: "In her sight there was Elysium; her smile was heaven; her voice was enchantment . . . for a little while I sat with the gods at their tables, I had tasted all of earth's bliss, 'both living and loving!' But now Paradise barred its doors against me."[69] The most fertile literary strand in the novel is not Pygmalion but Keats's *Lamia,* a fable of disillusionment closer to the temper of Hazlitt's narrative. Hazlitt swore, "by her dove's eyes and serpent-shape, I think she does not hate me,"[70] though he realized later that he had made the error of Lycius in Keats's poem: "It was a fable. She started up in her own likeness, a serpent in place of a woman . . . Seed of the serpent or of the woman she was divine! I felt like she was a witch, and had bewitched me."[71] The final shattering of his illusion brought the story back to Pygmalion, however. Inevitably, the reader follows Hazlitt's narrative with the happy ending of Ovid's version of the Pygmalion myth in mind, as the statue metamorphoses into a real woman, warmed by the devotion of Pygmalion. In Hazlitt's bitter and ironic revision of the myth, a living woman becomes as dead and cold as a statue: "I saw her cold pale form glide silent by me, dead to shame as to pity. Still I seemed to clasp this piece of witchcraft to my bosom; this lifeless image, which was all that was left of my love, was the only thing to which my dead heart clung."[72] Hazlitt's Quixotic reading of myth meant that, in the novel as in his love, life was frozen into art, in a reversal of Galatea's awakening into life. "It is an instance of the truth and beauty of the ancient mythology," he wrote in his essay "On Personal Identity," "that the various transmutations it recounts are never voluntary, or of favorable omen, but are interposed as a timely release to those who, driven on by fate, and urged to the last extremity of fear or anguish, are turned into a flower, a plant, an animal, a star, a precious stone, or into some object that may inspire pity or mitigate our regret for their misfortunes."[73] Hazlitt's use of myth in the *Liber Amoris* may have allowed him to clarify and even excuse his predatory obsession into a self-pitying disenchantment, but it thereby did little to redeem myth for his own disenchanted age.

The subjectivism of Hazlitt's renovation of the Pygmalion myth was true to Shelley's construction of modern monstrosity, if not to her revival of ancient mythology. *Frankenstein* had presented the relationship between creature and creator as a psychodrama told in the voices of the participants rather than judged omnisciently from without. Shelley's novel thereby "served to depoliticize the monster tradition" inherited from the ideological debate around the French Revolution by internalizing "the clear definable melodrama of external ideological causes that informed writings of the 1790s" and individualizing the collective movements of the period.[74] Frankenstein's monster embodied the forces feared by counterrevolutionaries like Edmund Burke and the Abbé Barruel but, by embodying them, confined and even domesticated them. Polidori's *Ernestus Berchtold* recuperated the postrevolutionary politics Shelley had internalized by setting his modernized myth in republican Switzerland and by making his tragic hero both consciously insurrectionary and unwittingly incestuous, the victim and perpetrator of monstrous crimes, but not therefore a monster himself. Later, Hazlitt narcissistically politicized his fable of self-fashioning by identifying himself with Napoleon, that other "modern Prometheus" of the late 1810s, but only by evacuating Shelley's mythological method of its association with monstrousness in politics. *Frankenstein* attained political significance later in the nineteenth century, as the monster became a graphic metaphor for all kinds of political monstrosities: reformers, the working classes, and the Irish; industrialism, capitalism, and imperialism.[75] However, the first graphic allusion to the novel, found among the terrors, treatises, and teeth piled up in Cruikshank's "Tugging at a ~~High~~ Eye Tooth," 1821 (figure 40) rendered its horror at once comic, intimate, and bod-

Figure 40. George Cruikshank, *Tugging at a ~~High~~ Eye Tooth* (1821). © Copyright The British Museum.

ily, rather than subversive, public, and political, in an apt parallel to the novel's own domestication and interiorization of both monstrosity and myth.[76]

Frankenstein alone endured of the early British experiments with modernizing myth in the age of prose. Shelley created a fiction so daringly successful in its monstrosity that it came to seem natural for modernity to possess such renovated myths, and perhaps even paradoxically to be defined by its possession of them: "In the last analysis nothing is more modern than myth."[77] Her Promethean emblem of scientific creation as intellectual overreaching in turn

brought the scientific contexts of the novel into high relief and effectively reminded her readers that "monster" and "demonstration" share a common etymology, though they of course have followed very different historical trajectories. Monstrosity passed from providential theology through curiosity to
embryology and biology; demonstration, from logical proof through to the
visual presentations so characteristic of the burgeoning public cultures of science in the eighteenth century.[78] The intersection of those trajectories with a
politicized and naturalized mythography in the decades around the turn of
the nineteenth century helped to produce in *Frankenstein* modernity's primal
myth of monstrosity.

AFTERWORD

Anatomical Readings in the Early Modern Era

ANDREW CURRAN

The essays contained in *Monstrous Bodies/Political Monstrosities,* reveal the striking diversity of monstrosity in the early modern era. Taken as a whole, the collection speaks to a new impetus within the study of the monstrous: a desire to bring this Protean notion—the monster—into dialogue with the specific metaphysical and political ideologies that generated the trope of monstrosity in the first place. The point of departure for such an endeavor is the overarching yet unstated belief that a given era's inquiry into the monster can only be understood by the light of its preoccupations, ideologies, and methodologies. This axiom holds true for our era as well. Indeed, before looking back at the fluctuating early modern understanding of monstrosity, we must first come to grips with our own view of human malformations. In a sense we must work through our present in order to assess our past.

Contemporary scientific knowledge relative to human malformations is as vast as it is specialized. Catalogs of birth defects contain exhaustive information on thousands of anatomic variants as well as their etiologies.[1] Much of what is now known in this field—including the causes of specific variants on the human genome—was made possible by experimental teratology, by the controlled replication of various "monstrosities." This field of research—

which produces pathological developments by, among other methods, decreasing specific nutrients or introducing viruses or chemical agents—has allowed scientists not only to witness but to predict the earliest moments of embryonic malformation. Indeed, one might argue that present-day teratology has changed the locus and focus of the study of the monstrous, from the sphere of gross anatomy to the realm of the cellular.[2]

To the specialist of the early modern period, contemporary teratology may recall Denis Diderot's fantastic speculations on the etiology of monsters in *Le Rêve de d'Alembert* (c. 1769). In a famous scene from this series of philosophical dialogues, the vitalist doctor Théophile Bordeu and his beautiful interlocutor Mlle de L'Espinasse engage in a titillating thought-experiment in teratogeny:

> *Bordeu*: Now do mentally what nature sometimes does in reality. Take another thread away from the bundle—the one destined to form the nose—and the creature will be noseless. Take away the one that should form the ear and it will have no ears or only one ear, and the anatomist in his dissection won't find either the olfactory or auditory threads, or will only find one of the latter instead of two. Go on taking away threads and the creature will be headless, footless, handless. It won't live long, but nevertheless it will have lived.
> *Mademoiselle de L'Espinasse*: Are there any examples of this?
> *Bordeu*: Oh yes. And that isn't all. Duplicate some of the threads in the bundle, and the animal will have two heads, four eyes, four ears, three testicles, three feet, four arms, six fingers to each hand. Jumble up the threads in the bundle and the organs will be displaced: the head will be in the middle of the body, the lungs on the left, the heart on the right. Stick two threads together and the organs will run into each other: the arms will be stuck to the body, the thighs, legs and feet will be all in one piece. In short, you will have every imaginable kind of monstrosity.[3]

Teasing de L'Espinasse with a proliferation of pathological development scenarios based on his own speculative "embryology," Bordeu generates all major forms of physical monstrosity in order to demystify and, to a lesser extent, distinguish among various types of anomalous embryonic development. Like many facets of Diderot's thought, this one was prescient; while pure flight of the imagination, Bordeu's and de L'Espinasse's thought-experiment certainly hinted at the profitable side of making monsters.

The full potential of producing specific monstrosities would not be understood until some fifty years after Diderot had written *Le Rêve*. Moving from the realm of thought-experiment to that of real experimentation, Étienne Geoffroy Saint-Hilaire attempted to replicate particular malformations by altering the gestational environment of chicken and duck embryos.[4] The impetus for these experiments was a far cry from what Diderot had hoped to demonstrate in his dialogues, however. Instead of staging, as had the famous *philosophe*, the chaos of generation (reproduction), Geoffroy sought to emphasize the fact that, according to him, monsters resulted from an interruption during fetal development. This belief in the predictability, the regularity and, in sum, the order of monstrosity as a whole would become the foundation of his son Isidore Geoffroy's research, which in turn culminated in the massive *Traité de teratologie* (1832–37).[5] In this systematic description of monstrous bodies based on painstaking anatomical analysis, an enormous range of monstrosities was subjected to the same methodical scrutiny as other natural phenomena.[6] Like seashells, mammals, or plants, the monster was now placed into an orderly Linnean-type grid. The consequences of this revolution were significant. Monstrosity became, once and for all, a natural and predictable occurrence found within a continuum of possible human development scenarios. Henceforth the once-absolute categories of *nature* and *contra natura* (the categories that, for many, separated monstrosity itself from natural processes) would no longer exist. On a certain level, this radical reconceptualization of human malformations heralded the death of the category of monstrosity as it referred to anomalous births.[7]

Human "monstrosities" did not disappear with the Saint-Hilaires, of course. Although advances in prenatal and genetic screening certainly raise the possibility that malformations will one day be a thing of the past, for the moment, humankind shares a common set of monstrosities.[8] What is more, we as a species remain fascinated by profound exceptions or deviations in human morphology. This elemental and visceral reaction to monstrosity obviously contrasts with what we might call the sanctioned conception of the misshapen body. Stemming to a certain degree from the Geoffroy Saint-Hilaires, today's open-minded interpretation of anatomical anomalies reflects both the naturalization and, perhaps more ambiguously, the normalization of the monster. If the former process—the monster's transformation from supernatural marvel to natural occurrence—has been all but universally accepted, the monster's normalization is more complicated, and is carried out in different ways. On one level, scientists and members of the medical profession have made a huge effort to discursively normalize those people suffering from human anomalies. While malformed humans cannot be portrayed as symptomless (for many, the definition of normal), doctors and psychologists have humanized the patients themselves, treating their anomalies as separate from their overriding status as human beings. This enlightened view of human difference is actively supported by a range of organizations that include the March of Dimes and the Children's Craniofacial Association. Among the many services that such organizations perform, one of the most important is attempting to eradicate humankind's social and psychological aversion to profound physical difference. This aversion is, after all, one of the last vestiges of the category of the physically "monstrous."

Discursive normalization of human "monstrosity" is seconded by a different and more active form of normalization: surgical correction. In many parts of the world, surgeons now repair certain congenital defects and pediatric deformities as a matter of course. It is this ability to treat surgically an increasing number of anomalies that has ushered in the final conceptual normalization of many of these conditions. Similar to the way in which the first eighteenth-century cataract operations fundamentally changed the notion of blindness, surgery has now transformed the conceptual status of once-monstrous malformations, including certain craniofacial defects.[9] The possibility of reconstructive surgery has, in essence, rationalized these malformations, making them easier to accept as temporary aberrations.

Discursive or surgical normalization does not come readily for the most rare and acute forms of human anomaly, however. Severely malformed fetuses or infants, including anencephalous infants (born without a brain), cranio-thoracopagus twins (joined at the chest and head) or fetuses with cyclopia (born with one large eye positioned below a small horn-like nose on the fore-head) are usually stillborn, or seldom survive the first days after childbirth. These terribly deformed humans occupy a liminal space between human and inhuman, as well as between life and death. Not surprisingly, sensitivity to the parents of such infants has dictated institutional practice. Today, the birth of a severely deformed or malformed infant is effectively contained within the clinical and hermetically sealed institution in which the infant is born. In ad-dition to protecting the privacy of the parents of such infants, this protocol has—unintentionally?—removed the existence of such infants from the col-lective imagination. Ask yourself: Did you know, as people did in earlier cen-turies, that the human cyclops is based in fact, not pure fantasy?

Whether passive or active, the decision to remove the existence of such anomalies from the popular consciousness is one of the defining characteris-tics of our era's treatment of monstrosity. True human monstrosity is now that which cannot be shown or even known. Indeed, such pitiful humans, in other eras referred to as monsters, have not only been stripped of their traditional status as "warnings" (*monere*); they are no longer beings that "show," or are shown (*monstrare*).[10] Certain conjoined twins are perhaps the one notable ex-ception to this rule. Although numbering among the most extreme and rare human malformations, the live birth of conjoined twins today incites sensa-tionalistic coverage reminiscent of that in earlier eras. One of the reasons be-hind such a reaction is, of course, the legacy and viability of certain remark-able conjoined twins: Helene and Judith (1701–23); the original Siamese twins Chang and Eng (1811–74); Daisy and Violet Hilton (1908–69); and Lori and Reba Schappell (1961–). Yet there is an even more pressing reason, a reason that is particularly characteristic of our era. Indeed, although the doubled humanity of conjoined twins somehow remains beyond discursive normalization, living infants with such a malformation are, thanks to recent progress in surgical technique, very often able to be corrected; there is, in fact, no better example of science's ability to eradicate an extreme case of monstrosity in our era.[11] Every year some twenty sets of conjoined twins are born throughout the world; about half that number survive birth. In recent years, most of these infants are separated by teams of surgeons volunteering their time and expertise for operations that last twenty or more hours. Few other pathologic states incite such generosity and, from the outside of the medical establishment, praise. Indeed, one might be tempted to think that, on a certain level, the most sensational aspect of the birth of craniopagus twins (attached at the head) has shifted, from the monstrous body itself to the surgeon who corrects the anomaly. This transposition of the wonder of monstrosity is quite revealing: if public discourse must, at least officially, treat the infants themselves with a studied lack of wonder, the corrective process is not subject to such censorship.[12]

News reports regarding the surgical correction of conjoined twins generally reflect our era's complex and contradictory relationship to human monstrosity. On one level, there is, of course, the undeniable and appropriate recognition that such procedures can both save and improve the lives of children born with such a burden. On the other hand, the standard narrative of surgical correction—which quietly recognizes humankind's elemental aversion to such human forms—carefully if elliptically evokes the category of extreme alterity so as to better stage monstrosity's final correction and elimination by the surgeon's scalpel. Indeed, contemporary medicine's ability to correct many such anomalies often engenders a self-congratulatory tone, the tone used to relate the story of technology's normalizing victory over the caprices of nature.[13] Seen from this perspective, surgery becomes more than an empirically suitable solution to a particular pathology; it has an esthetic or moral purpose, and functions as a proportional response to the threat of anomaly. To this author's knowledge, no reasonable person has quibbled with the surgical separation of conjoined twins as being an unholy alliance between surgical normalization and ideological normativity. This is not the case, however, for all surgical treatments of congenital defects, particularly those related to hermaphrodism or intersexuality. Indeed, some intersexuals maintain that the normalization of their condition should take place discursively, not surgically.[14] Such a position recalls the original normalizing discourse of Geoffroy Saint-Hilaire, with one exception: in this case, it is the "monster" itself who pleads to have his/her condition normalized.

Despite the presence of powerful normalizing discourses and procedures, it is clear that our own era's view of human malformations—like that of all eras—fluctuates both epistemologically and ontologically. Roland Barthes summarized this phenomenon as an axiomatic truth, writing that "the *monstrous* is . . . never based on more than a shift in perspective."[15] Bataille went even further, asserting quite flatly that, notwithstanding their normalization, monsters "remain, no less positively, anomalies and contradictions."[16] Together, Barthes's and Bataille's respective views of monstrosity underscore two truths regarding the status of monstrosity today. The first is the failure of a supposedly irrefutable epistemology to impose itself, to eradicate the category of the monster. The second is the fact that vestiges of this category seem to surface during individual or more general attempts to define the borders of the human. In his famous essay "La monstruosité et le monstrueux," Georges Canguilhem sought to understand humankind's reliance on the notion of the monster, as well as the contradictory status of this concept in the twentieth century. While acknowledging the fact that the monster had been safely quarantined under the rubric of the pathological, Canguilhem emphasized the challenge that monsters pose for notions of normalcy and collective identity. Much of what he writes in this brilliant essay can be encapsulated in three maxim-like truths relative to the reality of monstrous forms. The first two underscore monstrosity's psychologically disruptive role, the third its positive value within our collective self-understanding:

The existence of monsters calls life [itself] into question, [especially] its ability to teach us order.[17]

Monstrosity is the accidental and conditional threat of unfinished formation or distortion in the formation of the form; it is the limitation, from the interior, the negation of the living by the non-viable.[18]

And finally . . .

On the one hand, monstrosity produces anxiety. . . . On the other, it valorizes: since life is capable of failures, all its successes are failures [that have been] avoided.[19]

Of these three maxim-like insights, Canguilhem's synthetic third proposition positions monstrosity as an ambiguous construct that, while unsettling, also brings human normalcy into stark relief. This understanding of the monstrous obviously had implications that extended far beyond the philosophy of medicine. Indeed, by identifying normalcy and normalization as the polemical or ideological by-products of monstrosity, Canguilhem prompted scholars working in intellectual history and the history of science to complicate the narrative charting the supposedly neutral or positive movement of monstrosity's rationalization; henceforth this story would have to include the possibility that monstrosity functioned didactically, teaching us who we should be.

Foucault's 1974–75 lectures on *Les Anormaux* at the Collège de France were the first "studies" on monstrosity to exploit the full implications of Canguilhem's work. As the editors of this volume pointed out in their introduction, Foucault built on Canguilhem's view that normalization and normalcy were anything but neutral concepts. According to Foucault, these notions were necessarily political and carried a "pretension to power" that was constructed on the level on which knowledge itself is produced.[20] In short, Foucault declared normalization to be much more than a neutral rejection of the category of the monstrous: it was now a generative process producing normative identities within academic disciplines and institutions. While Foucault's lectures on this particular facet of normalization remained unpublished until very recently, those present at the Collège de France were told that the study of monstrosity was undergoing a major transition; indeed, the monster was no longer a text to be read; it was, rather, the reflection of a context, a context indicative of societal structures of control or self-control, a partner in the system of "discipline-normalization."[21]

Although one now finds major methodological differences in recent scholarship on monstrosity, much of what Foucault affirmed regarding the ideologically based process of normalization has found its way into the study of the monstrous, including what we find in the present volume.[22] Indeed, if there is an underlying tendency among those scholars working on the problem of monstrosity, it is to envision the history of monstrosity discursively, as a discourse or series of discourses that one must access through institutional and/or ideological analysis.[23] Current scholarship has indeed reoriented our scholarly gaze from the monster itself to the numerous and incongruous backgrounds that generate the category of monstrosity in the first place. This branch of learning has had the effect of recognizing the myriad contexts (physical, moral, political, gender, and racial) that have informed the category of the monstrous over the centuries.

On a certain level, the edited volume—which brings together specialists working on various cases or types of monstrosity—is the genre most reflective of the complexity and contradictions of the subject during the early modern era. In addition to the present collection on political monstrosities, three other edited volumes dedicated to the intricate subject of early modern monstrosity have appeared in the last six years. The editors of each of these collections have all recognized the diversity of monstrosity, and they all, too, have envisioned the range of monstrosity (and its possible synthetic points) in various ways. In the introduction to *Faces of Monstrosity in Eighteenth-Century Thought,* Patrick Graille and I suggested that the concept of eighteenth-century monstrosity was irreducible, a polysemous and polycontextual construct that was almost impossible to define since the "norms themselves (moral, physical, and aesthetic) were so hotly debated."[24] Timothy Jones and

David Sprunger, the editors of the collection *Marvels, Monsters, and Miracles,* have also emphasized the specificity of various monstrosities, and have suggested that recent trends in historiography are producing multiple narratives, each documenting a particular construction of monstrosity linked to a particular set of circumstances: "As historians have expanded the questions and interest of history to include issues of gender, class, and ethnicity, to include the unorthodox, the marginalized, the hidden, and the silenced," they explain, "[scholars] have found not one history but many."[25] Helen Deutsch and Felicity Nussbaum, the editors of *"Defects": Engendering the Early Modern Body,* have seen monstrosity from another perspective. Far from tracing specific historical narratives, they argue that the exegesis of the monster should examine the "interconnections [of the monster] with other imagined communities" and should also be "complicated with the emergence of racial and gender difference."[26] Disability studies, as Deutsch and Nussbaum call this approach, is designed to bring together the multiplicity of various monstrosities, including "matters as diverse as femininity as monstrosity, ugliness as an aesthetic category, deafness and the theory of sign language, and the exotic deformed."[27] More forcefully than most, Deutsch and Nussbaum have underscored one of the major tendencies in "monster" or "disability" studies: recovering the shared historical and epistemological links among monstrosity, gender, and race. This is certainly fertile ground for innovative interdisciplinary studies, as their own collection testifies. Nonetheless, Deutsch and Nussbaum's endorsement of "ally[ing] deformity, disability, and gender studies during the [early modern period]"[28] seems to replace one master narrative with another. Indeed, by arguing that the aberrant—non-European races, women, intersexuals, and the working class—"cohere" into notions of "nation and modern body" during this era, Deutsch and Nussbaum have advanced an interpretative scheme that recalls the overdetermined history of science narrative that their own work implicitly rejects.[29]

All historians, even the most empiricist of them, abhor a narrative vacuum. And a confusing empty space is exactly what scholars confronting the problem of monstrosity encountered after Whig history treatments of the question of monstrosity—along with most history of science questions—fell out of favor.[30] As the editors of this collection have made clear, this was particularly true for Lorraine Daston and Katharine Park, two scholars who played an important role in the downfall of this paradigm. Evaluating their own previous scholarship on early modern monstrosity in the 1998 *Wonders and the Order of Nature*, Daston and Park consciously abandoned a narrative charting the monster's final rationalization in favor of a view of the monstrous that explained the question of monstrosity as a function of aesthetic reactions such as wonder, horror, pleasure, and repugnance as well as the multiple sensibilities that "overlapped and recurred like waves."[31] As many critics have affirmed, Daston and Park's synthesis of the question of monstrosity, which contextualizes monstrosity within the larger notion of wonder as well as within various interpretative spheres such as court and scientific culture, is a compelling and unequaled tour de force within the field. Nonetheless, Daston and Park's interpretive schema, much like Deutsch and Nussbaum's, occasionally has a tendency to impose their paradigm on individual thinkers. We find this in their account of certain materialist or naturalist treatments of monstrosity in the late eighteenth century, particularly Buffon's. Indeed, according to their interpretation of various thinkers' reactions (or lack thereof) to the notion of wonder, Buffon's short three-page assessment of monstrosity in the 1749 *Histoire naturelle* is

> loud testimony that [monsters] had been banished to the margins of natural history and natural philosophy. No longer objects of wonder and desire on the far eastern and western rims of the European world, or objects of power encased in reliquaries or displayed at the courts of princes, marvels had been exiled to the hinterlands of vulgarity and learned indifference. The passions of wonder and curiosity that had singled them out as objects of knowledge had been decoupled and transformed.[32]

Characterizing Buffon's view of monstrosity as indicative of a larger aesthetico-intellectual shift towards indifference during the era raises two concerns. First, while the tone in which Buffon chose to write on monstrosity may indeed reflect his view that monstrous births were statistically insignificant, his accompanying naturalist explanation for the existence of monstrous forms—which asserted that monsters were produced from shocks or accidents in the womb—produced anything but indifferent reactions among materialist philosophers. For Diderot, to name but one thinker, Buffon's accidentalist reading of monstrosity would have been seen as part of a larger heterodox reconceptualization of nature, a reconceptualization that, in another venue, could signal chaos and godlessness. While Buffon may have chosen indifference when speaking about what he deemed to be flukes of nature, Diderot chose to evoke these same haphazardly generated monsters in order to put forth a strident and polemical refutation of the teleological argument for God's existence (in the 1749 *Lettre sur les aveugles*). In short, mid-eighteenth-century treatments of monstrosity did not all tend toward reactions of "detachment."

But perhaps more important than such anecdotal objections—and this will bring us to the more politically focused "monstrous bodies"—Daston and Park's focus on specific registers of interpretation sidesteps elements in this narrative that are tangential but significant to the question of monstrosity. This is again apparent in their interpretation of Buffon. While Buffon himself stated that monsters were, as Daston and Park correctly affirm, conceptually stillborn, the dynamic worldview behind such a statement produced other, more troubling offspring, the most important being a new categorization of human beings into various races. Buffon's *Histoire naturelle* played a critical role in this respect by synthesizing a range of proto-ethnic data culled from travelogues, compilations, and other works of natural history into a great account of humankind's origins and present geographical breakdown. A semiregressive chronicle, this history of Man and his varieties posited an original white race from which all other varieties had degenerated as a function of different climates and other environmental conditions.[33] While it should be pointed out that Buffon's degeneration theory was, comparatively speaking, not dogmatic or essentialist (after all, his nonessentialist view of race posited the unity of the species and also left open the possibility that particular groups could improve their status in time if they lived in better conditions), it is clear that the links between race and monstrosity in this case are both epistemological and thematic. Epistemologically speaking, human races—like monsters—were now explained as a function of physical laws posited on an accidentalist view of nature; like monstrous human eggs, less than ideal human varieties were seen as having suffered a twisting or deleterious alteration as a result of physical forces over time. The clear relation between race and tropes of monstrosity, anything but apparent in Buffon's almost dismissive tone on the subject of the monster, is echoed structurally in the *Histoire naturelle*. Indeed, directly following the three-hundred-page chapter charting humankind's most extreme forms comes Buffon's short assessment of monstrosity.[34] The progression from Laplander or Negro to physical monster, while not as linear as some critics might make it out to be, is nonetheless there for all to see.

The editors of *Monstrous Bodies/Political Monstrosities* have challenged their contributors to find similarly hidden connections between monstrosity and other spheres, particularly the political. In their introduction, Knoppers and Landes forcefully distance themselves from narratives of epistemological, interpretative, or embryological "progress" in lieu of a framework that carefully charts the relationship between religious strife, political instability, and the appearance of monstrous births (or monstrous allegories). To a certain extent, Landes and Knoppers have borrowed from Daston and Park's noteworthy understanding of the monster as a dynamic construct that "feed[s] on the anxieties and the aspirations of the moment, [that draws] its power from conditions of acute instability."[35] And yet, the editors of *Monstrous Bodies* have also avoided any schema that might obscure the complicated etiology and narratives of early modern monstrosity. Indeed, the rubric of early modern monstrosity is here interpreted as a fluctuating concept, as a rhetorical tool deployed within specific historical settings by particular groups or ideologies. The volume's main preoccupation, as the editors themselves make clear, is to investigate to what extent "political exigencies—as much as epistemological frameworks—[have shaped] and produce[d] the monstrous."[36]

Aberrations in the body—and body politic—take many forms. Landes and Knoppers have broken down the volume's chapters into the loose categories of race and nationhood; forms of medical practice; apocalypticism and bestiality; and finally, mythological or allegorical representations of the monster. The thematic link among such rubrics stems from the general framework of the collection, which seeks to examine the relationship between assorted forms of political, ideological, or ethnic normativity and the particular forms of monstrosity they engender. A collection such as *Monstrous Bodies* can of course be read in many ways; the connections among essays are as innumerable as they are unforeseen. Given the methodological point of departure for this volume—which emphasizes the specific breeding grounds for monstrosity—chronological or geographical readings of monstrosity obviously come to mind. My own reading of this volume seemed to spring organically from what I found to be a significant and useful tension between more sweeping studies and specific case studies of twisted political morphology.

Peter Burke's essay on the "Frontiers of the Monstrous," for example, serves as a reminder that there seems to exist a universal psychological tendency among humans to assign monstrous tendencies to foreign ethnicities or cultures. Despite the fact, as Burke points out, that we find an increasing number of ethnically based views of other cultures after knowledge of the world expands exponentially in the fifteenth century, and despite the fact that eighteenth-century thinkers including Edward Long marshaled nascent race theory (and tropes of monstrosity) in their quest to justify the slave trade, this far-reaching study, which moves from Herodotus and Pliny to the early modern era, paints a polyvalent view of monstrosity based on individual perspective: Catholics, Protestants, Jews, the English, the French, Eastern Europeans, Spaniards, Africans, Asians, and Indians, not to mention different classes, all are painted as having monstrous features, physiognomies, or habits by those who are in a position to represent them. Lévi-Strauss summed up this seemingly ahistorical phenomenon most famously in *Race and Culture* when he wrote that "humanity ceases at the frontiers of the tribe, of the linguistic group, [and] sometimes of the village."[37]

Afterword

While the focus of Marie-Hélène Huet's chapter on "Monstrous Medicine" is a marked departure from Burke's, her essay also brings up larger questions regarding monstrosity in general. Although Huet is careful to acknowledge the link between specific historical moments (such as the Reformation) and an increasingly feverish interpretation of monstrosity, she also works more generally to refine our understanding of the primary (elite) interpreters of monstrosity during the Renaissance. By examining a varied group of physicians and surgeons—all of whom had accepted medicine's newfound right to interpret monstrosities in reference to a divinely guaranteed corporeal canon—Huet reveals how medical practice "was itself contaminated . . . by the monstrous, and intimately linked with the mysteries that surrounded the Creation." This framework for the interpretation of monstrosity, where "the physician was first and foremost a reader of signs,"[38] underscores the almost godlike position of those people involved in the exegesis of human malformations; after all, their proclamations signaled nothing less than an ability to decode the divine, the demonic, and the natural.

Huet's emphasis on the power of exegesis, a power which was harnessed for purposes that went far beyond the simple recounting of prodigious histories, can be usefully coupled with Timothy Hampton's meditation on the Renaissance "rhetoric of description" as it is applied to monstrosities. In this linguistic analysis of how monsters' resemblance to other known objects or animals is transformed into unequivocal political allegories, Hampton uncovers the discursive process by which malformation becomes monstrous on a textual level. While Hampton's essay is primarily concerned with the deconstruction of this rhetorical device by both Rabelais and Montaigne, his examination of the textual fabrication of monstrosity illuminates many of the other examples of politically constructed monstrosity found in this volume. Indeed, whether in Renaissance France, Reformation Germany, or revolutionary England, the effectiveness of a particular reading of monstrosity depended on the interpreter's ability to reconcile malformation with a given social or political context (as well as on his political capital). As R. Po-chia Hsia points out in his absorbing account of the divergent interpretations of monstrous births during the German Reformation, "it was not the quality of the prophecy or prodigy that mattered, but the quality of the prophet."[39]

Huet's and Hsia's work rightly reorients our focus towards the actual interpreters of malformations. These are, after all, the thinkers, writers, and artists who cast the monster as hieroglyph of the political present; these are the people who positioned themselves as the via media between different conceptual realms (the physical, metaphysical, and the political); and, above all, these are the people who attempted to forge a coherent worldview or, perhaps more precisely, who attempted to keep a worldview coherent in the face of a particular monstrosity. This last characteristic is worth bearing in mind: physicians, surgeons, or theologians who provided exegeses of things monstrous did so not only as a function of certain political exigencies, but also as a function of the perceived efficacy of their explanations. Hsia's study of sixteenth-century Germany suggests this quite clearly. During the first half of the sixteenth century, according to Hsia, Lutheran reformers were able to decode (quite dogmatically) prodigies as signs of the "depravity of the monastic estate"[40] while Catholics interpreted the same monsters as emblems of Protestant heresy. During the last twenty-five years of the century, however, the proliferation of explanations coupled with the opposing teratologies of Protestants and Catholics seem to have undermined the efficacy of prodigious prophecy, prompting explanations recognizing, among other things, humankind's ignorance regarding God's will in such matters. Like Hsia's essay, David Cressy's analysis of monsters born in sixteenth- and seventeenth-century England also points to an evolving set of conventions in the interpretation of monstrosity, conventions that surely have to do with the political power marshaled by particular interpretative schemes. In the pre–Civil War era, according to Cressy, prodigious births allowed their interpreters to preach a "generic . . . message of reformation," a "moderate Godly agenda." By the 1640s, monsters become a sign of a "social pathology and religious failing."[41]

In addition to chronicling the evolving relationship between an increasingly conflicted country and the trope of monstrosity in seventeenth-century England, Cressy's study underscores a change in the prescriptive content of monstrosity. If the monster often functioned as a de facto sign of regrettable behavior or beliefs, the trope of monstrosity could also signal a more aggressive call to arms, especially in times of crisis. This was actually more true for what we might call moral monstrosity, those ethical or religious "defects" that were so great that they constituted a vice or monstrosity. The possibility of a moral defect had, of course, long been a part of the European consciousness. Boaistuau had recounted "prodigious" stories of greed;[42] Shakespeare called Lear a monster; and Purchase reduced Mohammed to a "monster of irreligion."[43] As James Steintrager has put it, moral, political or religious failings equaled, rhetorically speaking, "the absolute limit of what is called human."[44] The 1694 *Dictionnaire de l'Académie Françoise* makes this perfectly clear. In one of the entries for the article monster, it is stipulated:

> the term may be employed figuratively for a denatured and cruel person: *Nero was a monster, a monster of nature, a monster of cruelty, this is a monster that we must smother.*[45]

One of the advantages of looking at a dictionary definition of moral monstrosity is that we can see the slippage of a figurative use of the term towards a persuasive definition, a definition that is created to "affect or to appeal to the psychological states of the party to whom the definition is given."[46] Here the call to kill or smother the monster obviously parallels one of the long-established reactions to the birth of a physical monster: in the same way that conjoined twins were quickly dispatched within Roman times, the monster evoked in political discourse was now worthy only of being "stifl[ed] . . . in its cradle," as Cressy's chapter made clear.[47] Not surprisingly, the prescriptive aspect of moral monstrosity took many forms, and drew on many tropes. This is underscored in Laura Lunger Knoppers's meticulous study of the complex uses of allegory and moral monstrosity during Oliver Cromwell's period of influence in England. In this era, according to Knoppers, the potential for a political, theological, and thus a moral monstrosity came into focus against competing apocalyptic readings of the era's tumult. Indeed, given the era's rhetorical fixation on the text of Revelation, both Cromwell and his detractors cast themselves (or were cast) as the avenging Archangel to an either sectarian or popish Whore of Babylon.

As several critics have demonstrated, the projection of moral monstrosity onto political foes would also become an integral part of the representation and self-representation of various political elements in revolutionary France.[48] In the present volume, Joan Landes creatively extends the notion of monstrous bodies in this era to include the *écorché,* the artfully posed body of flayed skin "created" by artists including Honoré Fragonard in the 1790s. According to Landes, these three-dimensional testaments to Vesalius reveal a new and paradoxical corporeal legibility of the human body at the dawn of modernity. Like all things monstrous, the *écorché* functions as an information-carrying entity, or sign. Ostensibly didactic, the *écorché* may have taught medical students about the circulation of the blood; for us, however, the *écorché* signals a particular desire to rationalize the body or, perhaps, to create life during an era of political death and rebirth. Not surprisingly, David Armitage has also emphasized this desire to create life in his essay on Frankenstein and his monster. Like the *écorché,* this monster of assemblage, which was given life in a time of great turmoil, is at the crossroads of epistemologies, ideologies, and eras. Not only is this being the "offspring of literary and scientific models whose roots lay in early modern (and even premodern) models of myth";[49] Frankenstein's monster also embodies and domesticates the external ideological causes (such as the threat of new revolutions) during Shelley's era.

The contributors to this volume have testified to the range of physical, moral, and political monstrosities found during the early modern era; on a certain level, the specificity and range of monstrosity found in this volume bear witness to a reluctance to reduce the era's "monster" to a coherent trope. If this is a form of skepticism, it is well founded. First and foremost, a sweeping history of the early modern monster runs counter to the conceptual status of monstrous bodies at the time. While one can indisputably point to the ebb and flow of various interpretive schemes during the era, the analysis of monstrosity before the latter part of the eighteenth century must keep one simple fact in mind, namely, that the interpretation of monstrosities during much of the early modern period was performed by thinkers who would never have been able to conceive of the monster as having a history.[50] To shed light on the significance of a malformed human in Renaissance Italy, for example, interpreters had to acknowledge the spatiotemporal specificity of the occurrence. Despite the monster's status as exception, deviation, and contradiction, each particular monster reflected—in a way that is difficult to understand today—a fundamental coherence and mirror image vis-à-vis its world. *Monstrous Bodies/Political Monstrosities* makes this fact evident: the early modern monster—whether physical or metaphorical—came into focus against various orthodoxies at specific points in time and for specific reasons. Accordingly, to envision the trope of monstrosity during the early modern era, we must shy away from generating an all-powerful history, except of course, a history of distinct disruptions in coherent universes, an *histoire prodigieuse.*

NOTES

Introduction

1. *Emblema vivente, ou, Noticia de hum portentoso monstro que da provincia de Anatolia foy mandado ao Sultaõ dos Turcos. Com a sua figura, copiada do retrato, que delle mandou fazer o Biglerbey de Amasia, re-cebida de Alepo, em huma carta escrita pelo mesmo autor da que se imprimio o anno passado* (Lisboa Occidental: Pedro Ferreira, 1727). This anonymous tract has also been attributed to José Freire de Monterroio Mascarenhas (1670–1760), who published a pamphlet (possibly the one referred to on *Emblema Vivente*'s title page) entitled *Relaçam de hum formidavel e horrendo monstro silvestre, que foy visto, e morto nas visin-hanças de Jerusalem. Traduzido fielmente de huma que se imprimio em Palermo no Reyno de Sicilia . . . como retrato verdadeiro do dito bicho por J. F. M. M.* (Lisboa: Joseph Antonio da Sylva, 1726). Mascarenhas also published a wide range of historical works, including accounts of battles, wars of succession, diplomacy, foreign relations, natural disasters, and astrology.

2. *Novum Organum*, in *Francis Bacon, Advancement of Learning, Novum Organum, New Atlantis,* vol. 30 of *Great Books of the Western World* (Chicago: Encyclopaedia Britannica, 1952), 152. An influential debate within the French Academy about the origins of monsters opposed the ideas of the anatomists Louis Leméry and Jacques Winslow, both of whom nonetheless agreed on the theory of the preexistence of "seed-germs," created by God. As Andrew Curran and Patrick Graille observe, the initial context for this debate was theological: "In essence, the real question at the Académie was: 'Is God responsible for the production of such creatures?' The battleground for such an inquiry was the realm of embryology, where, since the beginning of the century, providentialist thinkers (who believed the monster to be will-fully created by God in a preformed seed) clashed with accidentalist theoreticians (who maintained that deformation resulted from mechanical accidental shocks suffered in utero)." Andrew Curran and Patrick Graille, "The Faces of Eighteenth-Century Monstrosity," in *Faces of Monstrosity in Eighteenth-Century Thought,* ed. Andrew Curran, Robert P. Maccubbin, and David F. Morrill, special issue of *Eighteenth-Century Life* 21, no. 2 (1997): 4.

Leméry disputed Winslow's providentialist view that monsters were produced by God's design within a preformed seed, arguing that non-normal, monstrous outcomes resulted from mechanical or accidental causes following conception. While Leméry himself remained a preformationist, his acciden-talist position did end up undermining preformationism by reviving the notion of epigenesis (the theory of the gradual development of the embryo *in utero*). Also, his mechanical notion is thought to have paved the way for the more desacralized embryological views advanced by such thinkers as Maupertuis and Buffon. For the broader context of this debate, as well as the difference dividing those who believed in the preexistence or preformation of germs (either in the sperm or the egg), and epigenesists (who attributed embryonic development to secondary causes), see the following: Jacques Roger, *The Life Sciences in Eighteenth-Century French Thought,* ed. Keith R. Benson, trans. Robert Ellrich (Stanford, Calif.: Stanford University Press, 1997; first published in French, 1963); Patrick Tort, *L'Ordre et les monstres: Le Débat sur l'origine des déviations anatomiques au XVIIIe siècle* (Paris: Le Sycomore, 1980); Jean Ehrard, *L'Idée de nature en France dans la première moitié du XVIIIe siècle* (Paris: S.E.V.P.E.N., 1963); Andrew Curran, *Sublime Disorder: Physical Monstrosity in Diderot's Universe* (Oxford: Voltaire Foundation, 2001); and Michael Hagner, "Enlightened Monsters," in *The Sciences in Enlightened Europe,* ed. William Clark, Jan Golinski, and Simon Schaffer (Chicago: University of Chicago Press, 1999), 186–91; Marie-Hélène Huet, *Monstrous Imagination* (Cambridge, Mass.: Harvard University Press, 1993).

3. We thank Paul Harvey for his advice on the Latin etymology. On defining the monstrous, see Jean Céard, *La Nature et les prodiges: L'Insolite au XVIe siècle en France* (Geneva: Droz, 1977), 158; John Block Friedman, *The Monstrous Races in Medieval Art and Thought* (Cambridge, Mass.: Harvard University Press, 1981), 108–30.

4. "Ah Imperio Ottomano! Quanto receava eu a visinhança da tua decadencia." *Emblema Vivente,* 9. We are indebted to Julia Hewitt for translating this tract from the Portuguese.

5. See Daniel Goffman, *The Ottoman Empire and Early Modern Europe* (Cambridge: Cambridge University Press, 2002); and Justin McCarthy, *The Ottoman Turks: An Introductory History to 1923* (London: Longman, 1997), chapter 5.

6. In his speculation about cross-species couplings, Voltaire does remark that such matings would have no permanent effects, since, as with horses and donkeys, they would produce sterile offspring. See the introduction to Voltaire's *Essai sur les moeurs* (1769 edition), in *Dictionnaire de la pensée de Voltaire par lui-même,* ed. André Versaille (Paris: Éditions Complexe, 1994), 895. In his article on monsters in his *Dictionnaire philosophique,* Voltaire goes a long way toward desacralizing and relativizing the monster, insisting that the definition of monstrosity depends upon the viewpoint of the beholder. Regarding the four-breasted, cow-tailed woman, Voltaire also writes, "She was a monster, certainly, when she let her bosom be seen, and a respectable enough woman when she did not." (Elle était monstre, sans difficulté, quand elle laissait voir sa gorge, et femme de mise quand elle la cachait.) Voltaire, "Monstres," in *Dictionnaire philosophique,* in *Oeuvres complètes de Voltaire* (Paris: Garnier Frères, 1879), 20:109. Despite his ecumenical view of difference, Voltaire did not give up altogether on the term "monster," reserving it for particularly horrifying animals. However, Lorraine Daston and Katharine Park insist that Voltaire's visceral definition of monstrosity derived from the violation of social conventions, rather than a violated nature, thus establishing a different standard for the understanding of monstrosity, *Wonders and the Order of Nature, 1150–1750* (New York: Zone Books, 1998) 213. A different approach is proposed by both Andrew Curran and Patrick Graille, for whom Voltaire's discrepant use of the monstrous is less a problem to be explained than a challenge to the dominant positivistic methodological approach to eighteenth-century monstrosity. See Curran, *Sublime Disorder,* 151; Curran and Graille, "The Faces of Eighteenth-Century Monstrosity," 1–15.

7. Carolus Linnaeus, *Systema naturae per regna tria naturae,* 10th ed. (Stockholm: Impensis Direct. Laurentii Salvii, 1758), 22–25, as cited in Katharine Park and Lorraine J. Daston, "Unnatural Conceptions: The Study of Monsters in Sixteenth- and Seventeenth-Century France and England," *Past and Present,* no. 92 (August 1981): 54. Joseph-François Lafitau, *Moeurs des sauvages amériquains comparées aux*

moeurs des premiers temps (Paris: Saugrain l'aîné, C. E. Hochereau, 1724). On Lafitau, see Jean-Louis Fischer, "Monstre," in *Dictionnaire européen des lumiéres,* ed. Michel Delon (Paris: Presses Universitaires de France, 1997), 720.

8. Hagner, "Enlightened Monsters," 178–79. On monsters as objects of early modern collections, see Paula Findlen, *Possessing Nature: Museums, Collecting, and Scientific Culture in Early Modern Italy* (Berkeley: University of California Press, 1994); and Marjorie Swann, *Curiosities and Texts: The Culture of Collecting in Early Modern England* (Philadelphia: University of Pennsylvania Press, 2001).

9. Curran and Graille, "The Faces of Eighteenth-Century Monstrosity," 4.

10. Mary Baine Campbell argues in *The Witness and the Other World: Exotic European Travel Writing, 400–1600* (Ithaca, N.Y.: Cornell University Press, 1988) that the first-person eyewitness format is adopted in accounts of exotic lands or people not so much to verify as to present an experience in which the reader can participate. More recently, see Peter Burke, *Eyewitnessing: The Uses of Images as Historical Evidence* (Ithaca, N.Y.: Cornell University Press, 2001). Eyewitnessing was also an important part both of the "virtual experience" and of the verification of scientific experiments in the late seventeenth century. See Simon Schaffer, "Natural Philosophy and Public Spectacle in the Eighteenth Century," *History of Science* 21 (1983): 1–43; and Schaffer, "Self Evidence," *Critical Inquiry* 18 (Winter 1992): 327–62.

11. On the importance of visuality and print, see also Barbara Stafford, *Body Criticism: Imaging the Unseen in Enlightenment Art and Medicine* (Cambridge, Mass: MIT Press, 1991); and Joan B. Landes, *Visualizing the Nation: Gender, Representation, and Revolution in Eighteenth-Century France* (Ithaca, N.Y.: Cornell University Press, 2001), 26–27. More specifically on the visual and monstrosity, William Burns has suggested that resonance of the popular exhibition of monsters in seventeenth-century may carry over to metaphorical political monsters: both emphasizing monstrosity and placing the reader in the position of "normal" viewer, "The King's Two Monstrous Bodies: John Bulwer and the English Revolution," in *Wonders, Marvels, and Monsters in Early Modern Culture,* ed. Peter Platt (Newark: University of Delaware Press, 1999), 191–92. On the political applications of monstrous imagery in revolutionary and counterrevolutionary caricature during the French Revolution, see Antoine de Baecque, *La Caricature révolutionnaire* (Paris: CNRS, 1988); idem, "Robespierre, monstre-cadavre du discours thermidorien," in Curran, Maccubbin, and Morrill, *Faces of Monstrosity,* 203–21; idem, *The Body Politic: Corporeal Metaphor in Revolutionary France, 1770–1800,* trans. Charlotte Mandell (Stanford, Calif.: Stanford University Press, 1998); and Claude Langlois, *La Caricature contre-révolutionnaire* (Paris: CNRS, 1988).

12. *Emblema Vivente,* 6.

13. "A todos causou admiração a sua fórma horrivel e sem exemplo," ibid.

14. "E vòs vos admirareis tambem a vendo estampada no papel, que vos mando," ibid.

15. On issues of periodization, see William Kerrigan and Gordon Braden, *The Idea of the Renaissance* (Baltimore: The Johns Hopkins University Press, 1989);James A Parr, "A Modest Proposal: That We Use Alternatives to Borrowing (Renaissance, Baroque, Golden Age) and Leveling (Early Modern) in Periodization," *Hispania* 84 (2001): 406–16; and, more broadly, *The Challenge of Periodization: Old Paradigms and New Perspectives,* ed. Lawrence Besserman (New York: Garland, 1996).

16. On taboo and violation, see Mary Douglas, *Purity and Danger: An Analysis of the Concepts of Pollution and Taboo* (London: Routledge and Kegan Paul, 1966). In this tradition, see also Peter Stallybrass and Allon White, *The Politics and Poetics of Transgression* (Ithaca, N.Y.: Cornell University Press, 1986).

17. The author of the influential *Traité de Tératologie* (1832–37), Étienne Geoffroy Saint-Hilaire, states in his *Dictionnaire classique d'histoire naturelle:* "Monsters have their usefulness: they are means of study for our intellects"; quoted in Huet, *Monstrous Imagination,* 112. On Saint-Hilaire's interest in teratogenesis, or the systemic production of monsters in the laboratory by interrupting or altering normal development, see the afterword to this volume by Andrew Curran. In addition to the nineteenth-century study of monsters associated with Saint-Hilaire, this volume also refers to classical teratology, which inaugurated a long tradition of attention to the monstrous in European societies. In the latter sense, teratology means not only the study of embryonic pathology but, in addition, the discourse of prodigies and wonders.

18. Jacques Roger discusses the evolution of this notion from Aristotle to Descartes in *The Life Sciences in Eighteenth-Century French Thought.*

19. "Le XVIIIe s. marque le passage nécessaire entre le fin d'une représentation fabuleuse du monstre et la demonstration des anomalies, des malformations, and des anomalies." Fischer, "Monstre," 722. It is surprising, given Diderot's interest in the topic, that the *Encyclopédie* lacks a significant treatment of monstrosity. Indeed, the two *Encyclopédie* entries on the topic suggest both a scientific attitude as well as the collector's curiosity (Curran, *Sublime Disorder,* 149).

20. Étienne Wolff, *La science des monstres* (Paris: Gallimard, 1948), 27, cited in Jean-Claude Margolin, "Sur quelques prodiges rapportés par Conrad Lycosthene," in *Monstres et prodiges au temps de la Renaissance,* ed. Marie Thérèse Jones-Davies (Paris: Diffusion Jean Touzot, 1980), 42. See also Isidore Geoffroy Saint-Hilaire, *Histoire générale et particulière des anomalies de l'organisation chez l'homme et les animaux, ou, Traité de tératologie: Ouvrage comprenant des recherches sur les caractères, la classification, l'influence physiologique et pathologique, les rapports généraux, les lois et les causes des monstruosités, des variétés et vices de conformation* 3 vols.(Paris : J.-B. Baillière, 1832–37).

21. Georges Canguilhem, "La Monstruosité et le monstrueux," in *La Connaissance de la vie* (Paris: J. Vrin, 1992), 172. See also "Le Normal et le pathologique" ibid., 155–70.

22. Michel Foucault, *Les Anormaux: Cours au Collège de France (1974–1975),* ed. François Ewald et al. (Paris: Seuil/Gallimard, 1999), 46.

23. Hagner, "Enlightened Monsters," 214.

24. Foucault's breakdown of the monster question will strike many today as extremely schematic. The hermaphrodite, for example, fascinated people in the seventeenth and eighteenth centuries as well. See Patrick Graille, *Les Hermaphrodites aux XVIIIe et XVIIIe siècles* (Paris: Belles Lettres, 2001).

25. Foucault, *Les Anormaux,* 60–61.

26. See the broadly theoretical introduction to Jeffrey Cohen, ed., *Monster Theory: Reading Culture* (Minneapolis: University of Minnesota Press, 1996).

27. On the social context of science, in which questions of generation and monstrosity are considered, see Mary Terrall, "Salon, Academy, and Boudoir: Generation and Desire in Maupertuis's Science of Life," *Isis* 87 (1996): 217–29.

28. Park and Daston, "Unnatural Conceptions," 23. Park and Daston attribute this teleological view to other scholars, including Georges Canguilhem, "Monstrosity and the Monstrous," *Diogène* 40 (1962): 27–42; and Céard, *La Nature et les prodiges.*

29. Pioneering works on the monstrous in earlier periods drawn upon by Park and Daston include

Rudolph Wittkower, "Marvels of the East: A Study in the History of Monsters," *Journal of the Warburg and Courtauld Institutes* 5 (1942): 159–97; Friedman, *Monstrous Races;* E. Martin, *Histoire des monstres depuis l'Antiquité jusqu'à nos jours* (Paris: C. Reinwald, 1880); Céard, *La Nature et les prodiges;* Jurgis Baltrusaitis, *Réveils et prodiges: Le gothique fantastique* (Paris: Flammarion, 1988).

30. See Jean Céard, *La Nature et les prodiges;* Wittkower, "Marvels of the East"; Ernest Martin, *Histoire des monstres depuis l'antiquité jusqu'à nos jours* (Paris: Reinwald, 1880); Park and Daston, "Unnatural Conceptions."

31. Park and Daston, "Unnatural Conceptions," 24. For the work that launched the concept of "withdrawal," which Park and Daston utilize, see Peter Burke, *Popular Culture in Early Modern Europe* (New York: New York University Press, 1978).

32. Park and Daston give credit for this to the argument between preformationists and epigenesists, according to which the monster came to be disinvested of its miraculous associations. See note 2 above.

33. On the popular display of monsters, see Robert Bogdan, *Freak Show: Presenting Human Oddities for Amusement and Profit* (Chicago: University of Chicago Press, 1988); Michael Hagner, "Monstrositäten in gelehrten Räumen," in *Alexander Polzin: Abgetrieben,* ed. Sander L. Gilman (Göttingen: Wallstein, 1997), 11–30; Paul Semonin, "Monsters in the Marketplace: The Exhibition of Human Oddities in Early Modern England," in *Freakery: Cultural Spectacles of the Extraordinary Body,* ed. Rosemarie Garland Thomson (New York: New York University Press, 1996), 69–81; Mark Thornton Burnett, " 'Strange and woonderfull syghts': *The Tempest* and the Discourses of Monstrosity," *Shakespeare Survey* 50 (1997): 187–99; and, most recently, his *Constructing 'Monsters' in Shakespearean Drama and Early Modern Culture* (Basingstoke: Palgrave, 2002).

34. In particular, wonder has become a central category of recent analysis. See Mary Baine Campbell, *Wonder and Science: Imaginary Worlds in Early Modern Europe* (Ithaca: Cornell University Press, 1999); Platt, *Wonders, Marvels, and Monsters.*

35. Daston and Park, *Wonders,* 176.

36. Ibid., 209.

37. Ibid., 17.

38. Huet, *Monstrous Imagination,* 119.

39. Ibid.

40. Ibid, 126. On teratogeny, the study of malformations, monstrosities, or serious deviations from normality, see Evelleen Richards, "A Political Anatomy of Monsters, Hopeful and Otherwise: Teratogeny, Transcendentalism, and Evolutionary Theorizing," *Isis* 85 (1994): 377–411.

41. Dennis Todd, *Imagining Monsters: Miscreations of the Self in Eighteenth-Century England* (Chicago: University of Chicago Press, 1995). Monstrous births are also treated in David Cressy, "De la fiction dans les archives? ou le Monstre de 1569," *Annales: Économies, sociétés, civilisations* 48 (1993): 1309–29; idem, *Travesties and Transgressions in Tudor and Stuart England: Tales of Discord and Dissension* (New York: Oxford University Press, 2000), 29–50; Stephen Pender, " 'No Monsters at the Resurrection': Inside Some Conjoined Twins," in Cohen, *Monster Theory,* ed. Cohen, 143–67; and Dudley Wilson, *Signs and Portents: Monstrous Births from the Middle Ages to the Enlightenment* (London: Routledge, 1993).

42. Platt, *Wonders, Marvels, and Monsters.*

43. Julia V. Douthwaite, *The Wild Girl, Natural Man, and the Monster: Dangerous Experiments in the*

Age of Enlightenment (Chicago: University of Chicago Press, 2002). See also Nancy Yousef, "Savage or Solitary? The Wild Child and Rousseau's Man of Nature," *Journal of the History of Ideas* 62, no. 2 (2001): 245–63.

44. See Graille, *Les Hermaphrodites;* and Kathleen Perry Long, "Hermaphrodites Newly Discovered: The Cultural Monsters of Sixteenth-Century France," in Cohen, *Monster Theory,* 183–201.

45. Curran, *Sublime Disorder,* 151. On philosophical discourse, see also James A. Steintrager, "Perfectly Inhuman: Moral Monstrosity in Eighteenth-Century Discourse," in Curran, Maccubbin, and Morrill, *Faces of Monstrosity,* 114–32; Emily Jane Cohen, "Enlightenment and the Dirty Philosopher," *Configurations* 5, no. 3 (1997): 369–424. On monstrosity in Sade's work, see Jean-Marc Kehrès, "Libertine Anatomies: Figures of Monstrosity in Sade's *Justine, ou les malheurs de la vertu,*" in Curran, Maccubbin, and Morrill, *Faces of Monstrosity,* 100–113.

46. Zakiya Hanafi, *The Monster in the Machine: Magic, Medicine, and the Marvelous in the Time of the Scientific Revolution* (Durham, N.C.: Duke University Press, 2000), x. On the monstrous as machine, see also Jonathan Sawday, " 'Forms Such as Never Were in Nature': The Renaissance Cyborg," in *At the Borders of the Human: Beasts, Bodies and Natural Philosophy in the Early Modern Period,* ed. Erica Fudge, Ruth Gilbert, and Susan Wiseman (Basingstoke: Macmillan, 1999), 171–95.

47. Among the many important studies of the body in early modern Europe, see Mikhail Bakhtin, *Rabelais and His World,* trans. Hélène Iswolsky (Cambridge, Mass.: MIT Press, 1968); Jonathan Sawday, *The Body Emblazoned: Dissection and the Human Body in Renaissance Culture* (London: Routledge, 1995); and Stafford, *Body Criticism.*

48. On uses of the body as metaphor for the state, see Ernst H. Kantorowicz, *The King's Two Bodies: A Study in Mediaeval Political Theology* (Princeton, N.J.: Princeton University Press, 1981); Norman O. Brown, *Love's Body* (New York: Vintage, 1966); Lynn Hunt, ed., *Eroticism and the Body Politic* (Baltimore: Johns Hopkins University Press, 1991); and David Hale, *The Body Politic: A Political Metaphor in Renaissance English Literature* (The Hague: Mouton, 1971).

49. Historians of print agree that the revolution in print in the early modern period made the visual image a more ubiquitous and powerful tool of communication than ever before. See Elizabeth Eisenstein, *The Printing Press as an Agent of Change: Communications and Cultural Transformations in Early-Modern Europe,* 2 vols. (Cambridge: Cambridge University Press, 1979); Roger Chartier, "Political Persuasion and Representation: Introduction," in *The Culture of Print: Power and the Uses of Print in Early Modern Europe,* trans. Lydia G. Cochrane (Princeton, N.J: Princeton University Press, 1989).

50. Paul Freedman argues that the colonial power dynamic is absent during the Middle Ages, "The Medieval Other: The Middle Ages as Other," in *Marvels, Monsters, and Miracles: Studies in the Medieval and Early Modern Imaginations,* ed. Timothy S. Jones and David A. Sprunger (Kalamazoo, Mich.: Medieval Institute Publications, 2002), 1–26. Helen Deutsch and Felicity Nussbaum set out to show the imbrication of race and the monstrous, although the monstrous races per se remain outside of their geography of defect: see their introduction to *"Defects": Engendering the Modern Body* (Ann Arbor: University of Michigan Press, 2000), 8. On a very different reappearance of the monstrous races in the Renaissance, see Mary Baine Campbell's fascinating study of "The Nude Cyclops in the Costume Book," in Jones and Sprunger, *Marvels, Monsters, and Miracles,* 285–301.

51. On the monstrous in the political/religious conflicts of mid-seventeenth-century England, see David Loewenstein, "'An Ambiguous Monster': Representing Rebellion in Milton's Polemics and *Paradise Lost*," *Huntington Library Quarterly* 55 (1992): 295–315, and Burns, "The King's Two Monstrous Bodies," 187–204.

52. On women, gender, and science in the early modern period, see Londa Schiebinger, *The Mind Has No Sex? Women in the Origins of Modern Science* (Cambridge, Mass: Harvard University Press, 1989). Earlier scholarship attentive to gender and monstrosity includes Marie-Hélène Huet's *Monstrous Imagination*. Dennis Todd looks at how cultural anxieties are mapped onto the female body in the opening anecdote of *Imagining Monsters;* the editors and contributors to Deutsch and Nussbaum, *"Defects": Engendering the Modern Body,* are also concerned with how the history of defects and monstrosity must be complicated with the emergence of gender (as well as racial) difference.

53. See Bakhtin, *Rabelais and His World.*

54. See, for instance, Anne K. Mellor, "*Frankenstein:* A Feminist Critique of Science," in *One Culture: Essays in Science and Literature*, ed. George Levine (Madison: University of Wisconsin Press, 1987), 287–312; Mary Favret, "A Woman Writes the Fiction of Science: The Body in *Frankenstein,*" *Genders* 14 (1992): 50–65; Janice Caldwell, "Sympathy and Science in *Frankenstein,*" in *The Ethics in Literature*, ed. Andrew Hadfield, Dominic Rainsford, and Tim Woods (Basingstoke: Macmillan, 1998), 262–74; and Debra Benita Shaw, *Women, Science, and Fiction: The Frankenstein Inheritance* (New York: Palgrave, 2000).

55. "Guardou a Providencia para o nosso Seculo esta ultima fatalidade," *Emblema Vivente,* 10.

56. "Porèm Deos he grande, cheyo de clemencia e de Misericordia . . . aproveitemo-nos, Senhor, da sua Clemencia," *Emblema Vivente,* 10.

Chapter 1. Frontiers of the Monstrous

1. Bernadette Bucher, *Icon and Conquest: A Structural Analysis of the Illustrations of de Bry's Great Voyages,* trans. Basia Miller Gulati (Chicago: University of Chicago Press, 1981), 36.

2. Claude Lecouteux, *Les monstres dans la littérature allemande au moyen âge* (Göppingen: Kümmerle, 1982), 15–24 (wild men), 25–56 (giants), 57–73 (dwarves), and 74–90 (monstrous races).

3. David Williams, *Deformed Discourse: The Function of the Monster in Medieval Thought and Literature* (Montreal: McGill-Queens University Press, 1996). On the monstrous Other as an aid to European self-definition, see Peter Mason, *Deconstructing America: Representations of the Other* (New York: Routledge, 1990), especially 41–68, 97, and for a criticism of attempts to "reduce" imaginary races to "a misperception of some empirical reality," 114.

4. Michel de Certeau, *Heterologies: Discourse on the Other* (Minneapolis: University of Minnesota Press, 1986); Edmundo Magaña, "Hombres selvajes y razas monstruosas de los Indios Kaliña de Surinam," *Journal of Latin American Lore* 8 (1982): 63–114, and Mason, *Deconstructing America,* 7, 14, 108, 112.

5. Rudolf Wittkower, "Marvels of the East: A Study in the History of Monsters," *Journal of the Warburg and Courtauld Institutes* 5 (1942): 159–97; John Block Friedman, *The Monstrous Races in Medieval Art and Thought* (Cambridge, Mass.: Harvard University Press, 1981).

6. Joshua Trachtenberg, *The Devil and the Jews: The Medieval Conception of the Jew and Its Relation to Modern Anti-Semitism* (New Haven, Conn.: Yale University Press, 1943); Ruth Mellinkoff, *Outcasts: Signs of Otherness in Northern European Art of the Late Middle Ages* (Berkeley: University of California Press, 1993); Debra Hassig, "The Iconography of Rejection: Jews and Other Monstrous Races," in *Image and Belief: Studies in Celebration of the Eightieth Anniversary of the Index of Christian Art,* ed. Colum Hourihane (Princeton, N.J.: Princeton University Press, 1999), 25–37.

7. Olivier Christin, *Une Révolution symbolique: L'Iconoclasme Huguenot et la reconstruction catholique* (Paris: Minuit, 1991).

8. David Kunzle, *The Early Comic Strip* (Berkeley: University of California Press, 1973), 32; James Brodrick, *St. Peter Canisius* (London: Sheed and Ward, 1935), 419n; William Coupe, *The German Illustrated Broadsheet in the Seventeenth Century,* 2 vols. (Baden-Baden: Heitz, 1966–67), 213, plate 101; Thomas Middleton, *The Game at Chess* (1624), Act I, scene I; Phineas Fletcher, *Locustae sive pietas jesuitica,* 1627. On the Jesuit "bestiary" in the nineteenth century, Michel Leroy, *Le mythe Jésuite de Béranger à Michelet* (Paris: Presses Universitaires de France, 1992), 210–24.

9. Michael Camille, *Mirror in Parchment: The Luttrell Psalter and the Making of Modern England* (Chicago: University of Chicago Press, 1998), 210; Margaret Sullivan, *Bruegel's Peasants: Art and Audience in the Northern Renaissance* (Cambridge: Cambridge University Press, 1994).

10. Quoted in David Zaret, *Origins of Democratic Culture: Printing, Petitions, and the Public Sphere in Early Modern England* (Princeton, N.J.: Princeton University Press, 2000), 53.

11. Edmund Leach, "Anthropological Aspects of Language: Animal Categories and Verbal Abuse" (1964), in *Mythology,* ed. Pierre Maranda (Harmondsworth: Penguin Books, 1970), 39–67.

12. Bucher, *Icon and Conquest;* cf. Peter Hulme, "Columbus and the Cannibals," *Ibero-Amerikanisches Archiv* 42 (1978): 115–39; Carmen Val Julián, "Nouveau monde, noveaux monstres," in *Des Monstres* (Saint-Cloud: ENS, 1994), 153–66.

13. Frank Lestringant, *Cannibals: The Discovery and Representation of the Cannibal from Columbus to Jules Verne,* trans. Rosemary Morris (Cambridge: Polity Press, 1997; originally published, 1994).

14. Samuel Sumberg, *The Nuremberg Schembart Carnival* (New York: Columbia University Press, 1941), 112.

15. Richard Bernheimer, *Wild Men in the Middle Ages* (Cambridge, Mass.: Harvard University Press, 1952); Lynn Kaufmann, *The Noble Savage: Satyrs and Satyr Families in Renaissance Art* (Ann Arbor, Mich.: UMI Research Press, 1984).

16. Sumberg, *Nuremberg Carnival,* 98–105.

17. Lee E. Huddleston, *Origins of the American Indians: European Concepts, 1492–1729* (Austin: University of Texas Press, 1967); cf. Joan-Pau Rubiés, "Hugo Grotius's Dissertation on the Origin of the American Peoples," *Journal of the History of Ideas* 52 (1991): 221–44.

18. Giuliano Gliozzi, *Adamo e il nuovo mondo: La nascità dell'antropologia come ideologia coloniale: Dalle genealogoie bibliche alle teorie razziali (1500–1700)* (Florence: La nuova Italia, 1976), 378–81; Anthony Pagden, *The Fall of Natural Man: The American Indian and the Origins of Comparative Ethnology* (Cambridge: Cambridge University Press, 1982), esp. 15–26, 126–35, 163–68.

19. Quoted in Stuart Piggott, "Antiquarian Thought in the Sixteenth and Seventeenth Centuries," in *English Historical Scholarship,* ed. Levi Fox (London: Oxford University Press, 1956), 101.

20. [Francois Bernier], "Nouvelle division de la terre par les différents espèces ou races qui l'habitent," *Journal des Savants* (1684); Siep Stuurman, "Francois Bernier and the Invention of Racial Classification," *History Workshop Journal* 50 (2000), 1–22; Gliozzi, *Adamo,* 602–4.

21. Jean-Dominique Pénel, *Homo caudatus: Les hommes à queue d'Afrique centrale, un avatar de l'imaginaire occidental* (Paris: SELAF, 1982), 43. This study makes no reference to the literature on European *homines caudati.*

22. Edward Tyson, *Orang-outang sive homo silvestris* (1699).

23. Felipe Fernández-Armesto, *Millennium: A History of the Last Thousand Years* (London: Bantam, 1995), 135.

24. George Neilson, *Caudatus Anglicus: A Medieval Slander* (Edinburgh: G. P. Johnston, 1896); Peter Rickard, "Anglais coué," *French Studies* 7 (1953): 48–55.

25. Denys Hay, "Italy and Barbarian Europe," in *Italian Renaissance Studies,* ed. E. F. Jacob (London: Faber and Faber, 1960), 48–68.

26. Pasquier, *Recherches de la France* 1.102, quoted in Jacques Barzun, *The French Race: Theories of its Origins and their Social and Political Implications Prior to the Revolution*(New York: Columbia University Press, 1932), 67.

27. Larry Wolff, *Inventing Eastern Europe: The Map of Civilization on the Mind of the Enlightenment* (Stanford: Stanford University Press, 1994), 10–11, 19, 35.

28. John Florio, *First Fruits* (1578).

29. John Bodin, *Method for the Easy Comprehension of History* (1566), trans. Beatrice Reynolds (New York: Columbia University Press, 1945), 97.

30. Ibid., 124

31. Carlos García, *La Oposición y conjunción de los dos grandes luminaries de la tierra, o la antipatia de franceses y españoles,* ed. M. Bareau (Edmonton, Alberta: Alta Press, 1979). Cf. Johannes de Laet, *Hispania* (Leiden, 1629) with an anthology of comments on Spanish manners by Mariana, Botero, de Thou, Barclay, etc.

32. Paolo Nobili, "Grammatiche e circolazione di stereotipi nell'Europa del Sei-Settecento," in *Grammatiche, Grammatici, Grammatisti: Per una Storia dell'insegnamento delle lingue in Italia dal Cinquecento al Settecento,* ed. Carla Pellandra (Pisa: Libreria Goliardica, 1989), 121.

33. John Evelyn, *A Discourse on Medals* (London: B. Tooke, 1697), 315.

34. David Hume, *Essays* (London, 1748), no. 21.

35. J. Zahn, *Specula* (1696), discussed in Nobili, *Grammatiche,* 130.

36. A brief discussion in Jack Goody, *The Domestication of the Savage Mind* (Cambridge: Cambridge University Press, 1977), 153–55. Cf. Franz. K. Stanzel, ed., *Europäischer Völkerspiegel: Imagologisch-ethnographische Studien zu den Völkertafeln des frühen 18. Jahrhunderts* (Heidelberg: Carl Winter, 1999).

37. Evelyn, *Discourse,* 316.

38. Quoted in Michael Duffy, *The Englishman and the Foreigner* (Cambridge: Chadwyck-Healey, 1986), 13.

39. M. Dorothy George, *English Political Caricature* (Oxford: Clarendon Press, 1959), 87, 105; Duffy, *Englishman and Foreigner,* 28.

40. Janusz Tazbir, *La République nobiliaire et le monde* (Wroclaw: Ossolinski, 1986), 389; cf. Duffy, *Englishman and Foreigner*, 4, and Wolff, *Inventing Eastern Europe*.

41. Bulwer, quoted in Neilson, *Caudatus Anglicus*, 32.

42. Ibid., 22, 28.

43. Cf. Laura L. Knoppers, "Oliver Cromwell, Andrew Marvell, and the Apocalyptic Monstrous," in this volume.

44. Henryk Barycz, "Italofilia e Italofobia nella Polonia del Cinque– e Seicento," in *Italia, Venezia e Poloni tra umanesimo e rinascimento*, ed. M. Brahmer (Wroclaw: PWN, 1967), 142–48.

45. Paul Hazard, *The European Mind, 1680–1715* (1935; English trans. 1953, by J. Lewis May, reprint ed., Harmondsworth: Penguin Books, 1964), 73ff.

46. Barycz, "Italofilia"; Jean Balsamo, *Les Rencontres des muses: Italianisme et anti-italianisme dans les lettres françaises de la fin du XVIe siècle* (Geneva: Éditions Slatkine, 1992); Jean-François Dubost, *La France italienne: XVIe–XVIIe siècle* (Paris: Aubier, 1997).

47. J. Phillips (1656); anon., *Character of Spain* (1660); anon., *Old England for Ever* (1740), quoted in Duffy, *Englishman and Foreigner*, 23.

48. George, *English Political Caricature*, 85–86, 104.

49. Quoted in Duffy, *Englishman and Foreigner*, 14.

50. Ibid.

51. Bob Tadashi Wakabayashi, *Anti-Foreignism and Western Learning in Early Modern Japan: The New Theses of 1825* (Cambridge, Mass.: Harvard University Press, 1986), 21.

52. Hannah Arendt, "Race-Thinking before Racism," *Review of Politics* 6 (1944): 36–73; cf. Harold Pagliaro, ed., *Racism in the Eighteenth Century* (Cleveland: Press of Case Western Reserve University, 1973); Michael Banton, "The Classification of Races in Europe and North America, 1700–1850," *International Social Science Journal* 111 (1987): 45–60; Ivan Hannaford, *Race: The History of an Idea in the West* (Baltimore: The Johns Hopkins University Press, 1996).

53. Pénel, *Homo caudatus*.

54. L. Perry Curtis, Jr., *Anglo-Saxons and Celts: a Study of Anti-Irish Prejudice in Victorian England* (New York: New York University Press, 1968), 60.

55. Since this essay was first written, a study of this topic has appeared: Elaine L. Graham, *Representations of the post/human: Monsters, Aliens and Others in Popular Culture* (Manchester: Manchester University Press, 2001). Graham examines the roots of these creatures in Greek and Jewish myth, but does not discuss the Plinian races.

Chapter 2. Lamentable, Strange, and Wonderful

1. Born of Maltese parents at Manchester in August 2000, the conjoined twins nicknamed "Mary" and "Jody" dominated the English tabloid media for several months. The controversial surgery that separated them in December 2001 allowed one to live and the other to die.

2. Christopher Hill, "The Many-Headed Monster in Late Tudor and Early Stuart Political Thinking," in *From the Renaissance to the Counter-Reformation: Essays in Honor of Garrett Mattingly*, ed. Charles H. Carter (New York: Random House, 1965), 296–324.

3. Jerome Friedman, *The Battle of the Frogs and Fairford's Flies: Miracles and the Pulp Press During the English Revolution* (New York: St. Martin's Press, 1993), 51–52.

4. Pierre Boaistuau, *Certaine Secrete Wonders of Nature, containing a description of sundry strange things,* trans. Edward Fenton (London: H. Bynneman, 1569).

5. *A Wonder Woorth the reading, or A True and faithfull Relation of a Woman, now dwelling in Kent Street* (1617).

6. *The forme and shape of a Monstrous Child born at Maydstone* (1568).

7. See, for example, Edward Forset, *A Comparative Discourse of the Bodies Natural and Politique* (1606). According to James VI and I, "The head cares for the body, so doth the king for his people. As the discourse and direction flows from the head, and the execution thereunto belongs to the rest of the members, everyone according to his office, so it is betwixt a wise prince and his people," quoted in Robert Ashton, *The English Civil War,* 2d ed. (London: Weidenfeld and Nicolson, 1989), 4–5.

8. David Cressy, "Monstrous Births and Credible Report: Portents, Texts and Testimonies," in *Travesties and Transgressions in Tudor and Stuart England: Tales of Discord and Dissension* (New York: Oxford University Press, 2000), 29–50.

9. Peter Lake, "Puritanism, Arminianism and a Shropshire Axe-Murder, *Midland History* 15 (1990): 37–64; idem, "Deeds against Nature: Cheap Print, Protestantism and Murder in Early Modern England," in *Culture and Politics in Early Stuart England,* ed. Peter Lake and Kevin Sharpe (Stanford, Calif.: Stanford University Press, 1994). Alexandra Walsham, *Providence in Early Modern England* (Oxford: Oxford University Press, 1999).

10. So wrote a Mr. Poole in 1657, Cambridge University Library Ms. Dd.3.64, f. 136. Cf. John Taylor, *A Delicate, Dainty, Damnable Dialogue* (1642), Sig. A2, where diabolical conspirators gloat in verse: "We have sow'd false distrusts and iealousies, / Mad tumults, libells, base reports and lies: / And over all the land we caused to flee, / Ten thousand pamphlets (all as false as we)."

11. [John Locke], *A Strange and Lamentable Accident that happened lately at Mears Ashby in Northamptonshire* (1642), Sig. A3; [Edward Fleetwood], *A Declaration, of a strange and Wonderfull Monster: Born in Kirkham Parish in Lancashire* (1646), title page, 8.

12. *The Lofty Bishop, The Lazy Brownist, and the Loyal Author* (1640), broadsheet; Richard [or John] Bernard, *A Short View of the Praelaticall Church of England* (1641), 16; William Prynne, *A New Discovery of the Prelates Tyranny* (1641), 1.

13. [John Wilde], *The Impeachment Against the Bishops* (1641), 3; Mary Anne Everett Green, ed., *The Diary of John Rous, Incumbent of Santon Downham, Suffolk, from 1625 to 1642* (London: Camden Society, 1856), 102; "Dialogue between two Zealots" in *The Decoy Duck: Together with the Discovery of the Knot in the Dragons Tayle* (1642). (There is another copy of this dialogue in Durham University Library Special Collections, Mickleton-Spearman Ms. 9, vol. II, f. 102.) See also John Vicars, *Jehovah-Jireh. God in the Mount* (London: Paine and Simmons, 1644), 38, for further reference to "that monstrous et-cetera oath . . . happily stifled in the embryo of it, ere it could come to birth."

14. *The Lofty Bishop,* broadsheet; *Rules to Get Children By with Handsome Faces* (1642), Sig. A4.

15. *The Soundheads Description of the Roundhead* (1642), title page; Matthew Wren, "Of the Origin and Progress of the Revolutions in England," in vol. 1 of *Collectanea Curiosa,* ed. John Gutch (Oxford, 1781), 231.

16. British Library, Add. Ms. 11045, vol. V, f. 122, Rossingham newsletter, 7 October 1640; Edward Hyde, Lord Clarendon, *The History of the Rebellion and Civil Wars*, vol. 1. (Oxford: Clarendon Press, 1888), 188.

17. Durham University Library Special Collections, Mickleton-Spearman Ms. 9, vol. 2, f. 122.

18. Richard Parkinson, ed., *The Life of Adam Martindale, Written by Himself*, Chetham Society Publications, 4th ser. (Manchester: Manchester University Press, 1845), 184; Huntington Library Ms. HM 55603, "William Drake's Journal," December 1641. Cf. the regicide Sir Hardress Waller's characterization of Leveller protests in 1649 as "these late monstrous revolts," Folger Ms. X.d.483, no. 38.

19. British Library Ms. Stowe 184, f. 31.

20. *Heads of All Fashions* (1642), 2; *Soundheads Description of the Roundhead*, 2.

21. *Mistris Parliament Brought to Bed of a Monstrous Childe of Reformation* (1648), 8; *Mistris Parliament Presented in the Bed . . . in the Birth of her Monstrous Off-spring, the Childe of Deformation* (1648), title page. See also the mock list of forces raised on behalf of Parliament, which has Lord Kimbolton contributing "twenty horses without heads," Durham University Library Special Collections, Mickleton-Spearman Ms. 9, vol. II, f. 257.

22. Other reports include *Signes and wonders from Heaven. With a true Relation of a Monster borne in Ratcliffe Highway* (1645), and *The Most Strange and Wounderfull apperation of blood in a poole at Garraton . . . as also The true relation of a miraculous and prodigious birth in Shoo-lane, where one Mistris Browne a Cutlers wife was delivered of a monster without a head or feet* (1645).

23. David Cressy, *Birth, Marriage and Death: Ritual, Religion and the Life Cycle in Tudor and Stuart England* (Oxford: Oxford University Press, 1997), 124–48. For violent conflicts about baptism with the sign of the cross in an Essex parish in 1642, see Bodleian Library, Rawlinson Ms. D 158, ff. 43v–44.

24. Rough masons were the least literate of all occupations, and their wives were rarely able to read or write. David Cressy, *Literacy and the Social Order: Reading and Writing in Tudor and Stuart England* (Cambridge: Cambridge University Press, 1980).

25. William Prynne, *A New Discovery of the Prelates Tyranny* (London, 1641), 108; John Vicars, *A Looking-Glasse for Malignants: or, Gods hand against God-haters* (1643), 15–16.

26. For example, the Norfolk Quarter Sessions Rolls record that Rachel Mercy of Fakenham told her neighbors in 1643 that "there is no king, no laws, nor or justice . . . because the king was not where he should be." And in 1644 Miles Cushion of Fincham, by trade a knacker, said in his cups that "the king is no king, he is a bastard, and was crowned with a leaden crown." Norfolk Record Office, Norwich: C/S/34, bundles 3 and 4.

27. Cf. the illustration in John Geninges, *The Life and Death of Mr. E. Geninges* (St. Omer, 1614), reproduced in Cressy, *Birth, Marriage and Death*.

28. *The Ranters Monster: Being a True Relation of one Mary Adams* (1652), title page. No study has yet attempted to trace the local background of this report from Tillingham, Essex.

29. Malcolm Letts, ed., *Mandeville's Travels: Texts and Translations*, vol. 2, Hakluyt Society Publications, 2d ser., vol. 101 (London: Hakluyt Society, 1953), 479; P. Hamelius, *Mandeville's Travels* (London: Early English Text Society, 1919), 133. Pliny had written of the "Blemmyae," a headless race with faces in their chests; J. Newsome, ed., *Pliny's Natural History: A Selection from Philemon Holland's Translation*

(Oxford: Clarendon Press, 1964), 43. See also Othello's tales of "men whose heads do grow beneath their shoulders," William Shakespeare, *Othello,* Act I, scene 3.

30. [John Taylor], *The Diseases of the Times* [1641], Sig. A3v. On women petitioners, see Dorothy Gardiner, ed., *The Oxinden Letters 1607–1642* (London: Constable, 1933), 285.

31. "Pigg's Coranto," Durham University Library Special Collections, Mickleton-Spearman Ms. vol. II, p.136.

32. Historical Manuscripts Commission, *Seventh Report* (London, 1879), 439.

33. The claim of Parliamentary authorization is made in the pamphlet itself. No independent verification can be found, so the possibility remains that the pamphlet was an independent journalistic enterprise, capitalizing on the concerns of the moment.

34. Vicars, *Looking-Glasse for Malignants,* 15–16; idem, *Jehovah-Jireh,* 430–31. Another account, derived from previous publications, appeared in *Five Wonders Seen in England* (1646), 5–6 (also published by Jane Coe). The description—"without a head, as the midwife had said, only the child had a face upon the breast of it, two eyes near unto the place where the paps usually are, and a nose upon the chest, and a mouth a little above the navel, and two ears, upon each shoulder one"—is remarkably similar to that of the headless monster born in Gascony in 1562 depicted in Ambroise Paré, *Des Monstres et Prodiges* (Paris, 1573).

35. John Vicars, *Prodigies & Apparitions. Or Englands Warning Pieces* (1643), 5, 11, 20–26. Cf. Mr. Poole's scheme of 1657 to create a national register of "illustrious providences," free from "false and foolish and unwitnessed fictions," Cambridge University Library Ms. Dd.3.64, f. 136. For the American monsters, see *Newes from New-England* (1642); *Antinomians and familists Condemned* (1644); *A Short Story of the Rise, Reign, and Ruine of the Antinomians* (1644). Reports of alleged monstrous births to Mary Dyer and Anne Hutchinson also spread by oral report. See Richard S. Dunn and Laetitia Yeandle, eds., *The Journal of John Winthrop, 1630–1649* (Cambridge, Mass.: Harvard University Press, 1996), 253–55, 264–66; Anne Jacobson Schutte, "'Such Monstrous Births': A Neglected Aspect of the Antinomian Controversy," *Renaissance Quarterly* 38 (1985): 85–106.

36. Northamptonshire Record Office, ZA 3710, Manor Court Rolls of Mears Ashby, 1639–48; Victoria County History, *Northamptonshire,* vol. 4 (1937): 129–32; David Hall, *The Open Fields of Northamptonshire,* Northamptonshire Record Society publications, vol. 38 (Northamptonshire Record Society, 1995), 136, 177, 180; Northamptonshire Record Office, X2159, f. 135. George Lawson was vicar of Mears Ashby in the late 1630s, but plays no part in this story.

37. A. G. Matthews, *Walker Revised. Being a Revision of John Walker's Sufferings of the Clergy during the Grand Rebellion 1642–60* (Oxford: Clarendon Press, 1948), 281. Lawson was sequestered as a malignant in 1644, and was later examined for his privity to a Royalist rebellion.

38. Henry Isham Longden, *Northamptonshire and Rutland Clergy from 1500,* vol. 9 (Northampton: Archer and Goodman, 1938), 19; idem, *Addenda* (Northampton: Archer and Goodman, 1952), 89; William George Walker, *A History of Oundle School* (London: Hazell Watson and Viney, 1956), 126–27; Joan Wake, ed., *Quarter Sessions Records of the County of Northampton: Files for 6 Charles I and Commonwealth* Northamptonshire Record Society, 1 1924), 11; John Venn and J. A. Venn, *Alumni Cantabrigienses: a Biographical List of All Known Students, Graduates and Holders of Office at the University of Cam-*

bridge, from the Earliest Times to 1900, 2 pts. in 10 vols. (Cambridge: Cambridge University Press, 1922–1954).

39. Ovid, *Metamorphoses*, I, 7, describing the original chaos of the world.

40. Longden, *Northamptonshire and Rutland Clergy*, 2:27; Northamptonshire Record Office, X 2159, f. 132v; A. G. Matthews, *Calamy Revised: Being a Revision of Edmund Calamy's Account of the Ministers and Others Ejected and Silenced, 1660–2* (Oxford: Clarendon Press, 1934), 40.

41. Roy Sherwood, *The Civil War in the Midlands 1642–1651* (Wolfeboro Falls, N.H.: Alan Sutton, 1992) 21, 25, 87, 98, 146; *Calendar of State Papers Domestic, 1641–43,* 371–73, 379, 383–87.

42. *Mercurius Aulicus*, 12–23 December 1643, quoted in Joad Raymond, ed., *Making the News: An Anthology of the Newsbooks of Revolutionary England, 1641–1660* (New York: St. Martin's Press, 1993), 106–7.

43. Henry Fishwick, *The History of the Parish of Kirkham in the County of Lancashire* (Chetham Society, 1874), 26.

44. Ibid., 97. Plague deaths in 1631 were 304, including 193 in August and September, R. Cunliffe Shaw and Helen G. Shaw, eds., *The Records of the Thirty Men of the Parish of Kirkham in Lancashire* (n.p.: Kendal, 1930), 21.

45. Historical Manuscripts Commission, *Twelfth Report: The Manuscripts of the Earl Cowper*, vol. 2 (London, 1888), 77, 80.

46. Fishwick, *History of the Parish of Kirkham*, 36, 44, 72–74, 80; R. C. Shaw, *Kirkham in Amounderness* (Preston: R. Seed and Sons, 1949), 148–49; W. K. Jordan, *The Social Institutions of Lancashire: A Study of the Changing Patterns of Aspirations in Lancashire 1480–1660*, Chetham Society Publications, 3d ser., vol. 11 (Manchester: Manchester University Press, 1962), 57–58.

47. Fishwick, *History of the Parish of Kirkham*, 36, 101, 139; John Bossy, *The English Catholic Community 1570–1850* (London: Darton, Longman and Todd, 1975), 126, 182–94, 404–5.

48. House of Lords Record Office, Protestation Returns for Lancashire, Amounderness Hundred, Kirkham. David Cressy, "The Protestation Protested, 1641 and 1642," *The Historical Journal*, 45.2 (2002), 251–79.

49. Fishwick, *History of the Parish of Kirkham*, 77, 98–102; R. Cunliffe Shaw and Helen G. Shaw, eds., *Records of the Thirty Men* (n.p.: Kendal, 1930), 22–31; Borthwick Institute, York, Metropolitical Visitation 1633, Diocese of Chester, R. VI. A. 23, f. 205v.

50. Fishwick, *History of the Parish of Kirkham*, 77–80, 102; Shaw and Shaw, *Records of the Thirty Men*, 31–4; Lancashire Record Office, Quarter Sessions Recognizances, QSB/1/245/24, 36, 38.

51. R. Sharpe France, ed., *The Parish Registers of Kirkham: Part II, 1601–1653* (Preston: Lancashire Parish Register Society, 1960), 182, 184. The Recusant Houghtons do not appear in this register.

52. Fishwick, *History of the Parish of Kirkham*, 36, 76; Shaw, *Kirkham in Amounderness*, 154; House of Lords Record Office, Protestation Returns.

53. See the entry for More in the *Dictionary of National Biography*.

54. Fishwick, *History of the Parish of Kirkham*, 140. See also Charles Carlton, *Going to the Wars: The Experience of the British Civil Wars, 1638–1651* (New York: Routledge, 1992).

55. Fishwick, *History of the Parish of Kirkham*, 25–26; Ernest Broxap, *The Great Civil War in Lancashire 1642–1651* (Manchester: Manchester University Press, 1910), 86, 132; William Beaumont, *A Dis-*

course of the War in Lancashire, Chetham Society Publications, 62d ser. (Manchester: Manchester University Press, 1864), 20–38, 55–56, 61; Vicars, *Jehovah-Jireh,* 268–69.

56. Cf. Henry Burton, A *Divine Tragedie Lately Acted* (London?: n.p., 1641). By contrast, the conformist minister Nathaniel Ward wrote in 1641 that "I trust in God I shall burn at a faggot before I so far forget myself as to frame my tenets the presbyterical way," British Library, Ms. Stowe 184, f. 4, but he is not known to have met a martyr's end; Walsham, *Providence in Early Modern England,* passim.

Chapter 3. A Time for Monsters

1. I have used the following critical edition: Sebastian Brant, *Narrenschiff,* edited by Friedrich Zarncke (Darmstadt: Wissenschaftliche Buchgesellschaft, 1964).

2. "Das kind man oftenlich hatt gesehen / Das zwey kopf trug auff einem leib / Das mit an zaygt wie ich oben schreib / Die kurfursten hie vorzertrennt / wurden in einen leib verwendt / Vn das beyd haupt der welt gemeyn / Zusamen sollen kummen eyn / Vnd in ein leib sambt werden bracht." This broadsheet is reprinted in Irene Ewinkel, *De Monstris: Deutung und Funktion von Wundergeburten auf Flugblättern im Deutschland des 16. Jahrhunderts* (Tübingen: M. Niemeyer, 1995), 365.

3. "Das ich in sunders dar auff acht / Dan yetz bey Wurms gleich an die stat / Die der gemainen kristenhay / zu frid helffen vnnd eynikait . . . Ich gedenck es hab allain ein hirn / vnnd eyn verstentnuss in sein haubt / dar auff ich warlich hab geglaubt / Das got die zeit geben woll / das sich das reich verainen soll." Ibid.

4. On the military and diplomatic background, see Horst Rabe, *Deutsche Geschichte 1500–1600: Das Jahrhundert der Glaubensspaltung* (Munich: C. H. Beck, 1991), 178–82.

5. Ibid., 182ff. On the problematic of Imperial diets and political reforms, see Heinz Angermeier, *Die Reichsreform 1410–1555: Die Staatsproblematik in Deutschland zwischen Mittelalter und Gegenwart* (Munich: C. H. Beck, 1984).

6. Gerald Strauss, ed. and trans., *Manifestations of Discontent in Germany on the Eve of the Reformation* (Bloomington: Indiana University Press, 1971), 32–34.

7. On Brant's role in 1512, see Georg Schmidt, *Der Städtetag in der Reichsverfassung: Eine Untersuchung zur Korporativen Politik der Freien und Reichsstädte in der ersten Hälfte des 16. Jahrhunderts* (Stuttgart: Franz Steiner, 1984), 127, 202.

8. Brant, *Narrenschiff,* 14 and notes to 319–20.

9. For modern scholarship on the Drummer of Niklashausen, see the authoritative study by Klaus Arnold, *Niklashausen 1476* (Baden-Baden: Valentin Koerner, 1980) and the popular narrative by Richard Wunderli, *Peasant Fires: The Drummer of Niklashausen* (Bloomington: Indiana University Press, 1992).

10. See Dieter Wuttke, "Sebastian Brants Verhältnis zu Wunderdeutung und Astrologie," and "Sebastian Brant und Maximilian I: Eine Studie zu Brants Donnerstein-Flugblatt des Jahres 1492." Both collected in Dieter Wuttke, *Dazwischen: Kulturwissenschaft auf Warburgs Spuren,* 2 vols. (Baden-Baden: V. Koerner, 1996), 1:195–212, 213–250.

11. Brant, *Narrenschiff,* chaps. 88, 85: "Eyn narr ist, wer für wunder heltt / Das gott der herr, yetz strafft die welt."

12. Ibid., chap. 88: "Man sah alleyn an jüdisch landt / was sie durch sünd verloren hant / Wie dyck

sie gott vertriben hatt / durch sünden, vfz der heyligen statt / Die krysten hant das ouch verloren / Do sie verdienten gottes zorn."

13. Lorraine Daston and Katharine Park, *Wonders and the Order of Nature 1150–1750* (New York: Zone Books, 1998), 176.

14. Ibid., 187.

15. There is copious literature on this. Still a good introduction is Willy Andreas, *Deutschland vor der Reformation: Eine Zeitenwende,* 6th ed. (Berlin: Duncker & Humblot, 1972).

16. "Das ist nu diese letzte vnd unsere zeit / da das Evangelium erschollen ist / vnd schreiet wider den Bapst / das er verzweiuelt / weis nicht wie vnd was er thun sol." Hanz Volz, ed., *D. Martin Luther, Biblia: Das ist ganze Heilige Schrifft deutsch auffs new zugericht,* 3 vols. (Munich: dtv, 1974), 1530.

17. On Cochlaeus, see David V. N. Bagchi, *Luther's Earliest Opponents: Catholic Controversialists 1518–1525* (Minneapolis: Fortress Press, 1991). On the propaganda surrounding Luther, see also Mark U. Edwards, *Printing, Propaganda, and Martin Luther* (Berkeley: University of California Press, 1994).

18. Ewinkel, *De Monstris,* 365.

19. Ibid., 359.

20. The best book on Reformation propaganda remains Robert W. Scribner, *For the Sake of Simple Folk: Popular Propaganda for the German Reformation* (Cambridge: Cambridge University Press, 1981).

21. *D. Martin Luthers Werke, Kritische Gesamtausgabe: Tischreden 5. Band,* 101 vols. (Weimar: Böhlaus, 1883–), nos. 6379, 6380. Hereafter cited as *WA Tr* for *Tischreden* and *WA Br* for *Briefwechsel.*

22. *WA Tr* 4, no. 4773.

23. *WA Br* 11, no. 115.

24. *WA Tr* 6, no. 6779.

25. See Steven E. Ozment, *Homo Spiritualis: A Comparative Study of the Anthropology of Johannes Tauler, Jean Gerson, and Martin Luther (1509–1516)* (Leiden: Brill, 1969).

26. *WA Tr* 6, no. 6779.

27. The idea that monstrous progeny resulted from the disorder of the maternal imagination was attributed to Empedocles and transmitted in the writings of Aristotle. For the exposition of the theory of monstrosity as the creation of maternal imagination, see Marie-Hélène Huet, *Monstrous Imagination* (Cambridge, Mass.: Harvard University Press, 1993).

28. *WA Tr* 1, no. 323.

29. Cited in Jean Céard, *La Nature et les prodiges: L'Insolite au XVIe siècle en France* (Geneva: Droz, 1977), 83–84. "Lorsque Luther prit la religion / Des Augustins en humaine semblance / Son visage fut sans corruption / Qu'il a pollu par son oultre cuidance / Car ce monster demonstre sa presence / A tous humains difficile et estrange / Car il s'est mis de vices en la fange / Dont congnoissons, et saiges et sciens / Plus que pierres sont durs Saxoniens / Qui estiment que ce monster soit vain / Point ne lairront leurs pechez antiens / Tant qu'ilz sentient du hault juge la main."

30. *Ein wunderbarliche seltzame erschröckliche Geburt* (Augsburg: Michael Moser, 1561). Image and text reprinted, 175 and 374, in Petra Schöner, *Judenbilder im Deutschen Einblattdruck der Renaissance: Ein Beitrag zur Imagologie,* Saecula spiritalia 42 (Baden-Baden: Valentin Koerner, 2002).

31. *Warhafftige vnnd erschröckliche Geburt / so von einer Jüdin in der weitberümbten Statt Venedig den*

26 Maij / Anno 1575. geschehen vnnd entpfangen worden. Den Ehrliebenden Teutschen zu gutem / auss Italienischer sprach in Teutsch getrewlich versetzt (Heidelberg: Michael Schirat, 1575). Reprinted text and image in Schöner, *Judenbilder,* 176, 375.

32. Cited in Johannes Janssen, *Geschichte des Deutschen Volkes,* vol. 6 (St. Louis: Herder, 1917), 428.

33. Céard, *La Nature et les prodiges,* 265–72.

34. Cited ibid., 272. "Testis erit nobis, testis Germania: / quae cum se Christo opposuit perjuri fraude Lutheri, / Saxonia innumera monstrorum prole referta. / Condoluit, justas ac sensit numinis iras."

35. *Ecclesia Militans: Ein wunderbarlicher gegenwurff / der Euangelischen Fürbildung / was yetziger zeit / die bestreitbar / heilig / Christlich kirchen / von allerly Ketzern / jhren erczfeinden vnd grewlichsten widersachern / dultig erleidt / vnnd durch Gottes Gnad vberstehe etc.* ([Ingolstadt: Alexander Weissenhorn], 1569). Text and image reproduced in Schöner, *Judenbilder,* 206, 381–90.

36. See Robin B. Barnes, *Prophecy and Gnosis: Apocalypticism in the Wake of the Lutheran Reformation* (Stanford, Calif.: Stanford University Press, 1988).

37. Ewinkel, *De Monstris,* 298.

38. "Was aber Gott der Allmechtig mit disem wunderwerck / auch andern wunderzeichen / so wir taglich horen vnd sehen / deutet / ist im allein wissend."

39. Ibid., 300.

40. "Solche wunderbarliche vnd vbernaturliche erschrockliche Geburt / haben nicht allein die Kirchendiener vnd der Schultheiss obgemelts orts / sonder fast die gantze Gemeind doselbsten sampt andern vmbligenden Flecken vnd Dorffern / etlich hundert personen gesehen. Was aber solche seltzame vnd vbernaturliche Geburt bedeut oder anzeyg / konnen wir eygentlich nicht wissen / ist aber hoch zuvermuten / dieweyl sich auch sonst erschrockliche zeychen am himmel vnd andern elementen inn disem '69. Jar zugetragen / es werde ohn sonderliche bedeutung / straff vnnd vngluck nicht abgehn / Lasst derhalben vnns Gott der Herr durch solche zeychen warnen vnd zur Buss vermanen."

41. Ewinkel, *De Monstris,* 71.

42. Ibid., 79–80.

43. Ibid., 89.

44. See R. Po-chia Hsia, *Social Discipline in the Reformation: Central Europe 1550–1750* (New York: Routledge, 1989).

Chapter 4. "The Antichrist, the Babilon, the great dragon"

1. A transcription of all the texts and explanations of the meaning of the images in the engraving, in relation to the original drawing by Francis Barlow now in the Huntington, can be found in Robert Wark, *Early British Drawings in the Huntington Collection, 1600–1750* (San Marino, Calif.: The Huntington Library, 1969), 15–17. Although I differ from what he sees as the ambiguous, even subversive nature of the engraving, Bruce Lawson nonetheless offers detailed and helpful commentary in "The Body as a Political Construct; Oliver Cromwell's Image in William Faithorne's 1658 Emblematic Engraving," in *Deviceful Settings: The English Renaissance Emblem and Its Contexts,* ed. Michael Bath and Daniel Russell (New York: AMS Press, 1993), 113–38. Lawson argues that the beauty of the harlot upon whom

Cromwell stands undermines his heroism: I shall argue that her beauty is in fact a more dangerous because less discernable monstrosity than that of the dragon/serpent which Cromwell has also defeated.

2. On Cromwellian portraiture more broadly, see my *Constructing Cromwell: Ceremony, Portrait,
and Print, 1645–1661* (Cambridge: Cambridge University Press, 2000).

3. In an important recent book, Frances E. Dolan looks at uses of the Whore of Babylon in
seventeenth-century anti-Catholic polemic surrounding the Gunpowder Plot (1605), Queen Henrietta
Maria's advocacy of Catholicism in the 1630s, and the Popish and Meal Tub plots (1678–80). See *Whores
of Babylon: Catholicism, Gender, and Seventeenth-Century Print Culture* (Ithaca, N.Y.: Cornell University
Press, 1999).

4. Oliver Cromwell, *The Writings and Speeches of Oliver Cromwell*, ed. W. C. Abbott, 4 vols. (Cambridge, Mass.: Harvard University Press, 1937–47), 2:199.

5. Letter of 20 September 1650, in *Original Letters and Papers of State addressed to Oliver Cromwell*,
ed. John Nickolls (London: William Bowyer, 1743), 23.

6. Letter of September 1650, ibid., 24.

7. *A Declaration of the English Army now in Scotland, to the People of Scotland, especially those among
them, that know and fear the Lord* (1650), 3, 4.

8. Ibid., 7.

9. Steven C. A. Pincus, *Protestantism and Patriotism: Ideologies and the Making of English Foreign
Policy, 1650–1668* (Cambridge: Cambridge University Press, 1996). Some aspects of Pincus's ground-
breaking thesis have been challenged by Jonathan Israel, whose own work represents economic and commercial rivalries as central to the outbreak of hostilities. See Israel, *Dutch Primacy in World Trade, 1585–
1740* (Oxford: Clarendon Press, 1989), 197–213, and Israel's omnibus review, "England, the Dutch Republic, and Europe in the Seventeenth Century," *Historical Journal* 40, no. 4 (1997): 1117–21.

10. Cromwell, *Writings and Speeches*, 3:64.

11. John Rogers, *Dod or Chathan. The Beloved; or, The Bridegroom going forth for his Bride* (London,
1653), 5.

12. Ibid., 16.

13. On the Fifth Monarchists, see Bernard Capp, *The Fifth Monarchy Men: A Study in Seventeenth-
Century English Millenarianism* (Totowa, N.J.: Rowman and Littlefield, 1972).

14. On the widespread expectations of Christ's imminent return, continuing into the late seventeenth century, see Christopher Hill, *Antichrist in Seventeenth-Century England* (London: Oxford University Press, 1971) and William Lamont, *Richard Baxter and the Millennium: Protestant Imperialism and
the English Revolution* (London: Croom Helm, 1979).

15. Roger L'Estrange, *Dissenters Sayings, The Second Part* (London, 1681), 61.

16. "An intercepted Letter from London, 20 Oct. 1653," in *A Collection of the State Papers of John
Thurloe*, ed. Thomas Birch, 7 vols. (London, 1742), 2:534.

17. Ibid.

18. Ibid.

19. "An intercepted Letter of Sir W. Vane," 25 November 1653, Thurloe, *State Papers*, 1:612.

20. "An intercepted Letter," 2 December 1653, ibid., 621.

21. The text of the Instrument of Government is reproduced in *The Constitutional Documents of the*

Puritan Revolution, 1625–1660, ed. S. R. Gardiner (Oxford: Clarendon Press, 1906), 405–17. On this written constitution, see Austin Woolrych, *Commonwealth to Protectorate* (Oxford: Clarendon Press, 1982), 352–86.

22. *Strange and Wonderful Newes from White-Hall: or, The Mighty Visions Proceeding from Mistris Anna Trapnel* (London, 1654), 4.

23. Ibid., 5.

24. Ibid., 5–6.

25. "A Vindication against the Complaints of Mr. Rogers, addressed to Edward Dandy, Esq," 2 February 1655, Thurloe, *State Papers,* 3:136.

26. Ibid.

27. [John Hall], *Confusion Confounded . . . Wherein Is Considered the Reasons of the Resignation of the late Parlament, and the Establishment of A Lord Protector* (January 1654), 3.

28. *Strena Vavasoriensis, A New-Years-Gift for the Welch Itinerants, or, a Hue and Cry after Mr. Vavasor Powell* (January 1654), 5.

29. Andrew Marvell, in *The Poems and Letters of Andrew Marvell,* ed. H. M. Margoliouth, 3d ed., rev. Pierre Legouis with E. E. Duncan-Jones, vol. 1 (Oxford: Clarendon Press, 1971), 108–119. Cited by line number in the text.

30. Valuable political readings of Marvell's *First Anniversary,* albeit focused on domestic politics rather than international relations, include Derek Hirst, "'That sober Liberty': Marvell's Cromwell in 1654," in *The Golden and the Brazen World: Papers in Literature and History, 1650–1800,* ed. John M. Wallace (Berkeley: University of California Press, 1985), 17–53; M. L. Donnelly, "'And still new stopps to various time apply'd': Marvell, Cromwell and the Problem of Representation at Midcentury," in *On the Celebrated and Neglected Poems of Andrew Marvell,* ed. Claude J. Summers and Ted-Larry Pebworth (Columbia: University of Missouri Press, 1992), 154–68; Joad Raymond, "Framing Liberty: Marvell's *First Anniversary* and the Instrument of Government," *Huntington Library Quarterly* 62 (1999): 313–50; and David Loewenstein, *Representing Revolution in Milton and his Contemporaries: Religion, Politics, and Polemics in Radical Puritanism* (Cambridge: Cambridge University Press, 2001), 143–71. See also my *Constructing Cromwell,* 98–102.

31. Margarita Stocker posits a belief in the imminent return of Christ as central to this poem and to Marvell's work more broadly, in *Apocalyptic Marvell: The Second Coming in Seventeenth Century Poetry* (Brighton, Sussex: Harvester Press, 1986); extending this for the *First Anniversary,* Gayla S. McGlamery suggests that Marvell presents a complex vision, keeping one eye on immediate turbulent politics and the other on eternity, in "The Rhetoric of Apocalypse and Practical Politics in Marvell's 'The First Anniversary of the Government under O. C.,'" *South Atlantic Review* 55, no. 4 (1990): 19–35. Annabel Patterson points to the highly conditional language and the unusual placement to argue that the apocalyptic is contained, even undercut, by other elements of the poem, *Marvell and the Civic Crown* (Princeton, N.J.: Princeton University Press, 1978). Hirst, "That sober Liberty," however, points out that Cromwell's own conditional language echoes that of the biblical texts.

32. "Cromwellian foreign policy" is the phrase used in the recent book-length study of the subject by Timothy Venning; other historians prefer "New Model foreign policy" or "Protectoral foreign policy." Under the Instrument of Government, the Protector was responsible for foreign relations and could

declare war or peace, subject to the consent of the Council. The very rare Council minutes that survive show some debate on foreign policy. At times Cromwell's comments to foreign ambassadors indicated an independence in foreign affairs; but with no experience and little facility even in the languages of diplomacy, Cromwell likely relied heavily on his secretary of state, John Thurloe, and on the more experienced members of the Council.

33. A good overview of the critical history, structure, and content of Revelation, with particular attention to apocalypticism, can be found in Adela Yarbro Collins, "The Book of Revelation," in *The Encyclopedia of Apocalypticism,* ed. John J. Collins, vol. 1 (New York: Continuum, 1998), 384–414. Useful exegesis can be found in Frederick Murphy, *Fallen is Babylon: The Revelation to John* (Harrisburg, Pa.: Trinity Press International, 1998).

34. On the history of interpretation of Revelation, see Bernard McGinn, "Revelation," in *The Literary Guide to the Bible,* ed. Robert Alter and Frank Kermode (Cambridge, Mass.: The Belknap Press of Harvard University Press, 1987), 523–41.

35. On Luther and Revelation, see Hans-Ulrich Hofmann, *Luther und die Johannes-Apokalypse* (Tübingen: Mohr, 1982).

36. See Mary Douglas, *Purity and Danger: An Analysis of the Concepts of Pollution and Taboo* (London: Routledge and Kegan Paul, 1966); and Paul Duff, *Who Rides the Beast? Prophetic Rivalry and the Rhetoric of Crisis in the Churches of the Apocalypse* (New York: Oxford University Press, 2001), chapter 8. While Duff's argument that the monstrous imagery is primarily aimed at a prophetic rival, "Jezebel," may understate the threat and experience of the Roman Empire, he very usefully comments on the gender stereotypes and violation of taboos in Revelation.

37. On Babylon as economic critique, see Richard Bauckham, "The Economic Critique of Rome in Revelation 18," in *Images of Empire,* ed. Alexander Loveday (Sheffield: JSOT Press, 1991), 47–90.

38. On the Whore of Babylon and questions of gender in particular, see Adela Yarbro Collins, *The Combat Myth in the Book of Revelation* (Missoula, Mont.: Scholars Press, 1976), and her "Feminine Symbolism in the Book of Revelation," *Biblical Interpretation* 1 (1993): 20–33; Tina Pippin, *Death and Desire: The Rhetoric of Gender in the Apocalypse of John* (Louisville, Ky.: Westminster Press, 1992); and Barbara R. Rossing, *The Choice between Two Cities: Whore, Bride, and Empire in the Apocalypse* (Harrisburg, Pa.: Trinity Press International, 1999).

39. On the use of monstrous births in German Reformation polemic, see R. Po-chia Hsia, "A Time for Monsters," above.

40. See, for instance, Robin Bruce Barnes, *Prophecy and Gnosis: Apocalypticism in the Wake of the Lutheran Reformation* (Stanford, Calif.: Stanford University Press, 1988)

41. Mark U. Edwards, *Printing, Propaganda, and Martin Luther* (Berkeley: University of California Press, 1994), 27. The move into history and immediate polemical identification continued in illustrations that inserted contemporary political figures into the biblical text, for instance, showing Maximilian, Charles V, and the Archduke Ferdinand worshiping the Beast from the Sea in Revelation. See Barnes, *Prophecy and Gnosis,* 55; Robert Scribner, *For the Sake of Simple Folk: Popular Propaganda for the German Reformation* (Cambridge: Cambridge University Press, 1981), 69–75, 185–89.

42. The first Reformation Bible in English, William Tyndale's translation, was highly dependent on Luther in its layout and visual illustrations. David Daniell writes that "Anyone familiar with Luther's

splendid 1522 testament sees the resemblance at once. Though Tyndale's book is a small quarto, against Luther's handsome folio, he has the same page layout, similar woodcuts, parallel marginal texts, and an introductory list of New Testament books which is identical in order and layout," "William Tyndale, the English Bible, and the English Language," in *The Bible as Book: The Reformation,* ed. Orlaith O'Sullivan (London: British Library and Oak Knoll Press, 2000), 42. For commentary on the illustrations of English Bibles and on the possible significance of the omission of the papal tiara in these images, see Tatiana C. String, "Politics and Polemics in English and German Bible Illustrations," ibid., 137–44.

43. On this point, see Margoliouth, *Poems and Letters of Andrew Marvell,* 1:326–27.

44. See, for instance, the speculation of foreign correspondents in Thurloe, *State Papers,* 2:592, 595–96, 606–7, 642; 3:7, 11–12.

45. For historical commentary on the Western Design, see Charles P. Korr, *Cromwell and the New Model Foreign Policy: England's Policy Toward France, 1649–1658* (Berkeley: University of California Press, 1975), chap. 11; Karen Ordahl Kupperman, "Errand to the Indies: Puritan Colonization from Providence Island through the Western Design," *William and Mary Quarterly* 45 (1988): 70–99; Timothy Venning, *Cromwellian Foreign Policy* (New York: St. Martin's Press, 1995), chap. 5; David Armitage, "The Cromwellian Protectorate and the Languages of Empire," *Historical Journal* 35, no. 3 (1992): 537–44.

46. *The Clarke Papers,* ed. C. H. Firth, vol. 3 (London: Camden Society, 1899), 203–8.

47. Ibid., 205.

48. For the former, see Pincus, *Protestantism and Patriotism;* for Cromwellian policy regarding Spain and elsewhere as infused with both Protestant ideology and pragmatism, see Venning, *Cromwellian Foreign Policy,* chap. 1. This debate will be further discussed below.

49. Cited in Kupperman, "Errand to the Indies," 91.

50. Abbott, *Writings and Speeches,* 3:859–60.

51. Primary sources on the Western Design include C. H. Firth, ed., *The Narrative of General Venables* (London: Camden Society, 1900); Granville Penn, ed., *The Memorials of the Professional Life and Times of Sir William Penn,* 2 vols. (London, 1833); and I. A. Wright, ed., *Spanish Narratives of the English Attack on Santo Domingo, 1655* (London: Camden Society, 1926).

52. On the severe spiritual crisis that followed the defeat at Jamaica, see Blair Worden, "Oliver Cromwell and the Sin of Achan," in *History, Society and the Churches: Essays in Honour of Owen Chadwick,* ed. Derek Beales and Geoffrey Best (Cambridge: Cambridge University Press, 1985), 125–45.

53. On the Treaty of Westminster, see Korr, *Cromwell and the New Model Foreign Policy,* chap. 13; and Venning, *Cromwellian Foreign Policy,* 110–12.

54. See Venning, *Cromwellian Foreign Policy,* chaps. 4, 8, 9, and 10, and the details in James Breck Perkins, *France under Mazarin,* vol. 2 (Boston: Houghton Mifflin, 1886), esp. chap. 16, "The War with Spain and the Treaty with England," 246–301.

55. Slingsby Bethel, *The World's Mistake in Oliver Cromwell* (1668), reprinted in *The Harleian Miscellany,* vol. 7 (London: Robert Dutton, 1810), 347–60. While some early historians echo this bias, more recent assessments tend to find a mixture of ideology and national interest shaping foreign relations: see especially Venning, *Cromwellian Foreign Policy,* chap. 1; Roger Crabtree, "The Idea of a Protestant Foreign Policy," in *Cromwell: A Profile,* ed. Ivan Roots (New York: Hill and Wang, 1973), 160–89; and Michael Roberts, "Cromwell and the Baltic," *English Historical Review* 76, no. 300 (1961): 402–46.

56. See Korr, *New Model Foreign Policy*, and Venning, *Cromwellian Foreign Policy.*

57. Korr, *New Model Foreign Policy*, 164.

58. See Pieter Geyl, *The Netherlands in the Seventeenth Century, Part Two, 1648–1715* (London: Ernest Benn, 1964), esp. 38–43, and Venning, *Cromwellian Foreign Policy*, chaps. 11 and 12.

59. *Kort Bewerp vande dry Teghenwoordighe aenmerckens-weerdighe Wonderheden des Wereldts die wy in dese onsalighe ysere eeuwebeleven* (Cologne, 1656). For English translations of the Dutch text, I am grateful for the careful work of Harry Boonstra. To my knowledge, this tract has not previously been discussed by scholars of seventeenth-century England and its treatment in Dutch has been only cursory.

60. "Ten eersten, wordt probabel uyt Godts Woordt bewesen, dat wy het uytterste deel vande laetste Eeuwe des wereldts beleven, ende met ons voeten betreden. Ten tweeden, dat *Crom-ghewelt* op den rechten tijdt ghekomen is, te weten, als den oprechten *Anti-christ* aen de wereldt sich moet verthoonen, ende oock soo aerdigh de partije vanden *Antichrist* heeft beghinnen te spelen, met den Koningh van Sweden, ende *Mas-ruin,* als dat oyt ter wereldt iemandt voor hunnen tijdt ghespeelt heeft. Ten derden, wordt bethoont, hoe dat Godt de Godtsalighe bekeeringhe vande illustre *Christina Alexandrina Maria* Koninghinne van Sweden, in dese ysere Eeuwe oock ghestelt heeft op den Theater des wereldts, tot een over-tuyghende beschaemtmaeckinghe vanden Verbondt brekenden Koningh van Sweden, *Crom-ghewelt,* met *Mas-ruin,* ende alle de goddeloose des wereldts van dees y sere Eeuwe," *Kort Bewerp,* title page.

61. "De staeten van Hollant scriecken, voor t'Crom gewelt, / Om dat hÿ als Tÿran nu al de werelt quelt," *Kort Bewerp,* 3.

62. "Doch het volck, die haeren Godt kennen ende vreesen, sullen elckanderen vermaenen, ende de verstandighe inden volcke sullender vele andere leeren, ende daerom sullen sy door de creaturen vanden Antichrist door het vyer, svveerde, ende ghevangherisse vallen, ende gerooft ende gheplundert worden; ghelijck 't *Crom-ghewelt* in Enghelandt, Schotlandt, ende Yrlandt, oock aen de Hollanders, Vriesen, ende Zeeuvven ghedaen heeft, ende noch daghelijeks soeckte doen," *Kort Bewerp,* 16–17.

63. "En is het *Cromwel* niet, die ghelijck vanden Antichrist gheschreven staet, het H. daghelijcksche Sacrificie der Misse de gheheele wereldt door soeckt wegh te nemen door alle sijn creaturen?" *Kort Bewerp,* 17.

64. "Siet hoe Cromt Masruin dien steert vel boos venÿn / t'is Mazarin die seÿt t'moet noch al Crommer syn / Eer Ick de waere kerck kan tonders boven keeren / de staten van hollant naer fransche pÿpen leeren," *Kort Bewerp,* 3.

65. "En verheft hy hem oock niet als Godt, als hy sich van alle Princen ende Potentaten doet eeren ende aen-bidden als eenen Godt op der aerden. Want daer en is niet eenen Ambassadeur soo stoudt, die tot Olij in't vyer Cromt-wel soude dorven komen ter audientie, sonder dry mael voor Cromwel met hunne knien ende aenghesichten ter aerden te buyghen, ende als sy hun af-scheydt nemen, moeten sy achter waerts uyt-gaende met hun aenghesichten naer't Cromme dier ghekeert zijnde, voor dit seven-hoofdigh thien-hoornigh beest wederom dry-mael neder ter aerden buyghen," *Kort Bewerp,* 25.

66. "En ist het seven-hoofdigh thien-hornigh Dier van Enghelandt niet, die alle de af-vallighe vande Roomsche Kercke weet te verdooven, ende te betooveren met schoone woorden ende beloften, ende dreyghhementen, om daer door haer onder sijn tyrannigh Antichristisch ghevveldt te brenghen?" *Kort Bewerp,* 17.

67. "Want al draeght hy den tijtel van Cardinael, daerom en is hy noch gheen Priester Godts: maer ghelijck het seven-hoofdigh thien-hornigh krom-ghe wel-digh dier een vreesbaer verschrickelijck wonderlijck monstreus dier in Enghelandt is, dat het Christendom in ons onsalighe ysere Eeuwe doet schudden ende beven," *Kort Beworp,* 31.

68. "Desen is het tweede beest, den welcken hoornen draeght, ghelijck het lam, ende nochtans ghelijck den draeck sprack: ende sy doet alle de macht vand' eerste beest voor haer, ende sy maeckt dat de aerde, ende die daer in woonen, d'eerste beest aen-bidden, wiens doodelijcke wonde ghenesen was," *Kort Beworp,* 31.

69. A detailed account of Cromwell's relations with the Swedish ambassadors and his attitude toward Charles X can be found in Michael Roberts, introduction to *Swedish Diplomats at Cromwell's Court, 1655–1656,* Camden Society, 4th ser., vol. 36 (London: The Royal Historical Society, 1988). The letters of Peter Julius Coyet and Christer Bonde, translated and edited by Roberts in *Swedish Diplomats,* also provide a rich source of information on England's relations with Sweden and the ensuing tensions with the Dutch and others. As with Cromwellian foreign relations more broadly, the extent to which religious zeal shaped Baltic policies has been debated. Roberts sees pragmatic concerns as well as (not atypical) religious sentiments, in "Cromwell and the Baltic." See also Venning, *Cromwellian Foreign Policy,* chaps. 13 and 14.

70. "En heeft dat kromme Dier den Verbondt-brekenden Koningh van Sweeden met sijn slimme treken mede niet op sijn sijde ghekreghen, met intentie om het Koninghrijck van Polen, jae selfs het Roomsche Keyserrijck gantsch te vernielen, ghelijck hy alreede beghonnen heeft?" *Kort Beworp,* 18.

71. Abbott, *Writings and Speeches,* 4:713–14.

72. Marvell, *An Horatian Ode upon Cromwel's Return from Ireland,* in Margoliouth, *Poems and Letters of Andrew Marvell,* 1:91–93.

Chapter 5. Monstrous Medicine

1. Ambroise Paré, *Des Monstres et prodiges,* ed. Jean Céard (Geneva: Droz, 1971), 3.

2. Nancy G. Siraisi, *Medieval and Early Renaissance Medicine: An Introduction to Knowledge and Practice* (Chicago: University of Chicago Press, 1990), 101.

3. Ibid., 4.

4. Alison Klairmont Lingo, "The Rise of Medical Practitioners in Sixteenth-Century France: The Case of Lyon and Montpellier" (Ph.D. diss., University of California, Berkeley, 1980), 174–231.

5. Ibid., 217.

6. For a discussion of this trial, see Jean Céard's edition of Paré's *Des Monstres,* xiv–xix.

7. Lingo, "The Rise of Medical Practitioners," 208.

8. Paré, *Des Monstres,* 4.

9. Siraisi, *Medieval and Early Renaissance Medicine,* 129.

10. Sachiko Kusukawa, "*Aspectio divinorum operum,* Melanchthon and Astrology for Lutheran Medics," in *Medicine and the Reformation,* ed. Ole Peter Grell and Andrew Cunningham (New York: Routledge, 1993), 34.

11. See Siraisi, *Medieval and Early Renaissance Medicine*, 17–25.

12. See Marie-Hélène Huet, *Monstrous Imagination* (Cambridge, Mass.: Harvard University Press, 1993).

13. See Jurgis Baltrusaitis, "Monstres et emblèmes, une survivance du moyen-âge au 16e et 17e siècles," *Médecine de France* 39 (1953): 17–30; Jean Céard, *La Nature et les prodiges: L'Insolite au XVIe siècle en France* (Geneva: Droz, 1977); Katharine Park and Lorraine J. Daston, "Unnatural Conceptions: The Study of Monsters in Sixteenth- and Seventeenth-Century France and England," *Past and Present*, no. 92 (1981): 20–54; Huet, *Monstrous Imagination*, 13–35.

14. Paré, *Des Monstres*, 103.

15. Ibid., 8.

16. See Fortunii Liceti, *De Monstrorum Caussis, Natura et Differentiis* (Padua, 1616).

17. *Paracelsus, Selected Writings*, ed. and introd. Jolande Jacobi, trans. Norbert Guterman (Princeton, N.J.: Princeton University Press, 1973), 19.

18. Paré, *Introduction à la chirurgie, Animaux, monstres et prodiges* (Paris: Le Club Français du Livre, 1954), li.

19. Ibid.

20. Ibid., liii–iv.

21. *Paracelsus, Selected Writings*, 66.

22. Paré, *Introduction à la chirurgie*, lii. Of course, in the regular practice of medicine, experience—rather than sacred knowledge—prevailed. Yet, one observes close associations between medicine and religion when missionaries were sent to distant countries, continuing the medical role of the medieval clergy. As late as 1771, the *Dictionnaire des gens du monde*, a compilation of quotes and remarks from celebrated authors and popular literature, mentioned the importance of medicine in "the propagation of faith": "A missionary who adds to his zeal to save the souls the art of curing the body, is admitted among the powerful; and if he cannot convert them, he can obtain a protection that will allow him to work with more assurance and freedom towards the conversion of many others." The *Dictionnaire* also compares physicians to magistrates: "The physician is a natural magistrate, whose jurisdiction is the human body, and its elements. He removes from some excessive degrees of strength, and gives back to others the degrees of strength they lack. In so doing, he restores the beautiful cohesion among them that makes life sweet and pleasurable." *Dictionnaire des gens du monde, Historique, littéraire, critique, moral, physique, militaire, politique, caractéristique et social*, vol. 2 (Paris: Costard, 1771), 378.

23. Pietro d'Abano played an important role in the development of astrological medicine. He taught medicine and astrology at Padua, where he died in 1316. As Nancy G. Siraisi notes, in Pietro d'Abano's view, "in addition to the general influence of heavenly bodies, the horoscope at conception or birth was also considered to signal or predispose the physical and mental constitution of each individual down to the most minute detail; Pietro d'Abano held the stars responsible for his own dislike of, or possible allergy to, milk" (*Medieval and Early Renaissance Medicine*, 111).

24. Pietro d'Abano, *Traicté des Venins*, trans. from Latin by Lazare Boet (Lyon: Jean Huguetan, 1593), 124.

25. Siraisi, *Medieval and Early Renaissance Medicine*, 2.

26. D'Abano, *Traicté des Venins*, 124, 125.

27. Paracelsus, *Selected Writings*, 95.

28. Paré, *Des Venins et morsures des chiens enragés, et autres morsures et piquires de bestes venimeuses* (Paris: Club Français du Livre, 1954) 237, 238 (emphasis added).

29. It may be worth pointing out that a much-quoted example of monstrous births was that of a woman in Umbria who gave birth to a serpent. Isidore of Seville, who cited the event in his *Etymologies,* interpreted it as a *portentum.* This story too brought together the relationship between God and evil (God has specifically allowed such a birth), the woman's fateful role in the temptation of Adam, and the privileged role of the serpent in all knowledge connected with life and death, fear and hope. See Céard, *La Nature et les prodiges,* 32–33.

30. Claude-François Passerat de la Chapelle, *Recueil des drogues simples ou matière médicinale, con-tenant les remèdes et les préparations chymiques les plus usitées, leurs manières d'opérer, fondées sur l'oeconomie animale et sur les principes d'où procèdent leurs vertus, conformément aux sentiments des meilleurs auteurs* (Paris: D'Houry Père, 1753). Passerat de la Chapelle held the title of "Conseiller du Roi," and served as "Médecin des Hôpitaux Militaires de France."

31. Paré, *Des Venins,* 244.

32. Jean Clair, *Méduse* (Paris: Gallimard, 1989), 80.

33. Paré, *Des Venins,* 247.

34. See Danielle Jacquart and Claude Thomasset, *Sexualité et savoir médical au Moyen-Age* (Paris: Presses Universitaires de France, 1985), 103–5.

35. *Les Admirables secrets de magie naturelle du Grand-Albert et du Petit Albert* (Paris: Albin Michel, 1971), 67–68. This collection of medical secrets has been attributed to Albertus Magnus, and still circu-lated in the beginning of the twentieth century, making it the most durable and successful work of me-dieval medicine. The original medical notes were revised and augmented anonymously throughout the centuries. The *Grand-Albert* was often denounced by the Church which saw in its recipes an illegitimate recourse to quasi-supernatural knowledge.

36. Clair, *Méduse,* 26.

37. *Dictionnaire des gens du monde,* vol. 2, 84.

38. Paré, *Des Venins,* 244, 245.

39. Antonio Benivieni, *De Abditis Nonnullis Ac Mirandis Morborum Et Sanationum Causis,* trans. Charles Singer, with a biography by Esmond R. Long (Oxford: Charles Thomas, and Blackwell, 1954), 115.

40. Paré, *Des Venins,* 249.

41. Passerat, *Recueil des drogues simples,* 166.

42. William Cullen, *First Lines of the Practice of Physic,* vol. 1 (Edinburgh: Bell & Bradfute, and William Creech, 1796), 43.

43. Passerat, *Recueil des drogues simples,* 167. The crushed head of a serpent also had important reli-gious connotations, the Virgin Mary being sometimes represented crushing the serpent under her foot.

44. Charles Webster, "Paracelsus: Medicine as Popular Protest," in Grell and Cunningham, *Medi-cine and the Reformation,* 57.

45. Paracelsus, *Selected Writings,* 120.

46. Michel Foucault, *The Order of Things: An Archeology of the Human Sciences* (New York: Vintage, 1994), 17–45.

47. Paracelsus, *Selected Writings,* 122–23.

48. Ibid., 123.

49. *The hermetic and alchemical writings of Aureolus Philippus Theophrastus Bombast, of Hohenheim, called Paracelsus the Great: now for the first time faithfully translated into English,* ed. Arthur Edward Waite (Berkeley: Shambala, 1976), 171.

50. Ibid., 173.

51. See Huet, *Monstrous Imagination,* 13–35.

52. David Harley, "Spiritual Physic, Providence and English Medicine, 1560–1640," in Grell and Cunningham, *Medicine and the Reformation,* 101, 103, 108, 107–8.

53. *Selected Writings,* 81.

54. Benivieni, *De Abditis Nonnullis ac Mirandis Morborum et Sanationum Causis,* 36, 37.

55. Ibid., 99.

56. Paré, *Introduction á la chirurgie,* 45. This vocabulary would persist for many years among physicians. It is also interesting to note as that, as medical science progressed, diseases and monsters simultaneously would no longer be considered as *contrary* to nature, but as *deviations* from nature. William Cullen would redefine the Renaissance cosmic battle among elements that affect the human body as a strictly internal struggle between two factors. In his analysis of fevers, for example, he writes: "In every fever, there is a power applied to the body, which has a tendency to hurt and destroy it, and produces in it certain motions that deviate from the natural state; and, at the same time, in every fever which has its full course, I suppose, that, in consequence of the constitution of the animal economy, there are certain motions excited, which have a tendency to obviate the effects of the noxious power, or to correct and remove them," *First Lines of the Practice of Physic,* 105–6. This second effect, which Cullen invokes frequently in his *Practice of Physic,* is the *vix medicatrix naturae.*

57. See Jacques Roger, *Les Sciences de la vie dans la pensée française du XVIIIe siècle* (Paris: Armand Colin, 1963).

58. "The monster that you see represented here was found in an egg, with the head and face of a man, all the hairs being small live snakes, and the beard made of three snakes which came out of his chin," Paré, *Des Monstres,* 13.

Chapter 6. Revolutionary Anatomies

I am grateful to Colin Jones and the anonymous readers for the press for their many helpful suggestions on an earlier version of this essay.

1. For several versions of *The Patriotic Calculator,* see Claudette Hould, *Images of the French Revolution* (Quebec: Musée du Québec, 1989), 286–87.

2. On this topic, see Laurence Brockliss and Colin Jones, *The Medical World of Early Modern France* (Oxford: Clarendon Press, 1997); Dora B. Weiner, *The Citizen-Patient in Revolutionary and Imperial Paris* (Baltimore: Johns Hopkins University Press, 1993). For developments in natural history, see E. C. Scary, *Utopia's Garden: French Natural History from Old Regime to Revolution* (Chicago: University of Chicago Press, 2000).

3. Several commentators have pointed to the exploitation of monstrous rhetoric in revolutionary politics. See Antoine de Baecque, *La Caricature révolutionnaire* (Paris: CNRS, 1988); Claude Langlois, *La Caricature contre-révolutionnaire* (Paris: CNRS, 1988); Antoine de Baecque, *The Body Politic: Corporeal Metaphor in Revolutionary France 1770–1800,* trans. Charlotte Mandell (Stanford, Calif.: Stanford University Press, 1998); Marie-Hélène Huet, "Revolutionary Monsters," in *Animal Acts: Configuring the Human in Western History,* ed. Jennifer Ham and Matthew Senior (New York: Routledge, 1997), 85–102; Lynn Hunt, "The Many Bodies of Marie-Antoinette: Political Pornography and the Problem of the Feminine in the French Revolution," in *Eroticism and the Body Politic,* ed. Lynn Hunt (Baltimore: Johns Hopkins University Press, 1991), 108–30.

4. Originally named the "École pour le traitement des maladies des bestiaux," the world's first veterinary school was founded in 1761 by Claude Bourgelat, friend of Diderot and contributor to the *Encyclopédie.* Honoré Fragonard served as its director and chair of anatomy. In 1764, the school acquired its designation as the Royal Veterinary School. In 1765, Bourgelat was invited to found a royal veterinary school in Paris on the Lyon model, where Fragonard was again appointed director. See Alcide Louis Joseph Railliet and L. Moulé, *Histoire de l'École d'Alfort* (Paris: Asselin and Houzeau, 1908).

5. Michel Ellenberger, *L'Autre Fragonard* ([Le Mans]: Jupilles, 1981), 10. Thanks in good measure to the support of influential scientists such as Félix Vicq d'Azyr, Alfort's anatomy cabinet was preserved, though not as a unified collection, for which Fragonard had campaigned. The works were distributed between Alfort and two other new institutions founded during the Revolution, the School of Health and the National Museum of Natural History. After a long period during which he worked as a private anatomist, following his dismissal on pension from Alfort in 1771, Fragonard resumed a public career as an anatomist during the Revolution. He addressed the National Assembly in 1792, and served on the Jury of the Arts and the temporary Commission of the Arts charged with inventorying the anatomical cabinets of France. In 1795, he was appointed Chief Anatomist at the new School of Health. On his biography and his contribution, see Jonathan Simon, "The Theater of Anatomy: The Anatomical Preparations of Honoré Fragonard," *Eighteenth-Century Studies* 36, no. 1 (2002): 63–79.

6. Brousonnet, cited in Yvonne Poulle-Drieux, "Honoré Fragonard et le cabinet d'anatomie de l'École d'Alfort pendant la Révolution," *Revue d'histoire des sciences et leurs applications* (Paris: Presses Universitaires de France, 1962), 10.

7. Chaussart's letter appeared in [Prudhomme's] *Révolutions de Paris,* no. 27, 11 January 1790, 38–39. Chaussart's complaints—which he also addressed to the National Assembly in a *mémoire*—could be discounted as the grudge of a disgruntled employee. Yet he certainly piqued Prudhomme's interest by the manner in which he couched his arguments, indicting the collection as a glaring example of old regime privilege: one in which the monarchy, as the Royal Veterinary School's protector, was also implicated.

8. Cited in Ellenberger, *L'Autre Fragonard,* 9.

9. According to Süe, "It would be ridiculous to think that one who merely dissects could learn all the details of Anatomy with the full assiduity and penetration of mind assumed of him. It is necessary also to draw from the illumination that our predecessors have left us, without which progress would not be possible. It is in joining theory and practice, reading and lessons, that one can reach not only perfect knowledge of the parts of the human body, but even the discovery of others, and the addition of a new

luster to art. In addition, he who would know his subject perfectly is in a better state than he who has only part of a confused idea to distinguish the healthy parts from those which are affected or disordered." M. Süe, *Anthropotomie, ou l'art d'injecter, de disséquer, d'embaumer et de conserver les parties du corps humain,* etc., 2d ed., revised and augmented (Paris: P. G. Cavelier, 1765), 3. Süe held positions in both the artistic and medical domains, as a member of the Royal Academy of Painting and Sculpture and of the Royal College of Surgery. He worked with wax as well as actual cadavers. His cabinet, further enriched by his son, Jean-Joseph Süe, the younger (1760–1830), was one of the most important in Paris before the Revolution. On the wide appeal of reformist arguments in the decades following 1730, see Colin Jones, "The Medicalisation of Eighteenth-Century France," in *Problems and Methods in the History of Medicine,* ed. Roy Porter and Andrew Wear (London: Croom Helm, 1987), 40–56. More generally, see Toby Gelfand, *Professionalizing Modern Medicine: Paris Surgeons and Medical Science and Institutions in the Eighteenth Century* (Westport, Conn.: Greenwood Press, 1980); Brockliss and Jones, *The Medical World;* Kathleen Wellman, *La Mettrie: Medicine, Philosophy, and Enlightenment* (Durham, N.C.: Duke University Press, 1992).

10. Another tradition derives the term monster from *monere,* to warn. For discussion of these competing etymological traditions, see: Marie-Hélène Huet, *Monstrous Imagination* (Cambridge, Mass.: Harvard University Press, 1993), 6; Zakiya Hanafi, *The Monster in the Machine: Magic, Medicine, and the Marvelous in the Time of the Scientific Revolution* (Durham, N.C.: Duke University Press, 2000), 3; Lorraine Daston and Katharine Park, *Wonders and the Order of Nature, 1150–1750* (New York: Zone Books, 1998), chap. 5.

11. Michael Hagner, "Enlightened Monsters," in *The Sciences in Enlightened Europe,* ed. William Clark, Jan Golinski, and Simon Schaffer (Chicago: University of Chicago Press, 1999), 180.

12. In his *Correspondance littéraire,* Grimm commented on Bihéron's artificial models: "After having for a long time followed the dissection of cadavers in different amphitheaters, she [Mlle Bihéron] conceived to make artificial anatomies, that is to say, to compose not only an entire body with all its internal and external parts, but also to make all the parts in them separately with the greatest perfection. If you ask me of what these artificial parts are made, I could not respond; what I do know is that they are not of wax, since fire has no effect on them; what I know further is that they have no odor, that they are incorruptible and possess a surprising truthfulness." *Correspondance littéraire, philosophique et critique addressé à un souverain d'Allemagne, depuis 1770 jusqu'en 1782,* 5 vols. (Paris: F. Buisson, 1813), 1:454. Bihéron achieved renown for the creation of realistic anatomical models, famous for their texture, color, and appearance, as well as the position of the organs. She sold only completed models, keeping secret her formula for their composition. Among her most accomplished works were gynecological models, used in teaching of midwifery. She presented her models before the Royal Academy of Science on more than one occasion, and was invited to visit Russia by the Empress Catherine and visited by the Swedish crown prince on his journey to Paris in 1771. See Lemire, *Artistes et mortels,* preface E. A. Cabanis (Paris: Chabaud, 1990) 80–85.

13. Hagner, "Enlightened Monsters," 180.

14. "Frederik Ruysch" in http://www.whonamedit.com/doctor.cfm/1142.html. For an entrance fee, Ruysch displayed his preparations, which were sometimes referred to as "the Eighth Wonder of the

World." His cabinet attracted numerous foreign visitors, including Peter the Great of Russia, who purchased the collection from Ruysch in 1717 for thirty thousand guilders. Ibid.

15. Bernard Le Bovier de Fontenelle, *Éloges des académiciens* (The Hague: Isaac van der Kloot, 1740).

16. Simon, "The Theater of Anatomy," 70.

17. On Ruysch, see also José Van Dijck, "Bodyworlds: The Art of Plastinated Cadavers," *Configurations* 9 (2001): 99–126; Julie V. Hansen, "Resurrecting Death: Anatomical Art in the Cabinet of Dr. Frederick Ruysch," *Art Bulletin* 78, no. 4 (1996): 663–79.

18. For example, as Zakiya Hanafi states, "a monster is whatever we are *not;* so as monsters change form, so do we, by implication." Zakiya Hanafi, *The Monster in the Machine,* viii.

19. In addition to references to the classical hydra, prominent in Reformation polemics, the figure of a monstrous animal may also derive from popular accounts of a beast in the region of the Gévaudon terrorizing the surrounding population during the 1760s. On the latter, see: Xavier Pic, *La Bête qui mangeait le monde en pays de Gévaudan et d'Auvergne* (Paris: Albin Michel, 1971).

20. Mikhail Bakhtin, *Rabelais and His World,* trans. Helene Iswolsky (Bloomington: Indiana University Press, 1984), 317

21. The description is drawn from Cat. 68 in *French Caricature and the French Revolution, 1789–1799* (Grunwald Center for the Graphic Arts, Wight Art Gallery, University of California at Los Angeles, 1988), 181–82.

22. [L. -M.] Prudhomme [Louise-Felicité Keralio-Robert], *Les Crimes des reines de Marie-Antoinette d'Autriche dernière reine de France, avec les pieces justificatives de son procès* (Paris, II [1793–1794]), 446, cited in Michel Foucault, *Les Anormaux: Cours au Collège de France (1974–1975),* ed. François Ewald et al. (Paris: Seuil/Gallimard, 1999), 90.

23. Abbé Barruel, *Histoire du clergé,* vol. 1 (London, 1797), 287.

24. Edmund Burke, *Reflections on the Revolution in France* (Garden City, N.Y.: Doubleday, 1961).

25. This description accompanies the image *La Panthère autrichienne voué au mépris et à l'exécration de la nation française dans sa postérité la plus reculée* (Paris: chez Villeneuve [1792 or 1793]), Map and Picture Collection of Carolina Rediviva, Uppsala University Library.

26. *La Chasse aux bêtes puantes et féroces, qui après avoir inondé les bois, les plaines, &c., se sont répandues à la cour & à la Capitale.* (Paris: l'Imprimerie de la Liberté, 1789); *Fureurs utérines de Marie-Antoinette, femme de Louis XVI* (Paris, 1791).

27. *Vie de Marie-Antoinette d'Autriche, reine de France, femme de Louis XVI, roi des Français, depuis la perte de son pucelage jusqu'au premier mai 1791.* Paris, I [1791], cited in Foucault, *Les Anormaux,* 90–91. Cf. *La Vie privée, libertine et scandaleuse de Marie-Antoinette d'Autriche, ci-devant reine des Français, depuis son arrivée en France jusqu'au detention au Temple* (n.d.). Michel Foucault's prescient discussion in his 1975 lectures at the Collège de France of monstrosity in the anti-Royalist pamphlet literature (*Les Anormaux*) clearly anticipated subsequent research on the queen in the pamphlet literature. See Chantal Thomas, "L'Architigresse d'Autriche: La Métaphore animale dans les pamphlets contre Marie-Antoinette," and Antoine de Baecque, "Le Récit fantastique de la Révolution: *Les monstres aristocratiques* des pamphlets de 1789," in *La Révolution du Journal, 1788–1794,* ed. Pierre Rétat (Paris: CNRS, 1989); Chantal Thomas, *The Wicked Queen: The Origins of the Myth of Marie-Antoinette,* trans. Julie Rose (New

York: Zone, 1999); Lynn Hunt, *The Family Romance of the French Revolution* (Berkeley: University of California Press, 1992); Elizabeth Colwill, "Just Another *Citoyenne?* Marie-Antoinette on Trial, 1790–1793," *History Workshop* 28 (Autumn 1989): 63–87.

28. P. A. L. Maton (de la Varenne), *Les Crimes de Marat et des autres égorgeurs, ou Ma Résurrection. Où, parmi quelques matériaux précieux pour l'histoire, on trouve la prevue que Marat et d'autres scélérats, membres des autorités publiques, ont provoqué tous les massacres des prisonniers,* 2d ed. (Paris: Chez André, III [1795]), 94.

29. See: A. Granier de Cassagnac, *Histoire des girondins et des massacres de septembre d'après les documents officiels et inédits,* vol. 2 (Paris, 1860), 224–27. Granier credits another work by Mathon as the source for this event, *Histoire particulière des événements pendant les mois de juin, juillet, d'août et de septembre 1792, et qui ont opéré la chute du trône royal* (Paris, 1806). As if to acknowledge the reader's suspicions about the veracity of the story of Mademoiselle de Sombreuil, Granier insisted on Mathon's credibility as an historian: "The duty of the historian should be to doubt, but doubt becomes impossible in the presence of the following testimony, addressed to us by the sons of Mademoiselle de Sombreuil." Granier de Cassagnac, *Histoire des girondins,* 2:225.

30. On the theme of dismemberment, see Ronald Paulson, "The Severed Head: The Impact of French Revolutionary Caricatures on England," in *French Caricature and the French Revolution, 1789–1799,* ed. James Cuno (Los Angeles: University of California, Grunwald Center for the Graphic Arts, Wight Art Gallery, 1988), 55–66. On the scatological side of grotesque revolutionary imagery, see Albert Boime, "Jacques-Louis David, Scatological Discourse in the French Revolution, and the Art of Caricature," in Cuno, *French Caricature,* 67–82.

31. Antoine de Baecque, *Glory and Terror: Seven Deaths under the French Revolution,* trans. Charlotte Mandell (New York: Routledge, 2001), 102–3.

32. Cf., Paulson, "The Severed Head," 58.

33. "La scene se passe sur la place de la Révolution / Admirez de Sanson l'Intelligence extrême, / par le couteau fatal, il a tout fait périr / Dans cet affreux état que va t'il devenir? / Il se guillotine lui même." *Le Gouvernement de Robespierre ou le Bourreau se guillotine lui-même* (c. 1794). The various victims include the clergy, the Parlements, the nobility, the Legislature, and the people.

34. Galen, *On the Natural Faculties* 2.3, cited in Barbara Maria Stafford, *Body Criticism: Imaging the Unseen in Enlightenment Art and Medicine* (Cambridge, Mass.: MIT Press, 1991), 47.

35. Vesalius's *De Humani Corporis Fabrica,* published in 1543, is generally credited with ushering in a new era in the history of medicine and marking the beginning of modern anatomy. T. V. N. Persaud, *A History of Anatomy: The Post-Vesalian Era* (Springfield, Ill.: Charles C. Thomas, 1997), 9.

36. It has been argued that "the dissection of the dead and decaying human body stood in stark contrast to the classical humanism of the Renaissance." Ibid., 9. For the view that spiritual values reigned supreme over material things in the Renaissance, see E. A. Cassirer, "The Place of Vesalius in the Culture of the Renaissance," *Yale Journal of Biological Medicine* 16 (1943), 109–19; C. Singer, "To Vesalius on the Fourth Century of His *De humani corporis fabrica,*" *Journal of Anatomy* 77 (1943), 261–65.

37. David Le Breton, *La Chair à vif: Usages médicaux et mondains du corps humain* (Paris: A. M. Métailié, 1993), 141. See also Thomas A. Kselman, *Death and the Afterlife in Modern France* (Princeton, N.J.: Princeton University Press, 1993).

38. Félix Vicq d'Azyr, *Traité d'anatomie et de physiologie, avec des planches coloriées représentant au naturel les divers organes de l'homme et des animaux* (Paris: de l'Imprimerie de France, Amb. Didot l'Aîné, 1786), 1.

39. Bakhtin, *Rabelais and his World,* 27, 20–21, 25–26.

40. Julia Kristeva, *Powers of Horror: An Essay on Abjection,* trans. Leon S. Roudiez (New York: Columbia University Press, 1982), 9. Cf. Mary Douglas, *Purity and Danger* (New York, Praeger, 1966); Sigmund Freud, *Civilization and Its Discontents,* trans. James Strachey, intro. Peter Gay (New York: W. W. Norton, 1989).

41. Vicq d'Azyr, *Discours sur l'anatomie,* 2.

42. On this theme see two works by Rembrandt, *The Anatomy Lesson of Dr. Nicolaes Tulp* (1632) and *The Anatomy Lesson of Dr. Jan Deijman* (1656), as well as Adriaen Backer's *The Anatomy Lesson of Dr. Fredrik Ruysch* (1670), and Jan Van Neck's *The Anatomy Lesson of Dr. Fredrik Ruysch* (1683), all reproduced in Martin Kemp and Marina Wallace, *Spectacular Bodies: The Art and Science of the Human Body from Leonardo to Now* (London: Hayward Gallery; Berkeley: University of California Press, 2001). For a reading of Rembrandt's opus within the broader culture of dissection of early modern Europe, see Jonathan Sawday, *The Body Emblazoned: Dissection and the Human Body in Renaissance Culture* (New York and London: Routledge, 1995), 146–158.

43. Lemire, *Artistes et mortels,* 4. In fact, it was not Paris but Montpellier that was in the avant-garde of human autopsy in France, inaugurating its anatomical theater in 1556 almost a century before Paris. The first rudimentary theater in the capital was built in 1604, lasting a few years. In 1608, the Faculty of Medicine of Paris bought a large house at the corner of the rue du Fouarre, which became the Riolan Amphitheatre, inaugurated in 1620. Ibid.

44. Mercier cited in Philippe Ariès, *The Hour of Our Death,* trans. Helen Weaver (New York: Knopf, 1981), 365, 368. According to Ariès, "Dissection had become a fashionable art. A rich man who was interested in nature might have his own private dissecting room, just as he might have his own chemical laboratory. But this room had to be supplied with bodies. This explains a remark in the article on the cadaver in the *Encyclopédie:* 'Each family wants their deceased member to enjoy his burial service as it were, and rarely, if ever, allows him to be sacrificed to the cause of public education. At most, they may allow a body to be used for their own instruction or to satisfy their own curiosity.' This is the meaning of certain clauses in wills." Ibid., 366.

45. Lemire, *Artistes et mortels,* 80. Lemire notes that "the young student lunched with her teacher before making a demonstration on anatomical parts [avant de se faire 'démonstraire' sur pièces] like the brain, eye, ear, lungs, heart, stomach, intestines, bladder, muscles, veins, arteries, [although] the demonstration of the reproductive parts, reserved to men and married women, were forbidden to her." Ibid.

46. See: "Anatomie," in *L'Encyclopédie ou Dictionnaire raisonné des sciences, des arts et des métiers,* vol. 1 (Paris: A'Livourne, 1751–1765)

47. See: Sawday, *Body Emblazoned,* esp. 80; Roger French, *Dissection and Vivisection in the European Renaissance* (Aldershot: Ashgate, 1999).

48. Ariès, *The Hour of Our Death,* 369.

49. The works reside at La Specola Collection in Florence. See Georges Didi-Huberman, "Wax

Flesh, Vicious Cycles," in *Encyclopaedia Anatomica: A Compete Collection of Anatomical Waxes* (Cologne: Taschen, 1999), 72. See also Sylvie Hugues's excellent consideration of Zumbo and Fragonard in the context of baroque, neoclassical, and Romantic aesthetics, "Esthétique et anatomie: Science, religion, sensation," *Dix-huitième siècle* 31 (1999), 141–58.

50. Baecque, *Glory and Terror,* 4.

51. Ibid., 11.

52. See Brockliss and Jones, *The Medical World of Early Modern France;* E. Haigh, *Xavier Bichat and the Medical Theory of the Eighteenth Century* (*Medical History,* supplement No. 4; London, 1984); Matthew Ramsey, *Professional and Popular Medicine in France, 1770–1830* (Cambridge: Cambridge University Press, 1988); Scary, *Utopia's Garden;* Dorinda Outram, *Georges Cuvier: Vocation, Science, and Authority in Post-Revolutionary France* (Manchester: Manchester University Press, 1984).

53. According to Sawday, "it was not just that anatomy as a discipline benefited from the scaffold through the provision of corpses, but that the explorers of the human body were themselves the executioners. . . . [Hence] there was very little distance between the ritual of execution and the opening of the body to knowledge," *Body Emblazoned,* 80.

54. Ellenberger, *L'Autre Fragonard,* 9. Cf. E. Leclainche, *Histoire de la médecine vétérinaire* (Toulouse: Office du Livre, 1936).

55. Barbara M. Stafford et al., "Depth Studies: Illustrated Anatomies," *CADUCEUS: A Humanities Journal for Medicine and the Health Sciences* 8, no. 2 (1992): 40.

56. René Descartes, *Méditations métaphysiques* (Paris: PUF, 1970), 39.

57. Sylvie Hugues, "Esthétique et Anatomie," 151–52; she quotes Bichat, *Recherches physiologiques sur la vie et sur la mort* (1800). Hugues argues that given the refutation of materialism in new conceptions of irritability and sensibility, Fragonard is using an already outmoded language. She sees the dominance of aesthetic discourse in this work as troubling its scientific aspect. "Esthétique et Anatomie," 152.

58. Although not pictured in this particular photograph, the figure's attentiveness is mimicked by his penis's turgidity.

59. See John Cody, M.D., *Visualizing Muscles: A New Écorché Approach to Surface Anatomy* (Lawrence: University Press of Kansas, 1990), 1.

60. Georg Ludwig Rumpelt, *Notes Vétérinaires et Économiques, recueillies dans un voyage à travers quelques provinces d'Allemagne, de Hollande, de France et de Suisse* (Dresden, 1802), cited in Pierre-Louis Verly, *Honoré Fragonard: Anatomiste, Premier Directeur de l'École d'Alfort* (Alfort: École nationale d'Alfort, 1963), 30.

61. Rumpelt, *Notes Vétérinaires et Économiques,* cited in Ellenberger, *L'Autre Fragonard,* 26.

62. K. A. Rudolphi, *Bemerkungen aus dem Gebiet der Naturgeschichte, Medicin und Thierarzneykunde auf einer Reise durch einen Theil von Deutschland, Holland und Frankreich,* 2 vols. (Berlin, 1804–5), cited in Lemire, *Artistes et mortels,* 172.

63. Rudolphi, *Bemerkungen,* cited in Simon, "The Theater of Anatomy," 72.

64. On the link between public spectacle and eighteenth-century experimental science, see Simon Schaffer, "Natural Philosophy and Public Spectacle in the Eighteenth Century," *History of Science* 21 (1983): 1–43; and Schaffer, "Self-Evidence," *Critical Inquiry* 18 (1992): 327–62.

65. In her discussion of the "animated statue models" by which Enlightenment authors such as Condillac, Buffon, and Bonnet portrayed the awakening of a statue to thought, one sense at a time, Julia V. Douthwaite draws an important connection between the topos of the animated statue and the use of the *écorché* in anatomy. She writes: "Coming alive *ex nihilo*, like Locke's 'blank sheet,' the statue represented the logical point of departure for a psychology based on sequential development. As a means of visualizing the invisible, the figure also conjured up the technologies used to demonstrate hidden bodily functions, like the *écorchés* of human musculature in the *Encyclopédie* article 'anatomy,' the gynecological wax model (or *femme invisible*) of Marie-Catherine Bihéron, and Vaucanson's automated digesting duck." Julia V. Douthwaite, *The Wild Girl, Natural Man, and the Monster: Dangerous Experiments in the Age of Enlightenment* (Chicago: University of Chicago Press, 2002), 70. See also J. L. Carr, "Pygmalion and the *Philosophes:* The Animated Statue in Eighteenth-Century France," *Journal of the Warburg and Courtauld Institutes* 23, nos. 3–4 (1960): 239–55.

66. Ellenberger, *L'Autre Fragonard*, 32.

67. Lemire, *Artistes et mortels,* 185. Jonathan Simon concludes that the question itself is misplaced, a result of the imposition of a disciplinary division between art and science that made no sense in the eighteenth-century. "The Theater of Anatomy," 76. Yet Thouret's eulogy, previously discussed, points to the fact that even in Fragonard's lifetime questions were raised about his "science."

68. André-Pierre Pinson, an artist/modeler in wax, had exhibited at the Academy of Sciences in the 1770s, as well as at the Louvre. Like Fragonard, he was trained as a surgeon, though unlike the former, his surgical experience was quite extensive. He served as surgeon to the Hundred Swiss Guards and later as chief surgeon at the military hospital of Saint-Denis in 1794, subsequently transferring to the hospital of Courbevoie where Jean-Joseph Süe then practiced. Pinson was the creator of the former duke of Orleans's celebrated collection of anatomical pieces in wax, which was acquired by the nation following the latter's death. Like Fragonard and Lemonnier, a painter-draftsman and former academician in painting, Pinson joined the Paris School of Health, where he assisted Fragonard in building a cabinet of anatomy, dissecting specimens of pathological anatomy. He also made models of fungi, plants, and animals for the Museum of Natural History, which were utilized by Georges Cuvier in his studies of comparative anatomy.

69. Lemire, *Artistes et mortels,* 184.

70. "Le désir de nous unir à la chose publique." Documents in Yvonne Poulle-Drieux, "Honoré Fragonard et le cabinet d'anatomie de l'École d'Alfort pendant la Révolution," *Revue d'histoire des sciences et de leurs applications* 15 (1962): 153.

71. The members of the commission were elected and remunerated by the Convention. The other members of the commission were: Thillaye (surgeon and professor of anatomy at the École Pratique de Chirurgie), Vicq d'Azyr (former first physician of the queen, successor of Buffon at the Royal Academy of Science, perpetual secretary of the Royal Society of Medicine), Corvisart (physician and head of a famed clinic, future first physician to Napoleon), and Portal (doctor and professor of anatomy at the Collège de France), all some ten to twenty years younger than Fragonard.

72. Ellenberger, *L'Autre Fragonard*, 23.

Chapter 7. Signs of Monstrosity

1. "I mostri altro non sono che misteriosi ieroglifici e imagini facete figurate da [Natura] o per ischerno o per documento degli uomini." Emanuele Tesauro, *Cannochiale Aristotelico* (1654), ed. Ezio Raimondi (Torino: Ricciardi, 1987), 24. Unless otherwise indicated, translations are mine.

2. "Il fut engendré à Ravenne mesme un monstre ayant une corne en la teste, deux aesles, un pied semblable à celuy d'un oyseau ravissant et avec un oeil au genoil." Pierre Boaistuau, *Histoires prodigieuses,* ed. Gisèle Mathieu-Castellani (Geneva: Slatkine, 1996), 425. For a reading of Paré and the Ravenna monster as portent, see Marie-Hélène Huet, "Monstrous Medicine," in this volume. On Boaistuau, Rabelais, and numerous other writers about Renaissance monsters, see the magisterial study by Jean Céard, *La Nature et les prodiges: L'Insolite au XVIe siècle en France,* 2d ed. (Geneva: Droz, 1996).

3. "Par la corne estoit figuré l'orgueil et l'ambition: par les aesles, la legereté et inconstance: par le deffault des bras, le deffault des bonnes oeuvres: par le pied ravissant, rapine usure et avarice: par l'oeil qui estoit au genoil, l'affection des choses terrestres," Boaistuau, *Histoires prodigieuses,* 425.

4. Aristotle, *The Generation of Animals,* book 4, 769bl, cited from the *Complete Works of Aristotle,* ed. Jonathan Barnes, trans. A. Platt, vol. 2 (Princeton, N.J.: Princeton University Press Bollingen Series, 1995), 1191.

5. Ibid., 1186.

6. See Heinrich Lausberg, *Elementi di retorica,* trans. Lea Ritter Santini (Bologna: Il Mulino, 1969), 222ff.

7. Aristotle, *The "Art" of Rhetoric,* trans. J. H. Freese, Loeb Classical Library (Cambridge, Mass.: Harvard University Press, 1982), 3.3.4, 367.

8. "Cicero," *Ad Herennium,* trans. H. Caplan, Loeb Classical Library (Cambridge, Mass.: Harvard University Press, 1964), 4.49.63, 385.

9. Cicero, *De Oratore,* trans. H. Rackham, vol. 2, Loeb Classical Library (Cambridge, Mass.: Harvard University Press, 1960), 3.38.156, 123.

10. Quintilian, *Oeuvres complètes,* ed. and trans. M. Nisard (Paris: Firmin-Didot, 1881), 8.4, 298.

11. Erasmus, "*Copia:* Foundations of the Abundant Style," in *Collected Works of Erasmus: Literary and Educational Writings 2,* trans. Betty I. Knott (Toronto: University of Toronto Press, 1978), 337.

12. Ibid., 337, 333.

13. The topic of resemblance was, of course, linked many years ago by Michel Foucault, in the opening sections of *Les Mots et les choses* (Paris: Gallimard, 1968), to the "episteme" of the Renaissance. Without revisiting Foucault's suggestive if reductive presentation, one can point to recent good work done on resemblance in the context of Rabelais. Especially important are Samuel Kinser's interesting study, *Rabelais's Carnival: Text, Context, Metatext* (Berkeley: University of California Press, 1990); and Michael Randall, *Building Resemblance: Analogical Imagery in the Early French Renaissance* (Baltimore: Johns Hopkins University Press, 1990), esp. chaps. 5 and 6. On the importance of analogy as a cast of thought see Céard, *La Nature et les prodiges,* 303ff.

14. My thinking about the reductive and potentially violent nature of allegory has benefited from Gordon Teskey's book, *Allegory and Violence* (Ithaca, N.Y.: Cornell University Press, 1996); see especially chaps. 2 and 4. On the question of allegory in Rabelais more generally, see Michel Jeanneret, "Signs

Gone Wild: The Dismantling of Allegory," in *François Rabelais: A Critical Reassessment,* ed. Jean-Claude Carron (Baltimore: Johns Hopkins University Press, 1995), 57–72.

15. François Rabelais, *Oeuvres complètes,* ed. Pierre Jourda, vol. 2 (Paris: Garnier, 1962), 163. Passages in English will be from the translation of J. M. Cohen, *Gargantua and Pantagruel* (Harmondsworth: Penguin, 1955). On occasion I have altered Cohen's version slightly to conform more closely to the original.

16. *Gargantua and Pantagruel,* 513. "Les ventricules d'icelle, comme une tirefond. L'excrescence vermiforme, comme un pillemaille. Les membranes, comme la coqueluche d'un moine. L'entonnoir, comme un oiseau de masson. La voulte, comme un gouimphe. Le conare, comme un veze," *Oeuvres complètes,* 2:127–28.

17. *Gargantua and Pantagruel,* 518. "S'il guygnoit des oeilz, c'estoient gauffres et obelies. S'il toussoit, c'estoient boytes de coudignac. S'il discouroit, c'estoient neiges d'antan"; *Oeuvres complètes,* 133–34.

18. *Gargantua and Pantagruel,* 518. "S'il souffloit, c'estoit troncs pour les Indulgences"; *Oeuvres complètes,* 134. On much of the background to Quaresmeprenant, in particular, see Kinser's *Rabelais's Carnival,* chap. 3.

19. Perhaps the best known of these images is Pieter Bruegel's *Fight between Carnival and Lent* (1559), which features an emaciated figure on a cart wielding an oar with fishes on it, surrounded by various symbols of culinary abstemiousness. Another Flemish artist of the same period, Frans Hogenberg, did something similar in an etching.

20. John Calvin, *Institutes of the Christian Religion,* trans. Henry Beveridge (Grand Rapids, Mich.: Eerdman's Publishing, 1989), bk. 4, ch. 12, sec. 20, 465. "[Jesus Christ] n'eust pas jeusné en façon humaine, comme il convenoit de faire, s'il eust voulu induire les hommes à son exemple: mais plustost par cest acte il a voulu se rendre admirable à tout le monde, que d'exhorter les autres à faire le semblable." Jean Calvin, *Institution de la Religion Chrestienne,* ed. Jean-Daniel Benoit, vol. 4 (Paris: Vrin, 1961), 255. Erasmus's discussion of "ceremonies" comes in his colloquy called "The Holy Feast," or "Convivium Religiosum." See *The Colloquies of Erasmus,* trans. Craig R. Thompson (Chicago: University of Chicago Press, 1965), 61–65.

21. "(Ils) présentent des signes et apparence extérieure, au lieu d'un coeur pur et net." Calvin, *Institutes,* 465, *Institution,* 254.

22. Jean Calvin, *Des Scandales,* ed. Olivier Fatio (Geneva: Droz, 1984), 70.

23. Ibid., 117.

24. Ibid., 79, 132.

25. Ibid., 62, 67.

26. "Or si c'est une chose monstrueuse qu'un homme soit converti en beste brute, telle maniere de gens sont d'autant plus à deplorer, quand ils ne sont point touchez de leur mal," ibid., 136.

27. Ibid., 140. In an account of the relationship between Calvin and Rabelais, Gérard Defaux has noted that their positions as regards ecclesiastical ceremonies would have been very close. See his *Rabelais Agonistes: Du Rieur au prophète* (Geneva: Droz, 1997), 473. See, as well, the useful discussion of Rabelais and Calvin in Kinser, *Rabelais's Carnival,* 87–92.

28. *Gargantua and Pantagruel,* 518–19. "Comme un ballon," "comme aureilles d'asne," "semblables aux talons"; *Oeuvres complètes,* 136.

29. *Gargantua and Pantagruel,* 520. "À toutes gens ecervelez et desguarniz de bon jugement et sens commun"; *Oeuvres complètes,* 137.

30. *Gargantua and Pantagruel,* 520. "Matagotz, Cagotz et Papelars; les Maniacles Pistolez, les Demoniacles Calvins, imposteurs de Geneve; les enraigez Putherbes . . . et aultres monstres difformes et contrefaicts en despit de Nature"; *Oeuvres complètes,* 137.

31. For a very good reading of several episodes in the *Quart livre* which brings out the ways in the book signals a breakdown in larger traditions of analogical thought, see Randall, *Building Resemblance,* chap. 6.

32. *Gargantua and Pantagruel,* 521. "Pantagruel de loing apperceut un grand et monstrueux physetere, venent droict vers nous, bruyant, ronflant, enflé, enlevé plus hault que les hunes des naufz"; *Oeuvres complètes,* 137.

33. *Gargantua and Pantagruel,* 521. "Leviathan descript par le noble prophete Moses en la vie du sainct home Job"; *Oeuvres complètes,* 138.

34. *Gargantua and Pantagruel,* 521. "Je croy que c'est le propre monstre marin qui feut jadis destiné pour devorer Andromeda"; *Oeuvres complètes,* 138.

35. *Gargantua and Pantagruel,* 522; "Ho, ho, Diable Sathanas, Leviathan!"; *Oeuvres complètes,* 139. There is much critical commentary on the encounter with the whale. Notable for the background it provides on the theological contexts of these episodes is Michael Screech's *Rabelais* (Ithaca, N.Y.: Cornell University Press, 1979), 367ff. For an exemplary allegorical reading that claims the episode as the central ideological moment in the entire book see Edwin Duval, *The Design of Rabelais's Quart Livre de Pantagruel* (Geneva: Droz, 1998), chap. 6. On Rabelais's dialogue with numerous "source" texts see Paul J. Smith, *Voyage et écriture: Étude sur le Quart livre de Rabelais* (Geneva: Droz, 1987), pt. 2, chap. 3.

36. *Gargantua and Pantagruel,* 524. "Adoncques mourant, le physetere se renversa ventre sus dours, comme font tous les poissons mors; et ainsi renversee, les poultres contre bas en mer, ressembloit au scolopendre, serpent ayant cent pieds comme le descript le saige ancien Nicander"; *Oeuvres complètes,* 142.

37. *Gargantua and Pantagruel,* 524; *Oeuvres complètes,* 139, 142.

38. *Gargantua and Pantagruel,* 524. "Le corps du physetere *sembloit* à la quille d'un guallion à troys gabies" (my emphasis); *Oeuvres complètes,* 142.

39. *Gargantua and Pantagruel,* 524. "Aultres assez pareilz, voyre encores plus enormes, avoit veu en l'Océan Gallicque"; *Oeuvres complètes,* 143.

40. *Gargantua and Pantagruel,* 524. "Et estoit chose moult plaisante à veoir"; *Oeuvres complètes,* 142. Duval (*Design,* 134) posits that the whale really is supposed to represent some type of evil figure, which Pantagruel, as a Christ substitute, defeats. He argues that Pantagruel shoots three initial arrows to represent the sign of the Trinity, or possibly a figure of the golden mean, "thus confirming his own moderate character and occasional role as moderator." The other arrows fired by the hero, he suggests, are simply sent to "make sport" (131) and amuse the company. This reading allegorizes the plot well enough. But I would want to try to account as well for the linguistic fabric of the episode. What is important here is, in fact, precisely the excess, the "extra" arrows and the extra meaning which adheres to the hero's exemplary deeds. For it is the dynamism of Rabelais's rhetoric which links the passage up to traditions of writ-

ing about monstrosity. And those traditions are never quite domesticated by allegory, even here. For an interesting consideration of the semiotic aspect of the episode see Michel Jeanneret, "Rabelais, les monstres et l'interprétation des signes (*Quart Livre* 18–42)," in *Writing the Renaissance: Essays on Sixteenth-Century French Literature in Honor of Floyd Gray,* ed. Raymond C. La Charité (Lexington, Ky.: French Forum, 1992) 65–78. In the same volume, Marcel Tetel offers helpful background to the figure of the "spouter." See his essay, "Le Phystère bicéphale," 57–64.

41. *Gargantua and Pantagruel,* 526. "Ces Andouilles venerables vous pourroient, par adventure, prendre pour Quaresmeprenant, quoy qu'en rien ne luy sembliez"; *Oeuvres completes,* 145.

42. For a good discussion of the representation of violence in this episode, and the curious shifting identity of the Andouilles, see Lawrence D. Kritzman, "Représenter le monstre dans le *Quart Livre* de Rabelais," *Études Rabelaisiennes* 33 (1997): 349–59.

43. *Gargantua and Pantagruel,* 531. "Mais je scays bien ce que je veidz"; *Oeuvres complètes,* 152.

44. In this regard one might place Rabelais's juxtaposition of mythical monstrosity with limited human perception at the beginning of a process of the translation of classical forms into human action that reaches its apogee and reversal in the romantic attempt to "remythologize" human experience some two and a half centuries later. For an account of one version of this romantic moment, see David Armitage's essay in this volume. On the breakdown of the authority of traditional genres in the genesis of the novel, the classic study remains M. M. Bakhtin's "Epos and Novel," in *The Dialogic Imagination,* trans. Caryl Emerson and Michael Holquist (Austin: University of Texas Press, 1981), 3–40. Erich Auerbach's discussion of Rabelais in *Mimesis* is still useful for its account of how Rabelaisian narrative explores the phenomenal world of objects. I have used the English version, translated by Willard Trask (Princeton, N.J.: Princeton University Press, 1953), chap. 11. On the history of the narrator as witness in early modern France, see the fine study by Andrea Frisch, *The Invention of the Eyewitness,* forthcoming from the University of North Carolina Press. For an eloquent account of the ways in which Rabelais's characters increasingly confront their own cognitive limitations as the books unfold, see Randall, *Building Resemblance,* chap. 6. Let me also note that the encounter with the Sausages continues through an entire battle scene which deploys multiple levels of complicated allegorical representation. Unfortunately, the limits of space keep me from discussing it in detail.

45. Lorraine Daston and Katharine Park, *Wonders and the Order of Nature, 1150–1750* (New York: Zone Books, 1998), 173ff.

46. On the complex links between these religious conflicts and the rhetoric of apocalyptic history at a slightly later historical moment, see the essay by Laura Lunger Knoppers in this volume.

47. Michel de Montaigne, *Oeuvres complètes,* ed. Thibaudet and Rat (Paris: Gallimard, Bibliothèque de la Pléiade, 1962), 690.

48. "Il estoit en tout le reste d'une forme commune, et se soustenoit sur ses pieds, marchoit et gasouilloit à peu pres commes les autres de mesme aage." Ibid., 690.

49. "Ses cris sembloient bien avoir quelque chose de particulier." Ibid., 690. It is worth recalling that "particulier" in French has a stronger sense of "strange" or "out of the ordinary," than does English "particular."

50. Ibid., 691.

51. "De peur que l'évenement ne le demente, il vaut mieux le laisser passer devant." Ibid., 691.

52. "Ce que nous appellons monstres ne le sont pas à Dieu, qui voit en l'immensité de son ouvrage l'infinité des formes qu'il y a comprinses." Ibid., 691.

Chapter 8. Monstrosity and Myth in Mary Shelley's Frankenstein

I am especially grateful to Marilyn Butler, Joyce Chaplin, James Delbourgo, Lynn Festa, and the late Jeremy Maule for their help and comments.

1. Compare Timothy Hampton, "Signs of Monstrosity: The Rhetoric of Description and the Limits of Allegory in Rabelais and Montaigne," in this volume.

2. Compare Joan B. Landes, "Revolutionary Anatomies," in this volume.

3. Chris Baldick, *Frankenstein's Shadow: Myth, Monstrosity, and Nineteenth-Century Writing* (Oxford: Clarendon Press, 1987), 1.

4. Michael Hagner, "Enlightened Monsters," in *The Sciences in Enlightened Europe,* ed. William Clark, Jan Golinski, and Simon Schaffer (Chicago: University of Chicago Press, 1999), 175–217; Lorraine Daston and Katharine Park, *Wonders and the Order of Nature, 1150–1750* (New York: Zone Books, 1998); Zakiya Hanafi, *The Monster in the Machine: Magic, Medicine, and the Marvelous in the Time of the Scientific Revolution* (Durham, N.C.: Duke University Press, 2000).

5. Frank Manuel, *The Eighteenth Century Confronts the Gods* (Cambridge, Mass.: Harvard University Press, 1959); Burton Feldman and Robert D. Richardson, *The Rise of Modern Mythology, 1680–1860,* 2d ed. (Bloomington: Indiana University Press, 2000); James Engell, "The Modern Revival of Myth: Its Eighteenth-Century Origins," in *Allegory, Myth, and Symbol,* ed. Morton W. Bloomfield (Cambridge, Mass.: Harvard University Press, 1981), 245–71.

6. Samuel Johnson, *The Lives of the English Poets,* ed. G. Birkbeck Hill, 3 vols. (Oxford: Clarendon Press, 1905), 2:294; William Wordsworth, *Ode to Lycoris* (1817), note; Samuel Taylor Coleridge, *Biographia Literaria,* ed. John Shawcross, 2 vols. (Oxford: Oxford University Press, 1907), 2:58–59; Johnson, *Lives of the English Poets,* 1:295, 3:436, quoted in Engell, "The Modern Revival of Myth," 245, 248, 249, 250.

7. William Hazlitt, "On the Living Poets," in *The Complete Works of William Hazlitt,* ed. P. P. Howe, 21 vols. (London: J. H. Dent, 1930–34), 5:161–62.

8. Hartley Coleridge, "On the Poetical Use of the Heathen Mythology," *London Magazine* 5 (February 1822): 113.

9. For example, Thomas Blackwell, *An Enquiry into the Life and Writings of Homer* (London, 1735); Blackwell, *Letters Concerning Mythology* (London, 1748).

10. Giambattista Vico, *The First New Science* (1725), 3.6, in Vico, *Selected Writings,* ed. and trans. Leon Pompa (Cambridge: Cambridge University Press, 1982), 145; Joseph Mali, *The Rehabilitation of Myth: Vico's "New Science"* (Cambridge: Cambridge University Press, 1992), 188–89, 199–200.

11. [William Godwin], *The Pantheon: Or Ancient History of the Gods of Greece and Rome. Intended to Facilitate the Understanding of the Classical Authors, and of the Poets in General. For the Use of Schools, and Young Persons of Both Sexes* (London: Thomas Hodgkins, 1806), v.

12. For example, Douglas Bush, *Mythology and the Romantic Tradition in English Poetry* (Cambridge,

Mass.: Harvard University Press, 1937); Edward B. Hungerford, *Shores of Darkness* (New York: Columbia University Press, 1941); Alex Zwerdling, "The Mythographers and the Romantic Revival of Greek Myth," *PMLA* 71 (1964): 447–56; Marilyn Butler, "Myth and Myth-Making in the Shelley Circle," *ELH* 49 (1982): 50–72; though see also Butler, "Druids, Bards and Twice-Born Bacchus: Peacock's Engagement with Primitive Mythology," *Keats-Shelley Memorial Bulletin* 36 (1985): 57–76.

13. John J. White, *Mythology in the Modern Novel: A Study of Prefigurative Techniques* (Princeton, N.J.: Princeton University Press, 1971), 14.

14. Erich Heller, "The Poet in the Age of Prose: Reflections on Hegel's *Aesthetics* and Rilke's *Duino Elegies*," in Heller, *In the Age of Prose: Literary and Philosophical Essays* (Cambridge: Cambridge University Press, 1984), 3–19.

15. Friedrich Hölderlin, "Brod und Wein" (1801), in Hölderlin, *Poems and Fragments*, trans. Michael Hamburger (Cambridge: Cambridge University Press, 1980), 248, 249.

16. John Keats, *Endymion* (1818), "Preface," in *The Poems of John Keats*, ed. Jack Stillinger (Cambridge, Mass.: Belknap Press, 1978), 103.

17. Robert Gittings, *John Keats* (Boston: Little, Brown, 1968), 172, 177.

18. Johnson, *Lives of the Poets*, 2:68.

19. M. D. George, *Catalogue of Political and Personal Satires Preserved in the Department of Prints and Drawings in the British Museum*, 11 vols. (London: British Museum, 1870–1954), 6 (1784–92), 6601 ("The Modern Colossus"), 7116 ("A Modern Hercules"), 7117 ("The Modern Venus"), 7210 ("The Modern Atlas"), 7580 ("The Modern Hercules Destroying the Hydra of Fanaticism"), 7840 ("The Modern Atlas"), 8257 ("A Modern Venus"); 7 (1793–1800), 8687 ("The Modern Hercules or a Finishing Blow for Poor John Bull"), 9374–80 ("The New Pantheon of Democratic Mythology"); 8 (1801–10), 10390 ("The Modern Hercules, Cleansing the Augean Stable"), 10590 ("Modern Atlas's Tottering under a Globe of their own Formation!!"), 10760 ("The Modern Atlas asking a favor of John Bull"), 11252 ("The Modern Circe Or a Sequel to the Petticoat!"); 9 (1811–19), 11879 ("The Modern Calypso; or the Matured Enchantress"), 12734 ("The Modern Phaeton or Hugely in Danger"), 12780 ("Hercules and Omphale, or Modern Mythology"), 13401 ("Modern Pegasus or Dandy Hobbies in Full Speed"). On Gillray as "the transmitter of other people's myths" see Ronald Paulson, *Representations of Revolution (1789–1820)* (New Haven, Conn.: Yale University Press, 1983), 210–11.

20. For an acute contemporary analysis of classical myth in graphic satire see the reading of Gillray, "Confederated-Coalition;—or—The Giants storming Heaven" (1804), in Christiane Banerji and Diana Donald, trans. and ed., *Gillray Observed: The Earliest Account of His Caricatures in 'London und Paris'* (Cambridge: Cambridge University Press, 1999), 169–84.

21. George, *Catalogue of Political and Personal Satires*, 9 (1811–19), 12299 ("The Modern Prometheus, or Downfall of Tyranny"), 12627 ("Le Promethée de l'Isle de Ste. Héléne"); Catherine Clerc, *Le caricature contre Napoléon* (Paris: Éditions Promodis, 1985), 301.

22. George, *Catalogue of Political and Personal Satires*, 9 (1811–19), 13055 ("Dandies—or—Monstrosities of 1818").

23. Anthony Ashley Cooper, third earl of Shaftesbury, *Characteristics, of Men, Manners, Opinions, Times* (1711), ed. Lawrence E. Klein (Cambridge: Cambridge University Press, 1999), 241; Immanuel Kant, *Fortgesetzte Betrachtung der seit einiger Zeit wahrgenommenen Erderschütterungen* (1756), in *Kants*

Werke, vol. 1: *Vorkritische Schriften I, 1747–1756* (Berlin: W. De Gruyter, 1968), 472; I. Bernard Cohen, *Benjamin Franklin's Science* (Cambridge: Mass.: Harvard University Press, 1990), 157.

24. Claude Lévi-Strauss, "The Structural Study of Myth," in Lévi-Strauss, *Structural Anthropology*, trans. Claire Jacobson and Brooke Grundfest Schoepf (Harmondsworth: Penguin, 1968), 210.

25. Baldick, *In Frankenstein's Shadow*, 4.

26. A. D. Harvey, "*Frankenstein* and *Caleb Williams*," *Keats-Shelley Memorial Bulletin* 29 (1980), 21–27; Jane Blumberg, *Mary Shelley's Early Novels: "This Child of Imagination and Misery"* (Basingstoke: Macmillan, 1993), 33–40.

27. Shelley alludes to Godwin's *Fables* in *The Letters of Mary Wollstonecraft Shelley*, ed. Betty T. Bennett, 3 vols. (Baltimore: Johns Hopkins University Press, 1980–88), 1:509.

28. Albert J. Kuhn, "English Deism and Romantic Mythological Syncretism," *PMLA* 71 (1956): 1094–115.

29. Godwin, *The Pantheon*, ix–x, vi, vii.

30. Ibid., 93–95.

31. Ibid., 93–94.

32. Ibid.

33. *Mary Shelley's Journals*, ed. Frederick L. Jones (Norman: University of Oklahoma Press, 1947), 43–47.

34. See generally J. L. Carr, "Pygmalion and the *Philosophes:* The Animated Statue in Eighteenth-Century France," *Journal of the Warburg and Courtauld Institutes* 23 (1960): 239–55.

35. Burton R. Pollin, "Philosophical and Literary Sources of *Frankenstein*," *Comparative Literature* 17 (1965): 100–101.

36. Stéphanie Felicité Ducrest de Saint Aubin, comtesse de Genlis, *Nouveaux Contes Moraux et Nouvelles Historiques,* 6 vols. (Paris: Maradan, 1819), 6:258: "Pour le reste de votre figure, [Pygmalion] ne s'est pas contenté d'un seul modèle, il en a pris cinq ou six; vous avez les pieds de la petite Aglaure, les bras de la jeune Cephise, et, ce qui pourra vous surprendre, vous avez mes mains et ma taille."

37. George Gordon, Lord Byron, "Prometheus" (1816), in Byron, *The Complete Poetical Works,* ed. Jerome J. McGann, 7 vols. (Oxford: Oxford University Press, 1980–93), 4:32.

38. Mary Shelley, *Proserpine* (1820), ll. 26–27, 47–49, in Shelley, *Matilda, Dramas, Reviews and Essays,* ed. Pamela Clemit (London: William Pickering, 1996), 74, 75; Alan Richardson, "*Proserpine* and *Midas:* Gender, Genre, and Mythic Revisionism in Mary Shelley's Dramas," in *The Other Mary Shelley: Beyond Frankenstein,* ed. Audrey A. Fisch, Anne K. Mellor, and Esther M. Schor (Oxford: Oxford University Press, 1993), 124–39.

39. Mary Shelley, *Frankenstein; or the Modern Prometheus* (1818 text), ed. James Rieger (Chicago: University of Chicago Press, 1982), 39.

40. T. S. Eliot, "*Ulysses,* Order and Myth," in Eliot, *Selected Prose,* ed. Frank Kermode (London: Faber, 1975), 177.

41. Mary Shelley, *Frankenstein; or the Modern Prometheus* (1831 text), ed. M. K. Joseph (Oxford: Oxford University Press, 1969), 129; Leslie Tannenbaum, "From Filthy Type to Truth: Miltonic Myth in *Frankenstein*," *Keats-Shelley Journal* 26 (1977): 101–13; John B. Lamb, "Mary Shelley's *Frankenstein* and Milton's Monstrous Myth," *Nineteenth-Century Literature* 47 (1992): 303–19.

42. Shelley, *Frankenstein*, 17, 139 (quoting *Paradise Lost* [hereafter *PL*], 12.646–47).

43. Thomas De Quincey, *Confessions of an English Opium-Eater* (1821), ed. Grevel Lindop (Oxford: Oxford University Press, 1985), 11 (*PL*, 12.647), 19 (*PL*, 12.646), 79 (*PL*, 12.644).

44. Shelley, *Frankenstein*, 57.

45. Percy Bysshe Shelley, *Prometheus Unbound* (1819), "Preface," in Shelley, *Poetical Works*, ed. Thomas Hutchinson (Oxford: Oxford University Press, 1970), 205.

46. Shelley, *Frankenstein*, 9.

47. Ibid., 211.

48. Shelley, *Prometheus Unbound*, "Preface," in Shelley, *Poetical Works*, 204–5.

49. Claude Brew, "A New Shelley Text: Essay on Miracles and Christian Doctrine," *Keats-Shelley Memorial Bulletin* 27 (1977): 10–28.

50. Mary Shelley, "The Necessity of a Belief in the Heathen Mythology to a Christian" (1821), MSS Shelley e. 274, 92 rev., Bodleian Library, Oxford, printed in Shelley, *Proserpine and Midas: Two Unpublished Mythological Dramas by Mary Shelley*, ed. A. Koszul (London: Humphrey Milford, 1922), xxiv; Emily Sunstein, "Shelley's Answer to Leslie's *Short and Easy Method with the Deists* and Mary Shelley's Answer, 'The Necessity of a Belief in the Heathen Mythology to a Christian,'" *Keats-Shelley Memorial Bulletin* 32 (1981): 49–54.

51. Shelley, "The Necessity of a Belief in the Heathen Mythology to a Christian," in Shelley, *Proserpine and Midas*, ed. Koszul, xxv, xxvi, probably referring to Aeschylus, *Prometheus Bound*, l. 323, and Acts 26:14.

52. Leigh Hunt to Mary Shelley, 9 March 1819, in *Shelley and His Circle, 1773–1822*, ed. Kenneth Neill Cameron and Donald H. Reiman, 8 vols. to date (Cambridge, Mass.: Harvard University Press, 1961–), 6:793.

53. Mary Shelley to Leigh Hunt, 6 April 1819, in *Letters of Mary Wollstonecraft Shelley*, 1:91; Timothy Webb, "Shelley and the Cyclops," *Keats-Shelley Memorial Bulletin* 23 (1972): 31–37.

54. "The New Frankenstein," *Fraser's Magazine* 17 (January 1837): 26; Baldick, *In Frankenstein's Shadow*, 141–42.

55. James Rieger, "Dr. Polidori and the Genesis of *Frankenstein*," *Studies in English Literature, 1500–1900* 3 (1963): 461–72; D. L. Macdonald, *Poor Polidori: A Critical Biography of the Author of "The Vampyre"* (Toronto: University of Toronto Press, 1991), 83–88; Judith Barbour, "Dr. John William Polidori, Author of *The Vampyre*," in *Imagining Romanticism: Essays on English and American Romanticisms*, ed. Deirdre Coleman and Peter Otto (Cornwall, Conn.: Locust Hill Press, 1992), 85–110.

56. John William Polidori, "Introduction," in Polidori, *Ximenes, The Wreath, and Other Poems* (London: Longman, Hurst, Rees, Orme, and Brown, 1819), xii.

57. Though Polidori's poetic tragedy *Ximenes* had originally been entitled *Count Orlando; or, The Modern Abraham* when he sent it to John Murray in July 1817: Macdonald, *Poor Polidori*, 26, 147, 211, 260 n. 30.

58. John William Polidori, *Ernestus Berchtold; or the Modern Oedipus* (London: Longman, Hurst, Rees, Orme, and Brown, 1819), v; also available in Polidori, *The Vampyre and Ernestus Berchtold; or, The Modern Oedipus: Collected Fiction of John William Polidori*, ed. D. L. Macdonald and Kathleen Scherf (Toronto: University of Toronto Press, 1994).

59. White, *Mythology in the Modern Novel*, 31.

60. Polidori, *Ernestus Berchtold*, 219.

61. Ibid., 275.

62. Polidori, *Ximenes, The Wreath, and Other Poems,* title page.

63. Duncan Wu, "Hazlitt's 'Sexual Harassment,'" *Essays in Criticism* 50 (2000): 211.

64. *The Letters of William Hazlitt,* ed. H. M. Sikes, W. H. Bonner, and G. Lahey (New York: New York University Press, 1978), 45 (Ovid), 52 ("Mr Dolounghpryée"), 110–11 ("Edward Baldwin").

65. Ibid.,231–32.

66. Ibid., 104; Hazlitt, *Liber Amoris; or the New Pygmalion* (1823), in Hazlitt, *Complete Works,* 9:117; Charles Nicholl, "'A Being Full of Witching,'" *London Review of Books,* 18 May 2000, 15–18.

67. Hazlitt, *Liber Amoris,* in Hazlitt, *Complete Works,* 9:103.

68. Ibid., 112.

69. Ibid., 122.

70. Ibid., 114.

71. Ibid., 157.

72. Ibid., 159.

73. Hazlitt, "On Personal Identity," in Hazlitt, *Complete Works,* 17:265.

74. Lee Sterrenburg, "Mary Shelley's Monster: Politics and Psyche in *Frankenstein,*" in *The Endurance of Frankenstein: Essays on Mary Shelley's Novel,* ed. George Levine and U. C. Knoepflmacher (Berkeley: University of California Press, 1979), 157; on the politicization of the monstrous during the French Revolution see Joan B. Landes, "Revolutionary Anatomies," in this volume.

75. Sterrenburg, "Mary Shelley's Monster," in Levine and Knoepflmacher, *The Endurance of Frankenstein,* 166–71; Baldick, *In Frankenstein's Shadow.*

76. George, *Catalogue of Political and Personal Satires,* 10 (1820–1827), 14311 ("Tugging at a ~~High~~ Eye Tooth"). This original allusion does not appear in Sterrenburg, "Mary Shelley's Monster"; in Baldick, *In Frankenstein's Shadow;* or in Donald F. Glut, *The Frankenstein Catalog* (Jefferson, N.C.: McFarland, 1984).

77. Theodore Ziolkowski, "Science, *Frankenstein,* and Myth," *Sewanee Review* 89 (1981): 56.

78. Marilyn Butler, "Introduction," in Shelley, *Frankenstein: 1818 Text,* ed. Butler (Oxford: Oxford University Press, 1994), xv–li; Simon Schaffer, "Natural Philosophy and Public Spectacle in the Eighteenth Century," *History of Science* 21 (1983): 1–43; Larry Stewart, *The Rise of Public Science: Rhetoric, Technology, and Natural Philosophy in Newtonian Britain, 1680–1750* (Cambridge: Cambridge University Press, 1992); Jan Golinski, *Science as Public Culture: Chemistry and Enlightenment in Britain, 1760–1820* (Cambridge: Cambridge University Press, 1992).

Afterword

I would like to thank Katherine Horowitz for her insightful comments on this essay.

1. Indeed, some specific genetic defects now function as signifiers, synecdoches, for a range of potential human malformations.

2. Although institutions like the Mütter Museum or the Musée de l'homme in Paris continue to display examples of human anomalies, this is a throwback to another era.

3. Denis Diderot, *Rameau's Nephew and D'Alembert's Dream,* trans. Leonard Tancock (New York: Penguin Books, 1966), 190.

4. This was an unsuccessful venture.

5. *Histoire générale et particulière des anomalies de l'organisation chez l'homme et les animaux: Ouvrage comprenant des recherches sur les caractères, la classification, l'influence physiologique et pathologique, les rapports généraux, les lois et les causes des monstruosités, des variétés et vices de conformation ou traité de tératologie,* 3 vol. (Paris: Baillière, 1832–1837).

6. Geoffroy was the first to use the system of Linnean binominal nomenclature to classify monsters. Isidore Geoffroy added a significant number of genera of monsters to this schema. See Patrick Tort, "La Logique du deviant: Isidore Geoffroy Saint-Hilaire et la classification des monstres," *Revue des sciences humaines* 188 (1982): 7–32.

7. The *Traité's* schema breaks with two competing interpretative frameworks used to explain monstrosity in the late eighteenth century: a metaphysical intervention by God (echoed in preformationist/providentialist views) on the one hand, and accidentalist or chaotic views (epigenesist and/or materialist) on the other.

8. Another more likely and more offensive possibility is that, like many other adversities, monstrosity will be a problem specific to the developing world.

9. The first successful attempts at surgically repairing the anomalous body began with cataract operations such as those performed by Grant in 1709 and Cheselden in 1728. At the time, a London newspaper, *The Tatler,* lauded Grant's achievement as "a matter 'of a yet higher consideration' than the history of princes, empires, and wars." William R. Paulson, *Enlightenment, Romanticism, and the Blind in France* (Princeton, N.J.: Princeton University Press, 1987), 27. Readers of Flaubert may also recall Charles Bovary's ill-fated operation of the clubfoot Hippolyte (congenital *talipes equinovarus*). See *Madame Bovary: Moeurs de province* (Paris: Garnier, 1951), 164–65.

10. It should be noted that the tradition of freak show, which has disappeared from public venues, continues to exist in book form and, increasingly, on the Internet.

11. The first such corrective surgeries took place in the late 1950s.

12. See David Cressy's comments in this volume on science's role in separating conjoined twins.

13. See, for example, an article published within days of the surgical separation of Patrick and Benjamin Binder, twins conjoined at the brain. The article, which is entitled "Surgeons Hopeful as Saga of Siamese Twins Continues" chronicles the intense preparation and skill of the surgical team, making no mention of the babies' postoperative status until the final paragraph. The last mention of the twins themselves appeared in the *New York Times* on 13 December 1987; five and a half years later, the paper featured a profile of one of the surgeons, Dr. Ben Carson, declaring him a "folk hero." See Jane E. Brody, "Surgeons Hopeful as Saga of Siamese Twins Continues," *New York Times,* 8 September 1987, C1.

14. According to its mission statement (www.isna.org), the Intersex Society of North America "is devoted to systemic change to end shame, secrecy, and unwanted genital surgeries for people born with an anatomy that someone decided is not standard for male or female."

15. "Image, raison, déraison," in *Univers de l'Encyclopédie*, ed. Roland Barthes, Robert Mauzi, and Jean-Pierre Seguin (Paris: Les Libraires Associés, 1964), 15, cited in Julia V. Douthwaite, *The Wild Girl, Natural Man, and the Monster: Dangerous Experiments in the Age of Enlightenment* (Chicago: University of Chicago Press, 2002), 206.

16. Georges Bataille, *Visions of Excess: Selected Writings, 1927–1939*, trans. Allan Stoekl, Carl R. Lovitt, and Donald M. Leslie, Jr. (Minneapolis: University of Minnesota Press, 1985), 55.

17. "L'existence des monstres met en question la vie quant au pouvoir qu'elle a de nous enseigner l'ordre." *La Connaissance de la vie* (Paris: J. Vrin, 1992), 171. Translations from Canguilhem are mine.

18. "Mais la monstruosité c'est la menace accidentelle et conditionnelle d'inachèvement ou de distorsion dans la formation de la forme, c'est la limitation par l'intérieur, la négation du vivant par le non-viable" (*La Connaissance de la vie*, 172–73).

19. "D'une part, il inquiète: . . . D'autre part, il valorise: puisque la vie est capable d'échecs, toutes ses réussites sont des échecs évités." Ibid., 173.

20. *Les Anormaux: Cours au Collège de France (1974–75)*, ed. François Ewald et al. (Paris: Seuil/Gallimard, 1999), 46, 48.

21. Ibid., 48

22. Given the recent publication date of *Les Anormaux*, many of these paradigms come from *Surveiller et punir: Naissance de la prison* (Paris: Gallimard, 1975) and *Histoire de la sexualité* (Paris: Gallimard, 1976).

23. Patrick Tort's important *L'Ordre des monstres* is a particularly good example of this phenomenon. His work on the great (and misunderstood) debate on monstrosity at the Paris Royal Academy of Sciences demonstrated clearly that the numerous Academy *mémoires* published on this subject during the early eighteenth century ultimately had as much if not more to do with a deep-rooted preoccupation with the extent of God's jurisdiction, than they did with anatomical analysis or embryology. While earlier history of science treatments of this long debate emphasize the contribution (or lack thereof) of the various Academy members to an emerging science of monsters, Tort's book meticulously examines the initial framework for this debate, the desire to reconcile doxa and paradoxa within the budding "science" of embryology. The willingness to engage and even decipher the implications of such epistemological syncretism is also at work in Patrick Graille's remarkable *Les Hermaphrodites aux XVIIe et XVIIIe siècles* (Paris: Belles Lettres, 2001). This study of a heretofore unexplored corpus of literary, scientific, and even theological texts relative to hermaphroditism underscores the early modern era's competing impulses to normalize, marginalize, deny, or even position as somehow perfect those individuals born between two sexes.

24. "The Faces of Eighteenth-Century Monstrosity," in *Faces of Monstrosity in Eighteenth-Century Thought*, special issue of *Eighteenth-Century Life*, ed. Andrew Curran, Robert P. Maccubbin, and David F. Morrill, 21, no. 2 (1997): 12.

25. *Marvels, Monsters, and Miracles: Studies in the Medieval and Early Modern Imaginations*, ed. Timothy S. Jones and David A Sprunger (Kalamazoo, Mich.: Medieval Institute Publications, 2002), xxiii.

26. *"Defects": Engendering the Modern Body*, ed. Helen Deutsch and Felicity Nussbaum (Ann Arbor: The University of Michigan Press, 2000), 1, 8.

27. Ibid., 1.

28. Ibid., 10.

29. Deutsch and Nussbaum argue, for instance, that the works of thinkers including Maupertuis "indicate the ways in which formulations of monstrosity connected with the racialization of the European character and were harnessed in the service of polygenetic theories" (ibid., 8). This powerful teleological narrative, while in some measure faithful to what transpires among race theorists, passes over several important facts. In the first place, Maupertuis was anything but a polygenesist. Indeed, to the extent that monstrosity and race function together in his *Vénus physique* (1745), and they do, the two concepts are combined within a larger rejection of racial essentialism. This simple fact forces us to rethink the association of monstrosity and nascent race theory (as we find them in authors like Maupertuis). Indeed, as Ann Thomson has argued, new dynamic theories of nature circulating in mid-eighteenth-century Europe (many of which were attached to theories of monstrosity) have not fully made their way into our understanding of eighteenth-century conceptions of monstrosity and their relationship to nineteenth-century race theory. See Thomson's article, "Diderot, le matérialisme et la division de l'espèce humaine," *Recherches sur Diderot et sur l'Encyclopédie* 26 (1999): 197–211.

30. This change in perspective, which has encouraged narratives that are less linear, less causal, has obviously allowed scholars to recover what were once thought of as the "dead ends" within the history of science narrative, such as the imaginative power of the womb or race theory among philosophers like Hume or Kant. Marie-Hélène Huet's *Monstrous Imagination* (Cambridge, Mass.: Harvard University Press, 1993) was among the first studies to provide a model for such interdisciplinary study. More recently, Julia Douthwaite's *The Wild Girl* has, in a similar fashion, brought the notion of the monstrous into dialogue with eighteenth-century constructions of gender and race.

31. Daston and Park, *Wonders and the Order of Nature* (New York: Zone Books, 1998), 11.

32. Ibid., 359–60.

33. See Andrew Curran, "Diderot and the *Encyclopédie's* Construction of the Black African," *SVEC,* Voltaire Foundation (forthcoming).

34. While it would be a historical fallacy to argue that materialism produced racism or that all eighteenth-century thinkers drew on tropes of monstrosity, for example, to justify chattel slavery, we can safely assert that elements of transformist thought in Buffon provided the epistemological link between the all-powerful trope of monstrosity and the power of an autonomous nature (which could now make mistakes).

35. Daston and Park, *Wonders and the Order of Nature,* 187. Daston and Park have advanced a historical narrative that equates the increasingly rationalized view of monstrosity during the early modern era with a consensus among elite culture that "increasingly rejected portents as politically and religiously volatile" (ibid., 176) rather than with humankind's inexorable march towards a more secular culture.

36. Above, 00.

37. "L'humanité cesse aux frontières de la tribu, du groupe linguistique, parfois même du village." Claude Lévi-Strauss, *Race et histoire* (Bussière à Saint-Amand: Denoël, 1987). My translation.

38. Above, 128, 134.

39. Above, 70.

40. Above, 80.

41. Above, 47.

42. Pierre Boaistuau, *Histoires prodigieuses* (Paris: Editions Slatkine, 1996).

43. Samuel Purchas, *Purchas his Pilgrimage. Or, Relations of the world and the religions observed in all ages and places discouered from the creation unto this present. In foure partes* (London: Printed by W. Stansby for H. Fetherstone, 1613), 51.

44. Steintrager, "Perfectly Inhuman: Moral Monstrosity in Eighteenth-Century Discourse," in Curran, Maccubbin, and Morrill, *Faces of Monstrosity,* 116.

45. *Dictionnaire de l'Académie Françoise,* vol. 2 (Paris: Chez la Veuve de Jean-Baptist Coignard, 1694), 47.

46. Robert Audi, ed., *Cambridge Dictionary of Philosophy* (Cambridge: Cambridge University Press, 1995), 186.

47. Above, 48.

48. Critics have rightly portrayed the era of the French Revolution as remarkably rich in politically monstrous discourses and iconography, as Landes shows in Chapter 6.

49. Above, 200–201.

50. To a certain degree, this is even true for materialist thinkers' treatment of monstrosity. Writing in an era where the norm against which monstrosity was defined was neither statistical nor entirely morphological, materialist thinkers both denied the monstrous form any particular significance and maintained that its twisted nature was a confirmation (sign) of their own antiteleological view of the universe. Seen from this latter perspective, the monster served as a living testament to a proto-Epicurean belief that nature was spewing forth new malformations over time. Accordingly, while materialists may have seen monsters as being part of the continual movement of nature, they did not attribute a historical sense, meaning, "order," or "evolution" to human malformations.

CONTRIBUTORS

DAVID ARMITAGE is Professor of History, Columbia University. He is the author of *The Ideological Origins of the British Empire* (Cambridge University Press, 2000), and the editor of *Theories of Empire, 1450–1800* (Ashgate, 1998), of *Bolingbroke: Political Writings* (Cambridge University Press, 1997), with Michael J. Braddick, of *The British Atlantic World* (Palgrave, 2002), and, with Armand Himy and Quentin Skinner, of *Milton and Republicanism* (Cambridge University Press, 1995).

PETER BURKE is Professor of Cultural History and Fellow of Emmanuel College at the University of Cambridge. His many books on early modern Europe include *Eyewitnessing: The Uses of Images as Historical Evidence* (Cornell University Press, 2001), *The European Renaissance: Centres and Peripheries* (Blackwell, 1998), *Varieties of Cultural History* (Cornell University Press, 1997), *The Fortunes of the Courtier: The European Reception of Castiglione's Cortegiano* (Pennsylvania State University Press, 1995), *The Art of Conversation* (Cornell University Press, 1993), and *The Fabrication of Louis XIV* (Yale University Press, 1992).

DAVID CRESSY is Professor of British History, Ohio State University. He has published widely on early modern England, including *Travesties and Transgressions in Tudor and Stuart England: Tales of Discord and Dissension* (Oxford University Press, 2000), *Birth, Marriage, and Death: Ritual, Religion, and the Life-Cycle in Tudor and Stuart England* (Oxford University Press, 1997), *Bonfires and Bells: National Memory and the Protestant Calendar in Elizabethan and Stuart England* (University of California Press, 1989), and *Literacy and the*

Social Order: Reading and Writing in Tudor and Stuart England (Cambridge University Press, 1980).

ANDREW CURRAN is Assistant Professor of French at Wesleyan University. He is the author of *Sublime Disorder: Physical Monstrosity in Diderot's Universe* (Voltaire Foundation, 2001) and the guest editor, with Robert Maccubbin and David Morrill, of a special issue of *Eighteenth-Century Life* entitled *Faces of Monstrosity in Eighteenth-Century Thought* (May 1997).

TIMOTHY HAMPTON is Professor of French, Comparative Literature, and Italian Studies at the University of California, Berkeley. He is the author of *Literature and Nation in the Sixteenth Century: Inventing Renaissance France* (Cornell University Press, 2001) and *Writing from History: The Rhetoric of Exemplarity in Renaissance Literature* (Cornell University Press, 1990), and co-translator of Giovanni Bocaccio's *Amorosa Visione* (University Press of New England, 1986).

R. PO-CHIA HSIA is Edwin Erle Sparks Professor of History and Religious Studies, The Pennsylvania State University. His publications on Reformation history include *The World of Catholic Renewal, 1540–1770* (Cambridge University Press, 1998), *Trent 1475: Stories of a Ritual Murder Trial* (Yale University Press, 1992), *Social Discipline in the Reformation: Central Europe, 1550–1750* (Routledge, 1989), and *The Myth of Ritual Murder: Jews and Magic in Reformation Germany* (Yale University Press, 1988).

MARIE-HÉLÈNE HUET is M. Taylor Pyne Professor of French, Princeton University. She is the author of *Mourning Glory: the Will of the French Revolution* (University of Pennsylvania Press, 1997), *Monstrous Imagination* (Harvard University Press, 1993), *Rehearsing the Revolution: The Staging of Marat's Death, 1793–1797*, trans. Robert Hurley (University of California Press, 1982), *Le Héros et son double: Essai sur le roman d'ascension sociale au XVIIIe siècle* (J. Corti, 1975), and *L'histoire des voyages extraordinaires: Essai sur l'oeuvre de Jules Verne* (Minard, 1973).

Contributors

LAURA LUNGER KNOPPERS is Professor of English and Director, Institute for the Arts and Humanities, The Pennsylvania State University. She is the author of *Constructing Cromwell: Ceremony, Portrait, and Print, 1645–1661* (Cambridge University Press, 2000) and *Historicizing Milton: Spectacle, Power, and Poetry in Restoration England* (University of Georgia Press, 1994), and editor of *Puritanism and Its Discontents* (University of Delaware Press, 2003).

JOAN B. LANDES is Professor of Women's Studies and History at The Pennsylvania State University. She is the author of *Visualizing the Nation: Gender, Representation, and Revolution in Eighteenth-Century France* (Cornell University Press, 2001) and *Women and the Public Sphere in the Age of the French Revolution* (Cornell University Press, 1988), and editor of *Feminism, the Public and the Private* (Oxford University Press, 1998).

INDEX

Index

Index

gender (*continued*)
    Cromwell, Oliver, and, 95
    disability and, 236
    imagination and, 11, 131
    nationhood and, 15
    serpents and, 138–39
    Whore of Babylon and, 95, 117, 122
The Generation of Animals, 181–82
Genlis, Comtesse de, 213–14
Geoffroy Saint-Hilaire, Étienne, 229, 250 n.17
Geoffroy Saint-Hilaire, Isidore, 229
Gillray, James, 160, *161*
Gnidias, Matthias, 73, *76*
God
    births, monstrous, and, 44, 45, 49, 50–51,
        55–56, 62–63, 129–34
    Creation and, 134–37
    Cromwell, Oliver, and, 96–98
    embryology and, 247 n.2, 290 n.23
    healing and, 143–45
    medicine and, 128–47, 198, 241
    portents and, 3, 49, 50–51, 62–63, 70, 82–83,
        89–91, 129–34, 143–44
    Reformation and, 82–83
Godwin, William, 204, 211–13
Graille, Patrick, 5, 12, 235, 247 n.2, 248 n.6
Great Albert, 138–39
Great Dragon. *See* Beast of Revelation
Greenacres, Isabel. *See* Gataker, Mrs.
Grimm, Melchior, Baron de, 274 n.12
grotesque, the, 165–70
Guérin, Pierre-Narcisse, 168–69
guillotine, 160–63. *See also* execution

Hagner, Michael, 5, 7–8
Hanafi, Zakiya, 12–13, 275 n.18
Harley, David, 143
Harriet, 168
Hazlitt, William, 203, 222–24
heads, monstrous
    births, monstrous, and, 41–44, 48, 49, 52–56,
        62–63, 67–70, 85–87
    English Civil War and, 41–44, 48, 49, 52–54,
        55–56, 62–63
    hydra and, 154–55, *156*

portents and, 67–70
    Reformation and, 67–70, 73–77, 85–87
healing, 143–45. *See also* medicine
Hegel, Georg W. F., 204–5
Histoire naturelle, 30, 237–39
Histoires prodigieuses, 179–81, 183–84
Hölderlin, Friedrich, 205
Holland, 98–100, 114–23. *See also* Dutchmen
Holy Roman Empire, 67–71, 72
Houghton, Mrs., 41, 51–54, 59, 62–63
Houghton, Sir Gilbert, 61–62
Houghton, William, 52, 59
Huet, Marie-Hélène, 11–12
Hugues, Sylvie, 170, 278 n.57
Hume, David, 32–33
Hunt, Leigh, 219
hydra, 154–55, *156*

imagination, 11–12, 45–46, 80, 131
Initia doctrinae physicae, 130
Institutes of the Christian Religion, 187
instrumentalization, 7–8
Introduction à la Chirurgie, 134–35
Ireland, 96
Irishmen, 39
Islam, 3–4. *See also* religion
Italians, 35

Johnson, Samuel, 202, 205
Jones, Timothy, 235–36
Judaism, 82–83. *See also* religion
Julius II, 31, 131
Jupiter, 212–13

Keats, John, 205, 223
Kirkham parish, 58–62
Knoppers, Laura Lunger, 239–40
Kristeva, Julia, 166
Kusukawa, Sachiko, 130

Lamia, 223
"La Monstruosité et le monstrueux," 233–34
Landes, Joan B., 239–40
Las Casas, Bartolomé de, 29
Lawson, George, 56, 259 n.36

Index

Index

Index